A COMPANION TO ANGUS
CHUANG TZU

The Society for Asian and Comparative Philosophy Monograph Series was started in 1974. Works are published in the series that deal with any area of Asian philosophy, or any other field of philosophy examined from a comparative perspective. The aim of the series is to make available scholarly works that exceed article length, but may be too specialized for the general reading public, and to make these works available in inexpensive editions without sacrificing the orthography of non-Western languages.

MONOGRAPH NO. 20
SOCIETY FOR ASIAN AND COMPARATIVE PHILOSOPHY

A COMPANION TO ANGUS C. GRAHAM'S *CHUANG TZU*

The Inner Chapters

Harold D. Roth

UNIVERSITY OF HAWAI'I PRESS, HONOLULU

07 06 05 04 03 02   6 5 4 3 2 1

Library of Congress Cataloging-in-Publication Data
Roth, Harold David.
  A companion to Angus C. Graham's Chuang Tzu : the Inner chapters / Harold D. Roth.
  p. cm. — (Monograph ... of the Society for Asian and Comparative Philosophy ; no. 20)
Includes bibliographical references and index.
ISBN 0-8248-2643-4 (pbk. : alk. paper)
  1. Zhuangzi. Nanhua jing. I. Title: Inner chapters. II. Graham, A. C. (Angus Charles)
III. Zhuangzi. Nanhua jing. English. Selections. IV. Title. V. Series.

BL1900.C576R67 2003
299'.51482—dc21

2002045415

Chapters 1–5 of the present work are reprinted with permission of the following publishers: Chapter 1: Textual Notes to *Chuang Tzu: The Inner Chapters.* © 1981. Reprinted with permission of the School of Oriental and African Studies. Chapter 2: How Much of *Chuang Tzu* Did Chuang Tzu Write? Originally published in a special *Journal of the American Academy of Religion* thematic volume, *Studies in Early Chinese Thought,* Henry Rosemont, Jr. and Benjamin Schwartz, eds. © 1979. Reprinted with permission of the American Academy of Religion, www.aarweb.org. Chapter 3: Chuang Tzu's Essay on Seeing Things As Equal. Originally published in *History of Religions.* © 1970. Reprinted with permission of University of Chicago Press. Chapter 4: Two Notes on the Translation of Taoist Classics. Originally published in *Interpreting Culture Through Translation,* Roger Ames, ed. © 1991. Reprinted with permission of Chinese University of Hong Kong Press. Chapter 5: Taoist Spontaneity and the Dichotomy of "Is" and "Ought." Originally published in *Experimental Essays on the Chuang Tzu,* Victor Mair, ed. © 1983. University of Hawai'i Press.

Camera-ready copy for this book was prepared by EdIndex.

Printed by Versa Press, Inc.

For Gus
and the
"Children of Angus"

Contents

Preface

Throughout a long and distinguished career, Angus C. Graham (1919–1991) was known both for the depth of his Chinese textual scholarship as a philologist, grammarian, and translator, and equally for the breadth of his philosophical interpretations of those texts against the background of the Western intellectual heritage in which he was originally trained.

Both of these dimensions of his work are especially evidenced in his studies of the *Chuang Tzu* (*Zhuangzi*), for whose author(s) Graham had a deep respect and affection. His translation of the text, *Chuang-tzu, the Seven Inner Chapters: and other writings from the book 'Chuang-tzu'* (Allen and Unwin, 1981), was the culmination of many years of study and reflection thereon, and fairly quickly became the benchmark for all readings and interpretations of the book.

The demand for Graham's translation continued after it went out of print in England. Thanks to the efforts of Dr. Jay Hullett and Ms. Deborah Wilkes of the Hackett Publishing Company, the book was reprinted from the original—save for the correction of a few minor typographical errors—in an inexpensive paperback edition in 2000, making it readily available again, this time to a wider audience.

Graham's subtitle is slightly misleading, for he actually translated over 80% of the Chinese text, omitting only those sections he believed merely duplicative, or corrupted beyond linguistic and philosophical reconstruction. But because he believed there were several distinctive philosophical voices in the different chapters of the work—and even within the same chapter on occasion—that had been indiscriminately collocated by later authors and editors, Graham also rearranged the standard order of the received text so that each of the several voices could be heard distinctly. To justify his omissions, emendations, translations, and rearrangements, he wrote extensive textual notes, but his original publisher did not want to include them in the book; they were published separately in 1982 as a supplement to the *Bulletin of the School of Oriental and African Studies*, and they, too, have long been unavailable.

Everyone interested in the *Chuang Tzu* and Graham's work on it, therefore, must be deeply indebted to Professor Harold D. Roth for rescuing these valuable notes from obscurity, and seeing to their reissuance. Further, he has gathered together and edited all of Graham's earlier writings on the *Chuang Tzu* so that all future scholars can trace the development of Graham's thoughts about what he considered the most significant philosophical and literary work produced in classical China.

And more: Roth has also taken Graham's philological, historical, and philosophical investigations and speculations several steps further in a closely but clearly crafted Colophon that concludes the present work. This Colophon is a significant contribution to the field of early Chinese textual studies in its own right, and is thereby simultaneously a most fitting tribute to the scholarship of Angus Graham.

Other scholars who have profited from, and significantly advanced Graham's work—and who have contributed to keeping his writings in print—are acknowledged by Roth in his Editor's Introduction, which follows immediately. It remains to thank the Chiang Ching-Kuo Foundation for International Scholarly Research for a generous subvention to defray the costs of publishing this work, and to the Trustees of Brown University, and Gary Baker and Dawn Graham Baker for additional financial support for this volume in the SACP Monograph Series.

Henry Rosemont, Jr.
Newport, R.I.
27 May 2003

A COMPANION TO ANGUS C. GRAHAM'S
CHUANG TZU

Editor's Introduction

It seems one of those remarkable ironies over which Angus Graham so loved to marvel, that the fate of his most renowned book, *Chuang-tzu, the Seven Inner Chapters: and other writings from the book 'Chuang-tzu,'* was for almost a decade in the hands of Rupert Murdoch, the Australian publishing magnate whom—I would surmise—didn't lose a great deal of sleep over whether to reprint the book with or without Chinese characters. Yet in one of those typical "big fish swallows little fish" corporate acquisitions, the small British scholarly press, Allen and Unwin (the book's original publisher), had been taken like Jonah into the belly of the corporate whale, HarperCollins, which gained rights to all of its publications including Graham's translation. In the spring of 1991 following Graham's untimely death at the age of 71, his literary executor, Henry Rosemont—accompanied by friends Roger Ames and myself—paid a visit to their corporate headquarters in Hammersmith to see if they could be convinced to relinquish their rights to the book to a more scholarly press who might be more likely to keep it in print. However, they had just done a fresh reprinting of the book and told us to wait until all 3000 new copies had been sold out. Long after this happened and the book had been out of print for some time, they finally cut it loose and this resulted in the new Hackett Publishing Company edition to which the present volume is a companion.

About two years ago Henry contacted me with the news that Hackett would be reprinting *Chuang Tzu: The Inner Chapters* and asked me what I thought should be done with Graham's detailed textual notes that were originally written to be included in the book but were rejected by Allen and Unwin. I responded by reviving an old proposal I had once written to HarperCollins to incorporate them into a revised edition that was reorganized to more closely conform to the received recension of the text. After mulling it over we both realized that it would take a great deal of time to accomplish this task, and, moreover, the revisions I was suggesting might well not have been in accord with Graham's wishes. The book had been out of print and difficult to obtain for several years and it seemed best to reprint it as is and leave the textual notes to another venue. Henry invited me to put together a volume of Graham's articles on the *Chuang Tzu* to augment the textual notes and this I agreed to do.

The textual notes that Graham wrote to accompany his *Chuang Tzu* translation are extremely important because they explain in detail the rationale for his many textual emendations and give further insights into his significant reorganization of the text. When considered together with the other articles assembled herein the textual notes help to form a complete picture of his sometimes controversial scholarship on the *Chuang Tzu*. Indeed, this scholarship cannot be fully appreciated without reference to these notes and they were previously available only in a typescript of very limited circulation published in 1982 by Graham's employer, the School of Oriental and African Studies of London University.

The other articles in this collection present different aspects of Graham's engagement with the *Chuang Tzu*, including the text-critical, philological, and the philosophical. "How Much of *Chuang Tzu* did Chuang Tzu Write?" first published in 1976 in a *Journal of the American Academy of Religion* thematic volume edited by Rosemont, is a pioneering work in which Graham identified five distinct philosophical voices in the text and justified them using detailed philological arguments. "Chuang Tzu's Essay on Seeing Things As Equal," written for the Bellagio Conference on Taoist Studies in 1968 and published in a special volume of *History of Religions*, contains Graham's first attempt at a translation of a chapter of *Chuang Tzu* (chapter 2) and his first explanation of the intellectual milieu in which this chapter was written. Grounded in his work on the *Canons* and on the Logicians, it is filled with insights into the *Chuang Tzu*'s technical language that are essential to grasping the underlying meaning of the entire work. "Two Notes on the Translation of Taoist Classics" is an article synthesized from two earlier pieces in which Graham critiqued a number of other translations of the *Lao Tzu* and the *Chuang Tzu*. Written before he undertook his own translation, it helps to explain the rationale for the extensive reorganization of the text he undertook in it. Finally, "Taoist Spontaneity and the Dichotomy of 'Is' and 'Ought,'" published in Victor Mair's valuable collection *Experimental Essays on the Chuang Tzu* (Hawaii, 1983) gives another side of his scholarship, namely his normative interest in using the *Chuang Tzu* to answer some perennial problems in Western philosophy. Although few people know of them, Graham published two books on philosophy, *The Problem of Value* (Hutchinson's University Library, 1960) and *Reason and Spontaneity* (Curzon, 1985). This article is an excellent summary of the latter work.

I have followed these chapters with a Colophon of my own in which I attempt to analyze and appraise Graham's scholarship on the text of the *Chuang Tzu*. In the course of preparing this volume and re-reading the works I included within it, I had the chance to get a complete overview of his work and see it in the context of new research—some of it my own— that Graham's insights helped to generate. I present this appraisal in the hope of answering some of the questions Graham's work raised but did not answer, but I have probably just raised a new set of unanswered questions that someone else will want to answer somewhere down the road.

The preparation of this volume turned out to be much more complex and problematic than I ever envisioned. The technology for scanning Chinese characters is non-existent; all had to be entered individually. We also had a problem with incompatible versions of Microsoft Word, which removed some of the characters when switched from one version to another. We also decided to do a complete edit of the notes and articles for consistency and to remove "anglicisms" that we colonists look upon as quaint, although it was beyond our resources to track down and complete all of Graham's partial references, which remain as he left them for the most part. I could not have accomplished this without the invaluable assistance of two graduate students in Religious Studies at Brown University, Jianshe Kong and Judson Murray, who worked on the three most difficult chapters—the first three. In addition, Anne Holmes and her partner Rob Rudnick of EdIndex in Maine, did a splendid job of copy editing and of preparing the camera-ready copy and the invaluable index for the volume.

For a number of complex reasons, Graham directed relatively few doctoral dissertations. Indeed, I think only Dan Daor and Chris Cullen ever finished under him. The influence of his scholarship, however is immense; it is simply not possible to tally all of us whose work has been significantly impacted by Graham's. I was once talking to Chad Hansen at an AAS conference and it suddenly struck me that while you couldn't find two more divergent interpreters of early Taoism than he and I, that we were both where we were because of the intellectual influence of Angus Graham. Indeed, there are many in the field for whom this is true and they

represent an even wider range of scholarly viewpoints and interests than
Graham's own: from Roger Ames to John Major, Herbert Fingarette to
Robin Yates, Henry Rosemont to Victor Mair, Jean-Paul Reding to
Christoph Harbsmeier, Lisa Raphals to Bob Henricks, Sarah Allan to Lee
Yearley, Sarah Queen to Paul Thompson, and many, many others too nu-
merous to mention. In a very real sense we are all the intellectual progeny
of Angus Graham and it is to all the "children of Angus" that I dedi-
cate this volume.

Chapter 1

Textual Notes to *Chuang Tzu: The Inner Chapters*

A. C. GRAHAM

PART 1
INTRODUCTION

This article is a computer-produced reprint of the original typescript monograph published in 1982 by the School of Oriental and African Studies. Angus Graham wrote these notes while he was working on *Chuang-tzu, the Seven Inner Chapters: and other writings from the book 'Chuang-tzu'* and hoped to include them with the original publication. When the publisher was unwilling to do this, he arranged with the Publications Committee of the School to publish them in a separate monograph. In his original preface, Graham thanked "the Publications Committee of the School of Oriental and African Studies for meeting part of the cost of publication."

While this monograph was originally entitled "Textual Notes to a Partial Translation," Graham's translation included much more than the seven "inner chapters." In addition to these, ten other chapters were translated in their entirety and significant passages from the rest of the work were also included. In all about 80% of the Chuang Tzu was translated by

Graham, although it is sometimes difficult to locate material because of the unusual arrangement and numbering of chapters. Despite this difficulty, I have modified the organizational arrangement of the following textual notes to make them easier to locate in the Graham translation. The notes follow the order and divisions of the translation, for which the corresponding page number is noted in the margin. For each item on which Graham commented, the chapter and line location in the Chinese text in his source edition, *Chuang-tzu yin-te (Concordance to Chuang-tzu*; Harvard-Yenching Institute Sinological Index Series, Supplement No. 20), is also provided. This Harvard edition contains only the text (and not the commentaries) from the edition of Kuo Ch'ing-fan (1894), which, in turn was based upon the Ku-i ts'ung-shu reproduction of a Southern Sung edition. Other than a few alterations to the arrangement of these textual notes to make them easier to identify and to understand, I have left Graham's original work untouched.

Editorial Conventions

*X	X is an emended character.
(Y) *X	Read X for Y.
<X>	Insert X.
[X]	Delete X.
+X	X is a corrupt character.
(X)	X is parenthetic and a suspected gloss.

Abbreviations

BSOAS   *Bulletin of the School of Oriental and African Studies*

BSS   Basic sinological series (*Kuo-hsüeh chi-pen ts'ung-shu* 國 學 基 本 叢 書)

CTIC   *Chuang-tzu, the Seven Inner Chapters: and other writings from the book 'Chuang-tzu,'* translated by A. C. Graham, London: Allen and Unwin, 1981

CTCC   (*Wu ch'iu pei chai*) *Chuang-tzu chi-ch'eng* 無 求 備 齋 莊 子 集 成, edited by Yen Ling-feng 嚴 靈 峰

     (a) *Ch'u-pien* 初編, 30 volumes. Taipei, 1972
     (b) *Hsü-pien*, 續編, 43 volumes. Taipei, 1974

G   Graham, A. C.

HY   Harvard-Yenching Institute Sinological Index Series

HYCT   *Chuang-tzu yin-te (Concordance to Chuang-tzu)*. Harvard-Yenching Institute Sinological Index Series, Supplement No. 20

SPPY   *Ssu-pu pei-yao* 四部備要

SPTK   *Ssu-pu ts'ung-k'an* 四部叢刊

Finding List

Chang Ping-lin 章炳麟
    Chuang-tzu chieh-ku 莊子解故. CTCC (b) v. 40.

Ch'en Ku-ying 陳鼓應
    Chuang-tzu chin chu chin yi 莊子今註今譯. Taipei, 1975.

Ch'ien Mu 錢穆
    Chuang-tzu tsuan-chien 莊子纂箋. Hong Kong, 1951.

Chu Kuei-yao 朱桂曜
    Chuang-tzu nei-p'ien cheng-pu 莊子內篇證補. Shanghai, 1935. CTCC (a) v. 26.

Ch'üeh-wu 闕誤
    Ch'en Ching-yüan 陳景元, *Chuang-tzu Ch'üeh-wu* 莊子闕誤 (Tao-tsang 道藏 edition). CTCC (a) v. 5.

Fukunaga Mitsuji 福永光司
    (1) *Sōshi*, 莊子. Tokyo, 1956 ("inner chapters" only).
    (2) *Sōshi gaihen*, 莊子外篇. Tokyo, 1966.
    (3) *Sōshi zappen*, 莊子雜篇. Tokyo, 1967.

Graham, A. C.   (*) included in this volume
    G1: *Book of Lieh Tzu*. London: John Murray, 1960 (Repr. Columbia University Press, 1990).
    G2: "Chuang-tzu's 'Essay on seeing things as equal.'" History of Religions 9 (1969/70): 137–159. *
    G3: *Later Mohist logic, ethics and science*. Hong Kong and London: Chinese University Press, 1978.

G4: "A post-verbal aspectual particle in Classical Chinese: the supposed preposition *hu* 乎." BSOAS 41/2 (1978): 314–342.

G5: "The *Nung-chia* 農家 'School of the Tillers' and the origins of peasant utopianism in China." BSOAS 42/1 (1979): 66–100.

G6: "How much of *Chuang-tzu* did Chuang-tzu write?" *Studies in Classical Chinese Thought*, edited by Henry Rosemont, Jr. and Benjamin I. Schwartz. Journal of the American Academy of Religion Thematic Issue 47/3 (Sept.1979): 459–501. *

Han Fei Tzu 韓非子

Ch'en Ch'i-yu 陳奇猷, *Han Fei tzu chi-shih* 韓非子集釋. Peking, 1958.

Harvard-Yenching Institute

Chuang Tzu yin-te (Concordance to Chuang-tzu). Harvard-Yenching Institute Sinological Index Series, Supplement No. 20. Cambridge, Massachusetts, 1956.

Hsi T'ung 奚侗

Chuang-tzu pu chu 莊子補註. CTCC (b) v. 40.

Hsün Tzu 荀子

Liang Ch'i-hsiung 梁啓雄, *Hsün Tzu chien-shih* 荀子簡釋. Peking, 1956.

Huai-nan Tzu 淮南子

Liu Wen-tien 劉文典, Huai-nan hung-lieh chi-chieh 淮南鴻烈集解. Shanghai, 1933.

Kao Heng 高亨

Chuang-tzu chin chien 莊子今箋. Taipei, 1971. CTCC (b) v. 42.

Karlgren, Bernhard

Book of Odes. Stockholm, 1950.

Kuo Ch'ing-fan 郭慶藩

Chuang-tzu chi-shih 莊子集釋. Peking, 1961. CTCC (b) v. 38, 39.

Lau, D. C.

Confucius: the Analects. London, 1979.

Li Mien 李勉

Chuang-tzu tsung-lun chi fen-p'ien p'ing-chu 莊子總論及分篇評注. Taipei, 1973.

Liang Ch'i-ch'ao 梁啓超
 Chuang-tzu t'ien-hsia p'ien shih-yi 莊子天下篇釋義. In *Yin-ping-shih ho-chi* 飲冰室合集.

Lieh Tzu 列子
 Yang Po-chün 楊伯峻, *Lieh-tzu chi-shih* 列子集釋. Shanghai, 1958.

Liu Shih-p'ei 劉師培
 Chuang-tzu chüeh-pu 莊子斠補. CTCC (b) v. 40.

Liu Wen-tien 劉文典
 Chuang-tzu pu-cheng 莊子補正. Shanghai, 1947. CTCC (a) v. 28, 29.

Luan Tiao-fu 樂調甫
 Mo-tzu yen-chiu lun-wen chi 墨子研究論文集. Peking, 1957.

Lü-shih ch'un-ch'iu 呂氏春秋
 Hsü Wei-yü 許維遹, *Lü-shih ch'un-ch'iu chi-shih* 呂氏春秋集釋. Peking, 1955.

Ma Hsü-lun 馬敍倫
 Chuang-tzu i-cheng 莊子義證. Shanghai, 1930.

Morohashi Tetsuji 諸橋轍次
 Dai Kan-Wa jiten 大漢和辭典. Tokyo, 1955–1960.

P'ei Hsüeh-hai 裴學海
 Ku shu hsü-tzu chi shih 古書虛字集釋. Peking, 1954.

Pulleyblank, E. G.
 "Studies in early Chinese grammar," Part 1. *Asia Major* (New series) 8/1 (1960): 36–67.

Shih-chi 史記
 Chung-hua shu-chü edition. Peking, 1959.

Sun Yi-jang 孫詒讓
 Chuang-tzu cha-yi 莊子札迻. CTCC (b) v. 37.

Takeuchi Yoshio 武內義雄
 Rōshi genshi 老子原始. Tokyo, 1967.

T'ao Hung-ch'ing 陶鴻慶
 Tu Chuang-tzu cha-chi 讀莊子札記. CTCC (b) v. 40.

Teraoka Ryugan 寺岡龍含
   Tonkō hon Kaku Shō chū Sōshi Nanka shinkyō shūei 敦煌本郭象注莊子南華眞經輯影. Fukui kambun gakkai 福井漢文學會, 1960.

Tz'u-t'ung 辭通
   Edited by Chu Ch'i-feng 朱起鳳. Taipei, 1960.

Wang Hsien-ch'ien 王先謙
   Chuang-tzu chi-chieh 莊子集解. Hong Kong, 1960. CTCC (a) v. 26.

Wang K'ai-yün 王闓運
   Chuang-tzu nei-p'ien chu 莊子內篇註. CTCC (b) v. 36.

Wang Nien-sun 王念孫
   Tu-shu tsa-chih 讀書雜志. CTCC (b) v. 36.

Wang Shu-min 王叔岷
   Chuang-tzu chiao-shih 莊子校釋. Taipei, 1972.

Watson, Burton
   The Complete Works of Chuang Tzu. New York and London, 1968.

Wen Yi-to 聞一多
   (1) *Ku-tien hsin-yi* 古典新義. Peking, 1956.
   (2) *Chuang-tzu nei-p'ien chiao-shih* 莊子內篇校釋. CTCC (b) v. 42.

Wu Ju-lun 吳汝綸
   Chuang-tzu tien k'an 莊子點勘. CTCC (a) v. 26.

Wu Yen-hsü 武延緒
   Chuang-tzu cha-chi 莊子札記. CTCC (b) v. 40.

Yang Shu-ta 楊樹達
   Chuang-tzu shih-i 莊子拾遺. CTCC (a) v. 30.

Yen Ling-feng 嚴靈峰
   (1) *Lao Lieh Chuang san-tzu chih-chien shu-mu* 老列莊三子知見書目. Taipei, 1965.
   (2) *Tao-chia ssu tzu hsin pien* 道家四子新編.

Yü Hsing-wu 于省吾
   Shuang chien ch'ih chu-tzu hsin-cheng 雙劍誃諸子新證. Peking, 1962. CTCC (a) v. 30.

Yü Yüeh 俞樾
   Chu-tzu p'ing yi 諸子平議. Peking, 1954. CTCC (b) v. 36.

CTIC Part 2, Chapter 1 (*Chuang Tzu* 1)

43 HYCT 1/1 Measurement of *ta* 大 'size' is by circumference. (G3: 379)

1/2ff. The P'eng episode shows signs of textual confusion, due either to Chuang Tzu failing to tidy up his draft or to an editor expanding with interpolations of his own. The two phrases (南冥者天池也) (齊諧者志怪者也) look like afterthoughts of Chuang Tzu or later glosses. There are two more such additions, in HYCT 11/4, 19, which, like the second phrase here, seem to comment on sentences still to come, suggesting that they have entered the text too early.

1/3 諧 'tall story' Chu Kuei-yao, 5.

1/3 (野馬也，塵埃也，生物之氣相吹也。)
This is probably another addition incorporated too early in the text, for it seems to be describing what the P'eng sees below him, obscuring the earth and making it indistinguishable from the sky.

1/5...則已矣 1/19...斯已矣
"...then ceases (rises no higher)." Cf. also 19/59; 23/66. There is no evidence in *Chuang Tzu* of either being used as a mere particle combination like 而已矣 'only.'

1/7, 8, 12 乃今 'only now,' as also in 4/71; 7/1; 11/56; 14/61; 23/43.

44 1/8 槍榆枋 <而止> Ch'üeh-wu variant supported by early quotations, cf. Ch'en Ku-ying, 9.

1/13–17 In this lengthy parenthesis an editor may be introducing a parallel noticed by himself, or an alternative draft by Chuang Tzu, or an extract from Chuang Tzu's source found among his notes.

1/17 比＝庇 following Wu Ju-lun (as in 17/9).

1/19 Cf. 1/5 above.

1/19 (彼其於世，未數數然也) (雖然，猶有未樹也)
As in 1/2ff., the two phrases look like interpolations, the latter of which comments on what follows, implying that it has been incorporated in

the text too early. Comparison with 1/20 confirms that the former refers to Sung Jung but suggests that the latter applies to Lieh Tzu.

1/19, 20 *Shu-'shu-jan* 數 數 然

I know no other examples of this expression, and with an otherwise un-attested reduplicative one can only guess from context. Ssu-ma Piao's explanation (as *chi-chi* 汲 汲 'fretful') would no doubt be such a guess, although editors have continued to repeat it in the absence of anything better. When the interpolations in 1/19 are identified the context becomes plainer; it implies that *shu-shu-jan* is descriptive of the detachment from worldly concerns which Sung Jung failed to attain.

45   ### 1/23 夫 子 立 而 天 下 治

Literally, "While you, sir, 'stand,' the empire is well ordered." *Li* 立 'stand' might be expected to refer to the occupation of a throne or a court position. Yet it is difficult to accept the customary interpretation as a contra-factual "If you took the throne the world would be well ordered" (Watson, p. 32), since (1) The contra-factual seems to demand a stronger particle, such as *shih* 使 'supposing that,' not a mere *erh* 而. (2) The whole context suggests that the empire is already in order through Hsü Yu's influence, so that Yao's position has become a mere formality. Cf. 28/5, where an offer of the throne by Shun is refused with the words 予 立 於 宇 宙 之 中 "All Space and Time are the court in which I stand."

1/25 爲 (賓) *實 乎   following Yü Yüeh.

46   1/28 遷 庭 binome, 'outrageous,' following Chu Kuei-yao, 19ff.

1/32 The otherwise rare word *ch'i* 薪 is used frequently in *Chuang Tzu* of deep urges independent of the will (G4: 337ff.), so that there is no difficulty about understanding the phrase 世 薪 乎 亂 as "the age has an incessant urge towards misrule."

CTIC Part 2, Chapter 2 (*Chuang Tzu* 2)

48   2/4 *Wei wu* 唯 無 Chu Kuei-yao, 39ff., points out another example in 4/9. The comparison suggests that in *Chuang Tzu* (although not in *Mo Tzu*, where the same combination is frequent) *wei wu* means 'If only it would not....'

2/5 畏 佳 = 鬼 崔 Chu Kuei-yao, 41.

49 2/8 (刁) * 勺 Chu Kuei-yao, 44.

2/9 夫吹萬不同，而使其自已也咸 (= 緘)，其自取 <也> 怒者, 誰邪.

Literally "Who is the one who puffs out the myriad dissimilars, and causes that when they end themselves they are sealed away, when they choose themselves they burst forth?" Wen Yi-to (Wen 242) was the first to offer a convincing punctuation of this sentence by identifying the word *chien* 緘 'seal up' of 1/12, here written without the radical (咸) as in the Ssu-ma Piao text of HYCT 14/2. The word was previously assumed to be the preverbal particle *hsien* 咸 'all,' imposing a punctuation which hardly allows a coherent interpretation: 使其自 已也，咸其自取. But in any case *hsien* is a pre-classical particle superseded by *chieh* 皆 'all' (it was only later that it returned as an archaism borrowed from the *Book of Documents* sanctified as a classic). It is never used in *Chuang Tzu*, although it is once mentioned as a word (HYCT 22/47 周遍咸三者，異名同實 "*Chou, pien, hsien,* the three of them, are different names for one substance").

It is likely that the introductory poem of *Cycles of Heaven* in the "outer chapters" (HYCT 14/1–4) was originally the conclusion of the Tzu-ch'i episode (2/1–9). The Buddhist *Chih-kuan fu-hsing ch'uan-hung chüeh* 止觀輔行傳弘決 of Ching Hsi 荊溪 (A.D. 711–781) cites it as from the "inner chapters" (*Taishō Tripitaka* No. 1912, p. 440C). Since the Buddhist is distinguishing the themes of the "inner" and "outer" chapters and using the poem to illustrate the theme of spontaneity in the former, this can hardly be a mere slip. Presumably when Kuo Hsiang abridged *Chuang Tzu* he cut the poem out of the "inner chapters" as a duplicate of the opening section of *Cycles of Heaven*, where it would be immovable because it provides the chapter title. The poem fits very neatly onto the end of the Tzu-ch'i dialogue:

1. The final reply of Tzu-ch'i breaks off after a single sentence and can hardly be complete; one would expect the dialogue to lead up to a grand climax.

2. The poem carries on Tzu-ch'i's question about who it is that causes things to begin and end, with the same metaphor of a wind blowing through everything.

3. As in the first two episodes of chapter 2, the ending of things is described in terms of 'stopping of themselves' (14/2 自 止 ; similar to 2/9 自 已) and being 'sealed up' (14/2 緘, variant 咸 in Ssu-ma Piao's text; similar to 2/9 咸, 2/12 緘); we also find the metaphor of the trigger which starts things off (機 14/2 cf. 2/11).

50   2/9 炎 = 淡 Li text variant. (NB: Li text as cited in Lu Te-ming).

2/10 詹 詹 'verbose' Chu Kuei-yao, 47.

2/12 所 爲 之 Unless the sentence is corrupt, this must be taken as 'that in (/from) which it does it' (the source out of which the heart's activities come). Cf. note on 2/14.

2/12 厭 'stop up' Chu Kuei-yao, 50.

2/13 溢 'dry up' Ch'ien Mu, 10.

2/13 姚 佚 啓 態 Rather than force this into the pattern of pairs of contrasting words in the previous two phrases, it seems better to understand it as "frivolously start up attitudes" (of aimless emotions initiating behavior).

2/14 旦 暮 得 此 ， 其 所 由 以 生 乎 。 Literally, "Does it (the heart) get these morning and evening from that which it came from and thereby was born?"

51   2/18 (盡) *進 following Yen Ling-feng.

52   2/27, 29 I have argued elsewhere (G2: 143ff.) that *yin shih* 因 是 (2/28, 29, 37, 39, 55; 25/55) and *wei shih* 爲 是 (2/35, 36, 47, 55; 23/63; 27/3) are contrasted technical terms of the same type as *kung shih* 公 是 (24/39) and *yi shih* 移 是 (23/62, 63, 65). All four expressions are confined to *Chuang Tzu* chapter 2 and certain closely related fragments from the "mixed chapters." I proposed "adaptive 'That's it'" for *yin shih* and "contrived 'That's it'" for *wei shih*, but am now more inclined to connect them with the technical uses of *yin* and *wei* in the *Canons* and other remains of the literature of disputation. There *wei* is the object being 'deemed' to be X if it fits the name 'X,' while yin is to 'go by' certain parts or instances as the criterion for deeming to be X (G3: 117, 126, 209ff., 214–216, 462).

The translation of *shih* as 'That's it' in chapter 2 is an inconvenience required to show its connection with the pronoun *shih* 是 ('this / it' contrasted with *pi* 彼 'that / the other') and does not, I hope, disguise the fact the syntactically I take *yin shih* and *wei shih* as nominalized pairs of verbs in which the first is subordinate to the second. *Yin shih* has a close parallel in the technical term *yin jen* 因任 'giving responsibility going by qualifications' in a Syncretist essay (13/33), also found in *Han Fei Tzu* chapter 43, 50 (Ch'en 906/3; 1093/1), as a nominalization of the verbal phrase which we find in the fuller form 因而任之 'going by qualifications he gave them responsibilities' (chapter 5, 8. Ch'en Ch'i-yu 67/3; 121/1). The first example of *yin shih* in *Chuang Tzu* may even be understood as the original coining of the term by nominalization:

2/27, 29 是亦因彼…因是因非…亦因是也 "'It' likewise goes by 'Other'…If going by something else you affirm (judge to be 'it') then going by something else you deny…This too is to affirm going by something else."

2/37 因是已。已而…cf. 3/1 殆已。已而…The repeated pattern confirms that the word at the end of one sentence and start of the next is the full verb *yi* 已 'cease.'

54 2/43 The position of *ku* 故 in the sentence is verbal; it must be understood as in 17/15 終始無故 "Ending or starting there is no staying as it was" and 17/18 知終始之不可故也 "He knows that ending or starting it cannot be kept as it was."

55 2/47 圖 = 鄙 with Wen, 246.

57 2/55 有左有右 'There is left, there is right' is implausible as the first pair in the sequence of the Eight Powers, and in the resumptive passage which follows the first key word is *ts'un* 存 (2/56). I formerly proposed to read 有在有存 (G2: 155 n.13). But the *Shih-wen* notes that the Ts'ui text read 宥 for 右. Now the Primitivist chapter *Tsai yu* 在宥 begins obscurely with the sentence 聞在宥(= 囿) 天下 "I have heard of keeping the empire in its place and within bounds" (11/1). This would be intelligible at first sight only if *tsai yu* were already a current combination. I suggest that its source is this passage, which in the Ts'ui text is corrupted only by the addition of a single stroke to one character: 有(左)*在有宥 "There is locating as there, there is enclosing with a boundary."

2/59 嗛= 誠 Chu Kuei-yao, 67.

2/60 仁 常 而 不(成) *周 a *Ch'üeh-wu* variant.

2/62 (蓨) *瑤 光 with the parallel in *Huai-nan Tzu* chapter 8 (Liu 8/7A/4; from Wen, 247).

59 2/75, 84 Granted that as rough equivalents 'extravagant' will do for *meng-lang* 孟 浪 and 'extraordinary' for *tiao-kuei* 弔 詭, there is always the problem with such binomes that their precise shade of meaning is eluding us. In this case they have something to do with the curious attitude of the two speakers to the saying ascribed to Confucius. The saying is introduced with the remark that Confucius himself thinks it only a *meng-lang chih yen* 之 言 but that it seems very profound. Confucius would be thinking of it as something he did not intend to be taken very seriously, a 'flight of fancy.' The second speaker declares it a deep and enigmatic utterance which Confucius himself would be incapable of understanding, and says that the suitable name for it is *tiao-kuei*. *Tiao-kuei* seems to be an absolutely original thought, an inspiration so unconventional that it may be foreign to the man who has it, and unappreciated and misunderstood by him. The binome occurs twice more with the first element written 誂 (for the interchange of the phonetics, cf. Chu Kuei-yao, 80): 5/29 彼 且 蘄 以 誂 詭, 幻 怪 之 名 聞 "He has an urge to become famous for being original and extraordinary": 33/67 其 辭 雖 參 差, 而 誂 詭 可 觀。 "Although his style is irregular his originalities deserve a look" (of Chuang Tzu himself). Cf. also *Lü-shih ch'un-ch'iu* chapter 5/2 (Hsü 5/8A): 俶 詭 殊 瑰, 耳 所 未 嘗 聞, 目 所 未 嘗 見 "original and strange, what the ear has never heard, what the eye has never seen" (on degenerate music).

2/77 挾 = 浹 Cf. Morohashi, 12118 sense 2/2.

60 2/92 天 倪, variant of 天 研 (the latter graph has a graphic variant 硎) 'whetstone of Heaven' (Chu Kuei-yao, 81).

2/92 振 於 無 竟, 故 寓 諸 無 竟 "Be vibrated into motion by the Limitless, and therefore find them lodging places in the Limitless." Instead of choosing between alternatives, be moved spontaneously by Heaven; instead of judging from fixed standpoints, shift between temporary standpoints. We understand *chen* 振 'shake' in the sense 'be stimulated to move,' as in the *Yüeh-ling* of the *Li-chi* (SPPY 6/2A/1). 蟄 蟲 始 振 "The hibernating insects for the first time stir," having failed to find convincing early authority for the meanings proposed by the traditional commentators (Ts'ui 止也, Ch'eng 暢也). Cf. 7/21 萌乎不振不(正)*止 "As I go on sprouting I neither vibrate nor stop" (of the mind in perfect stillness). 25/10 復命搖作，而以天爲師 "He returns to Destiny, is reverberated into motion, and takes Heaven as his authority."

61　2/95 自喻適志與.

The *Shih-wen* notes take the verb *yü* 喻 as equivalent of *yü* 愉 'happy,' and the final particle as exclamatory: "In spontaneous joy he pleased his own fancy!" Kuo Hsiang already understood the sentence in this way, and he has been generally followed. However, throughout pre-Han classical literature the final particle *yü* is not exclamatory but interrogative, equivalent to *yeh hu* 也乎 ('Is it that...?'), and the verb *yü* has the sense of 'understand/cause to understand.' In *Hsün Tzu's* "Right use of names" the verb *yü* is employed more than once of names showing what something is, cf. *Hsün Tzu* chapter 22 (Liang 314/3) 單足以喻則單，單不足以喻則兼 "If a single one is sufficient to show what it is, let it be single; if a single one is not sufficient to show what it is, then compound." We find the same usage in the present chapter of *Chuang Tzu*: 2/31ff. 以馬喻馬之非馬 "by means of a horse show that horse is non-horse." I formerly translated the sentence "Was he showing himself what it would please him to be?" (G2: 159) but now prefer an interpretation close to that of the Ch'eng sub-commentary: "Was it that in showing what he was spontaneously he suited his own fancy?" No longer bound by the dichotomies of the logicians, ox and non-ox, horse and non-horse, Chuang Tzu can please himself whether he is a man or butterfly. Cf. 7/3 一以己爲馬，一以己爲牛 "At one time he deemed himself a horse, at another an ox." The sentence is parenthetic, and should perhaps be rejected as a gloss (with Liu Wen-tien).

CTIC Part 2, Chapter 3 (*Chuang Tzu* 3)

62　3/1 Cf. 2/37 above.

3/1ff. The brevity and scrappiness of chapter 3 suggest mutilation, and these lines look like the ruins of an introductory essay. Three more fragments (24/105–111; 32/50–52; 24/103–105) can be recognized tacked on to the ends of chapter 24 and 32 in the "mixed chapters." (I formerly proposed as a further fragment 25/51–54, cf. G6: 473, but have since lost confidence in it.) Apart from general similarities in theme, we may note the following links in phrasing between the fragments and between them and the start of chapter 3 (3/1ff.) and the next episode, the story of Cook Ting (3/2–12):

3/1 有 / 無 涯 'with/without confines'; cf. 24/109ff. 有 / 無 涯 'with/without confines.'

3/1 殆 'dangerous' (of knowledge); cf. 24/103 (of exercise of senses and heart).

24/107, 108, 109, 111 解 'unravel' (of problems); cf. 3/2, 6, 11 解 'dismember' (of an ox—but how to carve is for a Taoist a paradigmatic problem).

24/106 恃 其 所 不 知 "depend on what one does not know" (good); cf. 32/51 恃 其 所 見 "depend on what one sees" (bad).

3/6 神 / / 目 (daemon preferred to eye); cf. 32/51 神 / / 明 (daemon preferred to eyesight) and 24/103: 故 目 之 於 明 也 殆 "Therefore the eye's capacity for sight presents dangers."

63   On a transposed fragment, we may note: 24/111 頡 滑 The only firm evidence for the meaning of this phrase is 10/36 頡 滑 堅 白 ， 解 垢 同 異 "wrench apart (?) the hard and the white, jumble together (?) the same and the different," a stronger variation on the formula 合 同 異 ， 離 堅 白 (17/66) "combine the same and the different, separate the hard and the white."

24/111 揚 推 'total number, sum of all.' See the examples assembled in *Tz'u t'ung* 2298.

64   3/12 Both here and in the obscure 23/76 *Chieh*/* KĂD 介 has been understood as 'one legged' (an extension of its sense of 'single, unique') by editors ever since Kuo Hsiang and his contemporaries in the *Shih-wen*. The *Shih-wen* notes that some give it the reading *wu*/*ngwăt 兀 ('chop foot'), and that the two graphs appear as variant for each other here and in 5/23; 23/76. However, the phonetic difference and graphic resemblance of the two suggest that this can be no more than an accident of textual corruption. Is it really necessary to read the Kung-wen Hsüan story in the light of the tales of men with chopped feet in chapter 5? It makes much better sense if we take him as singular, unique in appearance or character. The meaning 'one-footed' has entered the

dictionary solely on the authority of *Chuang Tzu* (cf. Morohashi, 359 def. 19), although the meaning 'single' is well attested (def. 17, 18), and there is a case of it in 23/10 夫 函 車 之 獸 ， 介 而 離 山 ， 則 不 免 于 罔 罟 之 患 "The beast big enough to swallow a carriage, if it leaves the mountain by itself, will not escape the perils of the trap."

3/14 神 雖 王 不 善 也 "The daemon does not find even kingship good" (sees even occupying a throne as an imprisonment). This interpretation assumes that the pattern 雖...不 善 functions as in 31/25 雖 善 不 善 "Even the good he does not find good."

65   3/15 始 也 吾 以 爲 其 人 也 ， 而 今 非 也 "I used to think of him as the man, but now he is not" (expressing disappointment over Lao Tan). The rival interpretation "I used to think of him as a man..." (but in dying he has ceased to belong to humanity) is tempting, but the *ch'i* 其 becomes difficult to account for. A modal *ch'i* marking the preferred alternative is common in the "inner chapters," and Ma Hsü-lun notes a possible parallel: 3/12 天 與 ， 其 人 與 "Is it from Heaven? Or is it rather from man?" However, there the modal *ch'i* precedes a main clause; one would not expect it in an auxiliary phrase after *yi wei* 以 爲 'think of as.'

3/19 I understand this much debated passage in terms of the terminology of disputation:

1. *Chih* 指 'meaning,' what is pointed out by means of a name (G3: 458–460) cf. 22/47 周 遍 咸 ， 三 者 ， 異 名 同 實 ， 其 指 一 也 "*Chou, pien, hsien*, these three are different names for the same object, their meaning is one."

2. *Wei* 爲 be 'deemed' the thing the name of which it fits (cf. on 2/27–29 above). Then taking *chin* 盡 in the sense of 'cinders' (Morohashi, 23029 def. 9 燼), of which there is a probable example in *Canons* A 85 (G3: 332), we have 指 窮 於 爲 薪 ， 火 傳 也 ， 不 知 其 盡 也 "If the meaning is confined to what is deemed 'firewood,' when the fire passes on from one piece to the next we do not know that it is the 'cinders.'"

If we confine the meaning of 'living' to what we pick out from the constantly changing totality by means of the name 'living,' we find ourselves assuming that at death it comes to an end, do not recognize that it is the same as what at the next stage in the endless process of transformation we call the 'dead.'

CTIC Part 2, Chapter 4 (*Chuang Tzu* 4)

66   4/2 死 者 以 國 量，(乎 澤) *若 *燒 若 蕉 (= 焦) "The whole state is full of dead men, as though it had been ravaged by fire and slaughter." Chu Kuei-yao (101) identified the idioms in this corrupt passage, but no fully satisfactory emendation has been proposed. The present proposal is rather a case of cutting the Gordian knot; it incorporates two formulae illustrated by Chu Kuei-yao:

   1. Cf. *Huai-nan Tzu* chapter 13 (Liu 13/12A/3): 道 路 死 人 以 溝 量 "The ditches were full of men who died on the road"; and

   2. *Hsün Tzu* (chapter 10) Liang 127/2 天 下 敖 然，若 燒 若 焦. "The empire is ravaged as though it were burned up, as though it were scorched."

   However, it ignores a third (*Lü-shih ch'un-ch'iu* chapter 21/3, Hsü 21/7B 其 死 者 量 於 澤 矣 "The woodlands are full of dead men"). The corruption may have been caused by the wrong idiom leaping into the copyist's head, but very probably we have only the remains of a mutilated passage: 死 者 以 國 量，...量 乎 澤，...若 焦

4/3 願 以 所 聞 思 其 <所 行>，則...Restored from a *Ch'üeh-wu* variant.

4/5 且 若 亦 知 夫 德 之 所 蕩 而 知 之 所 為 出 乎 哉。德 蕩 乎 名，知 出 乎 爭。 "Besides do you after all understand that the thing by which the Power in us is dissipated is the very thing by which knowledge is made to issue forth? The Power goes on being dissipated in making your name, knowledge goes on issuing from strife."

When both X and Y are nominalized, the pattern 'X *erh* 而 Y' is only intelligible as: 'Being X, it is Y' / 'X is the very same thing as Y.' The use of *so* 所 for the agent before a passive verb is remarkable (cf. 2/15 不 知 其 所 為 使 "We do not know by what it is caused").

4/9 (詔) *詻 Ts'ui text variant.

67 4/12 以 [下] 拂 其 上 者 也 Delete with Ch'ien Mu, 28.

4/17 譽 'estimate, appreciate' Morohashi, 35344 def. 1/4.

68 4/19 蘄 The post-verbal aspectual particle *hu* is here inceptive: *ch'i-hu* 'get carried away by an urge' (G4: 337ff.).

4/23 (諜) *媒, emended following Kao Heng, 13 A.

4/24 有 <心> 而 爲 之 *Ch'üeh-wu* variant.

4/26 若 一 志 'Unify your intent.' Liu Wen-tien transposes the first two words. But cf. 4/73 若 無 言 "Don't speak, you!"

69 4/28 實 自 回 也 "The deed derives from Hui." Throughout this dialogue Hui is being warned against the temptation of pursuing a good name (名, 4/6, 7, 13, 14, 29) and great deeds (實, 4/14 three times). At first sight it may seem more natural to take the first word as the adverbial *shih* 'really.' But the adverbial *shih* does not exist in literature before *Han Fei Tzu*, and even there *shih* 'in reality' is almost always contrasting with *ming* 名 'in name,' the usage out of which the adverbial function may be assumed to have developed. The pre-verbal *shih* in texts down to the *Tso chuan* is an archaic demonstrative cognate with *shih* 是, used to resume and emphasize the subject (Pulleyblank op. cit). The *shih* 'really' in the standard text of *Mo Tzu* was substituted for *ch'eng*, 誠 to avoid a Sung taboo, as is regularly confirmed by pre-Sung quotations (Lüan T'iao-fu, 155).

4/30 (毒) *實 an emendation of Hsi T'ung.

4/32 闋 The meaning 'empty' has entered the dictionary (cf. Morohashi, 41430 def. 1/7) only on the authority of commentators on this instance, who have gone on repeating the explanation of Ssu-ma Piao. *Ch'üeh* 闋 is defined in the *Shuo-wen* as 'shut the door when business is over' 事 已 閉 門. It is most firmly attested of the concluding of musical performances (cf. def. 1/4). Cf. also *Songs* 191/5, 君 子 如 屆 ， 俾 民 心 闋 "If noble men are moderate, the hearts of the people are set at rest" (Karlgren). It may be noticed that the phrase 瞻 彼 闋 者 follows a common formula in the *Songs* (cf. *Songs* 33/3 瞻 彼 日 月 "Look up at that sun and moon"), and is the first of the four-syllable lines of a quatrain (although imperfectly rhymed). I propose to translate: "Look up at the easer of our toil" (the Tao seen after the analogy of a ruler bringing rest to his people).

4/32 夫且不止 "The about to be does not stay still." The topic-marker
fu 夫 seems to be marking off a nominalized *ch'ieh* 且 'the about to
be.' This may seem implausible, but Chuang Tzu is familiar with the art
of disputation, in which *ch'ieh* attracted attention as a concept; a Mohist
Canon (A 33) defines it and also uses it as a full verb: 方然亦且
"The just now so too is about to be." The quatrain is describing a state
of perfect stillness in which "the about to be does not stay still," and
this is what Chuang Tzu proceeds to name 坐馳 "going at a gallop
while you sit." Missing this point, commentators since Kuo Hsiang
have assumed that 'going at a gallop while you sit' is an undesirable
state of mental restlessness, in spite of clear evidence to the contrary in
Huai-nan Tzu chapter 6 (Liu 6/5A/5) 故卻走馬以糞，而車
軌不接於遠方之外。是謂坐馳陸沈。 (Of the sage's
government) "Therefore swift steeds are retired to manure the fields (cf.
Lao Tzu 46) and carriage ruts do not cross in distant regions (cf.
Chuang Tzu 10/34): this is called 'going at a gallop as you sit' and
'submerging on dry land'" (joining two metaphors for desirable states
from *Chuang Tzu*, the latter from 25/35). The 'about to be' is what you
are on the point of doing if you do not pause to reflect; cf. 12/38 且然
無間謂之命 "What is about to be so without an interval (that is,
without intervening thought) is Destiny." This concept throws light on
two obscure passages related in theme:

6/80 是自其所以乃且也，相與吾之耳矣。
   "It is simply that, all the way up from that by which they are 'about
   to,' being together with them he treats them as 'I.'"

23/50ff. 與物窮者，物入焉。與物且者，其身之
不能容，焉能容人。不能容人者，無親。無
親者盡人。

   "Whoever is with other things in having limits, other things enter inside [possessions or other people's opinions become part of him].
   Whoever is with other things in 'being about to' [in surrendering to
   spontaneity] has no room even for a self of his own, let alone for
   other men. Whoever has no room in him for other men is no more
   kin to one than another; whoever is no more kin to one than another
   leaves no-one out."

   Cf. also a sentence which from its context is plainly about spontaneously moving forward from day to day, but where the word seems at
   first sight to be *ts'u* 徂 'go to':

21/21 丘 以 是 日 徂 (Variant 疽), "In this way I am from day to day 'about to.'"

Here the radical may be ignored, because *ts'u* is a pre-classical word never used in *Chuang Tzu*, nor anywhere in pre-Han classical literature except in quotations from the *Documents* or *Songs*.

70 4/36 凡 事 若 小 若 大， 寡 不 (道) *迫 以 (懼) *勸 成。
"There are few enterprises great or small in which we are not under pressure to push for success." I propose this emendation on the evidence of an instance of 勸 成 'push for success' later in the same story (4/52).

CTIC Part 2, Chapter 5 (*Chuang Tzu* 5)

77 5/17 子 而 悦 子 之 執 政 而 後 人 者 也。

"It will be someone who, being you, is pleased that you are Prime Minister and turns his back on other people." The repeated *erh* deserves attention, not as a grammatical anomaly but as a feat of style.

78 5/18 乃 = 仍 Wang K'ai-yün.

5/18 今 子 之 所 取 (=最) 大 者，先 生 也。
"The one whom you now think greatest is the Master." Cf. 19/34 人 之 所 取 (*Ch'üeh-wu* variant 最) 畏 者 "The things which men most dread..."

5/19, 20 狀 = 妝 Kao Heng, 16B.

5/21 遊 於 羿 之 彀 中 [中 央 者 中 地 也] 然 而 不 中 者 命 也. "To stray within the range of Yi's bow and not be hit is destiny." The bracketed phrase ("The center is the central land") is surely a gloss. But it looks like a comment, not on the 'within' (中) of the present passage, but on 7/33 中 央 之 帝 爲 渾 沌 "The emperor of the center was Hun-t'un."

5/22...以 善 邪。 <吾 之 自 寤 邪> *Ch'üeh-wu* variant.

79 5/24–31 A troubling parenthesis in chapter 6 (6/17–19) is surely a commentary on this story of Confucius and the man with the chopped foot. Note especially the reference to Confucius, by his personal name *Ch'iu* 丘, and to "people who have their feet" (有 足 者). Its form,

with a series of propositions repeated and annotated one by one, has parallels in 4/17–22; 24/88–95; 27/1–10.

5/41–52 In this area there is considerable evidence of textual dislocation:

1. At the start there is nothing to prepare for the abrupt leap from coffin plumes and shoes to Imperial concubines and a new bridegroom illustrating an entirely new theme. At the end we have a closely related passage placed after the conclusion of the story (5/49–52); I propose to shift it to the gap at the beginning.

2. The final exchange in the dialogue (5/46ff.) is a disappointingly meager and scrappy answer to the culminating question. Now at the end of chapter 24 in the "mixed chapters" there is a string of fragments, the last five of which are apparently put together only because fortuitously they all begin with *ku* 故 'therefore…' (24/100ff., 101ff., 103–105, 105–111; a further *ku* in line 104 does seem integral to an argument). We have already identified the last two fragments as from the remains of the introductory essay of chapter 2. The two preceding bits (24/101ff., 102ff.) are appropriate to the gap here. So is a puzzling fragment embedded in the story of Lieh Tzu and the shaman in chapter 7 (7/26ff.), found in a longer form in the parallel in *Lieh Tzu* chapter 2 (Yang, 45/4–13). Yü Yüeh already recognized it (Yü, 310) as a misplaced strip, and suggested that the abridger of *Chuang Tzu* cut it down to give the illusion of fitting the context. (The fit is in fact so poor that I was surely wrong in G1: 51 in taking the opposite view that the *Lieh Tzu* version is an expansion.)

3. The final section of the chapter (5/52–60) starts with *ku* 故, a word which, although its scope ranges from the strict logical connection of English 'therefore' to the looser ones marked in English by 'so, thus, then,' certainly cannot introduce a new episode which (as seems to be the case here) has no connection at all with what precedes. Something must have been lost in the dislocation of 5/41–52, which I tentatively identify as another "mixed chapter" item, 23/66ff.

For 5/41–52, then, we substitute:

5/49–52	68 characters
5/41–47	194
24/101ff.	42

Lieh Tzu (Yang 45/4–13)	59
24/102ff.	19 (+59=78)
5/47–49	83
23/66ff.	42

Taking the number of characters to a strip as about forty, we could treat the *Lieh Tzu* piece and 24/102ff. as two strips with the second broken in the middle, and identify 5/49–52 as incomplete. The figure of forty is firmly attested for stages in the text of *Mo Tzu* and of the *Mu T'ien-tzu chuan* (G3: 89ff.). However, I nowadays have rather less confidence in these mathematical games than in the past. The Han strips from Wu-wei and Lin-yi show no preference for the figure forty and the numbers of graphs on successive strips of the same length vary widely. The fragments used in reconstructing the beginning of chapter 3 (which may of course have been dislocated in another manuscript) show no obvious mathematical regularity.

80 5/50, 51 其 脰 肩 肩 "Their necks were too scrawny." The repetition of the clause without variation is surprising, and the word 脰 'neck' is appropriate only to the second cripple, who has a goiter; in the former instance I emend it to *hsing* 脛 'leg.'

5/44 規 = 闚 Ma Hsü-lun.

5/45 *Tui* 兌 'opening' as in *Lao Tzu* 52, 56 (Ch'ien Mu, 44).

81 7/26 (=*Lieh Tzu* Yang 45/4–13), 24/102. In both passages the graph 審 evidently represents the same word, which in *Lieh Tzu* is written 潘 (also the reading of the Ts'ui text of 7/26). Both Ssu-ma Piao on 7/26 and the *Lieh-tzu shih-wen* identified the word as *p'an* 蟠 'coil round' (the metaphor is of a snake coiling all the way round a border) cf. 15/19 精神四達並流，無所不極，上際於天，下 蟠於地。 "The quintessential and daemonic streams in all directions and reaches everywhere, borders Heaven above and coils round earth below." I take the word to refer to the water filling the irregular contour of the ground.

5/45 不付入於靈府。使之和豫...

"They are not to be admitted to the Magic Storehouse. To ensure that it (what issues from the Storehouse) is in peace and joy..."

The jump from the Magic Storehouse, the reservoir of all inner resources, to what issues from it, is not too abrupt. Cf. 2/61:

此之謂天府。注焉而不滿，酌焉而不竭，而不知其所由來。

"It is this that is called the Storehouse of Heaven. Pour into it and it does not fill, draw out from it and it is not drained, and we do not know from what source it comes."

5/47 (脩) *= 循 The latter graph has the former as variant in 6/17; 12/9. The graphs are often confused in *Mo Tzu* (cf. G3: 81) and other texts at some stage written in 'clerk's script,' in which they are nearly indistinguishable.

CTIC Part 2, Chapter 6 (*Chuang Tzu* 6)

84   6/4 不(謨) (士) *謀 *事 "They did not plan affairs," with Chu Kuei-yao, 153.

6/9 (捐) *損 Chu Kuei-yao, 156.

6/10 (志) *忘 Wang Shu-min

85   6/11–24 This is another area of textual dislocation. There are three incongruous intrusions from elsewhere:

  1. 6/11–14, recognized as misplaced by Wen Yi-to (265ff.). It may be a comment on 6/82–89.

  2. 6/17–19, rejected by Fukunaga, 269ff., who is however mistaken in taking the references to punishment and rites as incompatible with Chuang Tzu's thought. They turn out to have no general application when the passage is recognized as a comment on the story of Confucius and Choptoes (cf. on 5/24–31 above).

  3. 6/22–24 The little episode of the fish on dry land (repeated in 14/59ff.) is much more appropriately placed in 6/73.

Among the fragments at the end of chapter 24 which we have already twice pillaged (cf. on 3/1ff., 5/41–52), there are a couple in reversed order which must belong here:

24/97ff. + 96ff.: 古之真人，以天待之，不以人入天。古之真人，／以目視目，以耳聽耳，以心復心。若然者，其平也繩，其變也循。

The evidence is in the conjunction of the phrases 古 之 眞 人 and 若 然 者, and in the rhythm of clauses grouped in threes, both characteristic of 6/1–20.

We arrange as follows:
6/1–11
6/14–17
24/97ff., 96ff.
6/19–22

6/12 天 時 reverse as 時(= 伺)天 (Ma Hsü-lun), as implied by Kuo commentary and Ch'eng sub-commentary.

6/14–17 One is tempted to ignore this rhapsody as unintelligible. The translation assumes the following identifications of obscure words, several very dubious:

line 14 義 = 峨, 朋 = 崩 Yü Yüeh

line 15 與 = 樏 Ch'en Ku-ying

　　　　崔 = 催 Ch'en Ku-ying

line 16 與 = 豫 Chu Kuei-yao

　　　　(厲) *廣 Ts'ui text variant

87　6/43 攖 寧 也 者，攖 而 後 成 者 也。

On the explanation of *ying* 攖 in the sub-commentary as 'disturb' (擾 動) we should have to translate something like "The 'stable in disturbance' is what comes about only after being disturbed." But this is a strange description of what seems to be the Tao itself, and in any case there is nothing about disturbance in the whole dialogue. The word *ying* in the sense of 'disturb' seems to be used primarily of intrusion into an already occupied space (G3: 314). In the geometrical *Canons* it is the word for 'coincide' (A 67–69), and is defined as 'occupy each other' (相 得), with the comment: "Hardness and whiteness in coinciding exhaust each other, countables in coinciding do not exhaust each other." (堅 白 之 攖 相 盡，體 攖 不 相 盡) It could well be said that there is no Way without something going along it, cf. 2/33 道 行 之 而 成 "The Way comes about in being walked." We translate: "The 'at home where it intrudes' is that which comes about only where it intrudes into the place of something else."

6/61 (友) *語

89 6/69 假 於 異 物 ， 託 於 同 體 "borrow right of way through the things which are different, put up for the night in the body which is the same" cf. 14/51 假 道 於 仁 ， 託 宿 於 義 "borrow right of way through Kindness, put up for the night in Duty."

90 6/72 *Tsao* 造 'make' seems to have originated in a causative usage of *ts'ao* 造 'go to,' and to retain the basic sense of 'set going.' Cf. *Songs* 250/4 :

乃 造 其 曹 ， 執 豕 于 牢 。 "He sent out his servants to take a swine from the pen" (Karlgren), and *Mencius* 8/14:

君 子 深 造 之 以 道 ， 欲 其 自 得 之 也 。

"When the gentleman makes it go deep in by means of the Way, it's that he wants to grasp it in himself."

I take Chuang Tzu's image to be of swarming fish spontaneously avoiding each other as they wind in and out; they "set each other's directions" (相 造). This makes it the perfect metaphor for the spontaneous harmony of the ideal Taoist community.

6/77 唯 簡 之 不 得 ， 夫 已 有 所 簡 矣 。

"If you merely simplify it (knowledge) you don't succeed, to get rid of it altogether does simplify something."

This interpretation takes the *fu* 夫 as marking *yi* 已 as topic, as with *ch'ieh* 且 in 4/32.

91 6/80 是 自 其 所 以 乃 且 也 相 與 吾 之 耳 矣 。

"It is simply that all the way up from that on which we depend for momentary tendency (lit. 'being about to') he is with him in recognizing him as 'I'."

This proposal of Chu Kuei-yao (185) is supported by the observations on 'being about to' under 4/32 above. Other editors punctuate after 其 所 以 乃 "the reason why it is like this," taking *nai* as a full verb, 'like this' (equivalent to 如 此). But even P'ei Hsüeh-hai (494), who admits this supposed meaning of *nai*, finds only two more highly dubious examples, both of them pre-verbal.

6/88 (義) *戻 with parallel in 13/12 (Yang Shu-ta).

92   6/90 仁義 is exchanged with 6/91 禮樂 in the parallel in *Huai-nan Tzu* chapter 12 (Liu 12/19B/1–3), a superior order for the development as narrative (Wang Shu-min).

CTIC Part 2, Chapter 7 (*Chuang Tzu* 7)

97   7/12 萌乎不震不正止

"As they went on sprouting they were without vibration but without pause."

Meng-hu 萌乎 'going on sprouting,' with post-verbal *hu* marking continuative aspect, is a verbal phrase preceding and dependent on the main verb. For this construction cf. G4: 326, example # 48. 止 for the last word is the reading of the Ts'ui text and of the parallel in *Lieh Tzu* chapter 2 (Yang 44/5).

7/15 化= 貨 Chu Kuei-yao, 201.

7/19 信= 伸 Wang Hsien-ch'ien.

7/22 (全) *灰然 with parallel in *Lieh Tzu* (Yang 44/4) "The ash is aflame" (然= 燃)

7/26 莫 (勝) *朕 with the parallel in *Lieh Tzu* (Yang 45/3).

7/26ff. Delete. Cf. 5/41–52 above.

7/29 (流) *隨 Ts'ui text variant, confirmed by rhyme.

98   7/31 紛而封 (哉) *戎

The emendation is a Ts'ui text variant, supported by the *Lieh Tzu* parallel (Yang 46/2), and confirmed by rhyme. But *feng-jung* 封戎 is an otherwise unattested binome (cf. *Tz'u t'ung* 0010), so that a translation of this four-word line of verse can hardly pretend to be more than a conjectural filling of the space.

CTIC Part 2, Chapter 8 (Passages Related to the "Inner Chapters")

101   24/46 蹢= 謫

24/46 束縛 'tie up (prisoner)' Morohashi, 14480/52.

24/47 遺類 'overlooked category.' In disputation *yi* 遺 is used for overlooking in argument (G3: 192–194).

102 27/12 而其<口雖言，其心>未之嘗言 Restored from parallel in 25/34ff.

25/53 且無所逃 "There will be nowhere you can escape from it (from the undivided totality)." Cf. 23/74: 以天下爲之籠，則雀無所逃
"If you treat the whole world as the cage for it, the sparrow has nowhere to escape to."

25/53 此所謂然與然乎 "Is this what one calls 'the alternative which is so together with the alternative which is so'?" Cf. 2/90ff. 然不然…然若果然也，然之異乎不然也無辯。

"Treat as so even what is not so…If the so is really so, there will no longer be a difference for disputation from what is not so." But if you *do* insist on distinguishing alternatives, both of them will have to be "so."

23/52 道通，其分也<成也> Restored from Kōzanji MS and parallel in 2/35.

103 23/43 人見其人，<物見其物> Restored from *Ch'üeh-wu* variant, supported by Kuo Hsiang commentary.

23/43 (脩) *循 Ma Hsü-lun. Cf. on 5/47 above.

104 23/61 (守) *宗 *Ch'üeh-wu* variant.

23/61 (戴) *代 Chang Ping-lin.

23/61 (甲) *屈 Ma Hsü-lun.

23/63 爲是舉移是 "A *shih* which deems picks out *shih* as it moves" cf. 2/35 : 故爲是舉莛與楹 "Therefore when a *shih* which deems picks out a stalk from a pillar…"

105 24/63 我必先之…若我而不 (有) *先之…Corrected on grounds of parallelism.

27/17 五年而<神>來 Ch'ien Mu, 230.

27/18ff. 生有 (=又) 爲死也。勘公，以其<私>死也。Restored from the *Ch'üeh-wu* variant, supported by both Kuo commentary and Ch'eng sub-commentary.

106 27/1 重 言 'Weighted saying,' saying for which the authority is the degree of experience behind the speaker. Modern editors tend to assume that it is cited from an ancient sage, but it is notable that the older commentators, Kuo Hsiang and Ch'eng Hsüan-ying, did not think so. The account in lines 3ff. is not of a sage but of a speaker whose credentials other than old age need critical examination. *Below in the Empire* distinguishes weighted saying from the other two types as the most 'genuine' (33/65 眞), which surely implies that the speaker is not citing but speaking in person. In any case Chuang Tzu is conspicuous as a writer who never backs his claims by quotations from the *Documents* and *Songs* or from commonly acknowledged sayings of Confucius and Lao Tzu. He delights in devising frankly imaginary conversations in which Confucius improbably expresses his own opinions, but this hardly amounts to hiding behind the sage's authority.

27/3 所 以 己 言 也 "It is what you say on your own authority." The textual tradition of *Chuang Tzu* has blurred the graphic distinction between *chi* 己 'self' and *yi* 已 'cease,' and different editions seem quite indiscriminate in which they choose in this sentence. But both Kuo Hsiang and Ch'eng Hsüan-ying read *chi*, which therefore has the oldest textual authority. Most modern editors read *yi* and understand the sentence as, "It is the means of putting an end to saying," but apparently without other guidance than the assumption that weighted saying has not one's own but a sage's authority. Cf. 4/19 以 己 言 "speak on one's own authority," 7/4ff. 以 己 出 經 式 義 度 "issue on one's own authority rules, conventions, forms and regulations."

107 27/6 ＜言＞無言。言無言，終身言，未嘗 [不] 言。Both emendations follow the Kōzanji MS.

108 32/12 Ti 翟 is the personal name of Mo Tzu. Kuo Hsiang and Ch'eng Hsüan-ying took it for the name of Huan's brother, but we would expect his name at first appearance, if at all. This is surely a frivolous reference to Mo Tzu by his personal name, as Confucius is so often called Ch'iu 丘.

32/12 使其弟墨…13 使而子爲墨者予也…14 彼，故使彼…15 自是，有德者以(= 己) 不知也

"It caused his younger brother to become a Mohist…The one who caused your son to become a Mohist was I myself…He treated as *pi*, therefore caused to treat as *pi*…. Treating oneself as *shih*, even one who has Power would not know how to do that…"

The passage contrasts the two alternatives *shih* and *pi* as in chapter 2, and uses the latter verbally as well as the former. Cf. 2/27 自 彼 則 不 見，自 知 則 知 之。

"If you treat yourself as *pi* they (*shih* and *pi*) do not appear, if you are aware of yourself you are aware of them."

26/37 彼 教 不 學，承 意 不 彼。

"Teaching which treats as *pi* he does not learn, he takes in the idea but does not treat as *pi*."

23/7ff. 唯 蟲 能 蟲，唯 蟲 能 天。全 人 惡 天，惡 人 之 天，而 況 吾 天 乎 人 乎。

"Only the animal is able to be animal, only the animal is able to behave heavenwise. The perfect man hates the heavenwise, hates the heavenwise in man, and above all the question 'Am I behaving heavenwise or manwise?'"

The verbal use of *t'ien* 'behave heavenwise' and *jen* 'behave manwise' is common enough in *Chuang Tzu*, but the invitation to hate the work of Heaven is quite unparalleled. Kuo Ch'ing-fan (831) tried to take *wu* 惡 as the interrogative *wu* 'where? how?,' and paraphrased by 全 人 惡 知 天…"How would the perfect man know about Heaven?…" Many have followed this example, for want of a better suggestion (quite recently, Ch'en Ku-ying, 676), but there is no escaping the facts that syntactically we should expect a verb after *wu* 'how?' and an affirmative clause before *k'uang* 'how much more…?'

108 25/56 The incidents of the bath and of the three wives seem to be separate. Cf. Ch'en Ku-ying, 750ff.

109 25/36 彼 知 丘 之 著 於 已 也

"He knows that I attract more attention than he does." Kuo Hsiang defines *chu* 著 by *ming* 明, which Ch'eng Hsüan-ying takes in the sense of 'aware of' (明 識) : "He knows that I am aware of him." But the ordinary pre-Han use of *chu* is as an ergative verb, 'become visible, attract attention,' and I have noticed no evidence of it coinciding with *ming* except in this sense.

110　24/96 煬 = 養 Hsi T'ung.

24/96 天 [下] Delete with Tun-huang MS and parallel in *Huai-nan Tzu* chapter 7. (Liu 7/6B/3ff).

PART 3
A 'SCHOOL OF CHUANG TZU' SELECTION

CTIC Part 3, Chapter 1 (Stories about Chuang Tzu)

118　20/65 (月) *日 *Shih-wen* variant.

20/67 從 其 (俗) *令 *Ch'üeh-wu* variant.

119　32/46 This is a mutilated scrap of the story preserved in a full version in *Shih chi* (chapter 63), 2145.

120　20/46 (正) *以 Ch'en Ku-ying, 565.

121　20/2...終 其 天 年 夫 [子]　Delete with *Shih-wen* main text (Ch'en Ku-ying, 546).

20/3 (烹) *享 Kuo Ch'ing-fan, 667.

CTIC Part 3, Chapter 2 (The Dialogues of Confucius and Old Tan)

128　13/49 物 愷 The first graph has a *Shih-wen* variant 勿. *K'ai* 愷 is rare except in binomes expressive of joy, 愷 慷 , 愷 悌 , 樂 愷 (*Tz'u tung* 0895, 1329, 1342); this *wu-k'ai* is presumably one of them.

13/51 (牧) *朴 with the parallel in 14/58 (Fukunaga, 255).

129　14/56 (播) *簸 Ma Hsü-lun.

14/57 (憒) *憒 *Shih-wen* variant.

14/57 吾 子 <若 欲> 使...吾 子 亦...

"If you wish to cause...may you too..." Restored from the close parallel in 13/50-52: 夫 子 若 欲 使...夫 子 亦...

14/49 *Chu* 主 'master' and *cheng* 正 'director.' This interesting pair of concepts recurs in 25/62; 29/79. In communication, what you say will pass right through me unless there is a *chu* in me which appropriates, assimilates it, makes it my own knowledge. Similarly what I say will miss you unless there is a *cheng* which steers it in your direction.

131　12/42 (成 思) *來 *藉 Dubiously restored from the parallel in 7/13.

12/41 相 放 'the mutually dependent,' correlatives such as 'more and less,' 'elder and younger,' described in *Canon* A 88 as "becoming dependent in interplay" (交 得 放). Cf. G3: 186ff.

132　22/31 皇 'house without walls' (Morohashi, 22701 def. 1/13), with Chang Ping-lin.

22/35 (匱) *遺 with *Ch'üeh-wu* variant.

22/30 有 倫 生 於 無 形 "What has *lun* (place within an arrangement) is born from the shapeless." The reference is to the sequence of birth and death, as can be seen from a sentence later in the episode: 22/41ff. 不 形 之 形，形 之 不 形…比 眾 人 之 所 同 論 也 "The shaping of the unshaped (birth) and unshaping of the shaped (death)…are what common men are alike in *lun* (placing within an arrangement)." For nominal and verbal *lun*, cf. G3: 194.

22/33, 36 比 其 道 與

22/35 彼 其 外 與

These clauses are syntactically ambiguous, and can be taken

1. as leading questions with modal *ch'i* ('Is not this the way?' 'Is not that the exterior?'), or

2. as simple questions with pronoun *ch'i* emphasizing and rendering possessive a demonstrative pronoun (cf. G3: 123): 'Would it be of these (natural things, not thinking man) that it is the Way?' 'Would it be of that (the true Way) that it is the exterior?'

Comparison of the three sentences in context supports 2. It may be noticed that except in the formulaic 此 之 謂…"It is this which is called…" of the last sentence (22/43), throughout this episode *tz'u* 此 seems always to refer to concrete things (22/32, 33, 36, 42). Indeed, in the first three instances it follows at a short interval and may be taken as resuming 萬 物 'myriad things' (22/30, 33, 35).

CTIC Part 3, Chapter 3 (The Advantages of Spontaneity)

137 19/10 是<形>色而已 *Ch'üeh-wu* variant.

19/10 則物之造乎不形而止乎無所化

This pair of clauses (botched when I translated the parallel passage in *Lieh Tzu* G1: 37) is hard to fit into the context and may be mutilated. But the main difficulty is in the word *tsao/ ts'ao* 造, which as in 6/72 I would now understand as *ts'ao* 'take a direction,' *tsao* 'set going in a direction':

6/72 魚相造乎水

"The fish go on setting each other directions through the water."

6/72 人相造乎道

"Men go on setting each other directions through the Way."

19/10 物之造乎不形

"Things going on finding their own directions through the Unformed."

19/12 以通乎物之所造

"…and thereby go on circulating round that through which things find their own directions."

This accounts for the invulnerability of the sage, the theme of this episode; he never collides with other things because all are spontaneously moving on the Way in the directions set by their interactions, like a shoal of fish in the water.

19/11 (合) *含 with *Lieh Tzu* chapter 2 (Yang 31/2).

138 19/21 (凝) *疑於神, with the parallel in *Lieh Tzu* chapter 2 (Yang 40). Cf. 19/59 疑 (= 擬) 神 "comparable with the daemonic."

19/23 數 = 速 Ma Hsü-lun.

19/62 蓋 = 盇 in the sense defined by 合 'fit.' Morohashi, 22980 def. 2, following Hsi T'ung.

139 21/45 揖 = 牒 Ma Hsü-lun.

22/69 (守) *道 Wang Nien-sun.

142 20/70 自賢之 (行) *心 Hsi T'ung.

CTIC Part 3, Chapter 4 (Rationalizing the Way: The 'Great Man')

144–
153 17/1–53; 25/59–82 These two dialogues expounding the rationalizing Taoism of the 'Great Man' (大人) with his 'Great Scope' (大方), centered on the distinction between the finite which is verbally communicable and the infinite which is not, are established as the work of a single hand by their style as well as their thought.

Table 1

	Chuang Tzu 17/1–53 (+22/16–21)	Chuang Tzu 25/59–82	Rest of Chuang Tzu
'entitle' 號	17/11 號 物 之 數 謂 之 萬	25/67 今 計 物 之 數 ，不 止 於 萬 而 期 曰 萬 物 者 ，以 數 之 多 者 號 而 讀 之 也 25/68	once (8/21)
計 X 之 Y	17/10, 11, 18	25/66	once (5/9)
殊	17/26, 36, 37 twice, 39 twice	25/62, 63 twice, 65	
差	17/30, 31, 39	25/65	
不 可 圍	17/20ff. 至 精 無 形 ，至 大 不 可 圍	25/76 精 至 於 無 倫 ，大 至 於 不 可 圍	
形 + 天 地 氣 + 陰 陽	17/9 自 以 比 形 於 天 地 ，而 受 氣 於 陰 陽 ，吾 在 天 地 之 間 ，猶 小 石 小 木 之 在 大 山 也	25/67 是 故 天 地 者 ，形 之 大 者 也 。陰 陽 者 ，氣 之 大 者 也 。	

	Chuang Tzu 17/1–53 (+22/16–21)	Chuang Tzu 25/59–82	Rest of Chuang Tzu
丘 山	17/31, 37	25/61	once (26/40)
江 河	17/8	25/61	
無 止	17/15 量 無 窮 時 無 止 17/17	25/79 twice 無 窮 無 止	once (14/21)
萬 物 +理	17/46; 22/18 萬 物 之 理 22/17 萬 物 有 成 理	25/63 萬 物 殊 理	once (33/13)

145　17/9 比 = 庇 Kao Heng, cf. 1/17.

　　17/13 (連) *襢 Wang Shu-min.

146　17/24 [察] 致

　　17/24–28 As Ch'en Ku-ying recognizes, this passage is out of context; we consider it under 149ff. (3) below.

148ff. 17/48–53 The end of this dialogue shows signs of mutilation, and before this passage we insert 22/16–21. The latter is a fragment or fragments intervening between two dialogues in a chapter which consists otherwise of clearly distinguished dialogues. Several points suggest a connection with the 'Autumn floods':

　　22/17ff. 達 萬 物 之 理　cf. 17/46 論 萬 物 之 理, 17/48 必 達 於 理.

　　22/18, 21 觀 於 X 'have a full view of X': cf. 17/6, 16.

　　22/20 終 身 不 故 : cf. 17/15, 18 終 始 無 故...終 始 之 不 可 故 也

　　22/21 此 之 謂 本 根，付 以 觀 於 天 矣 : cf. 17/50 本 乎 天

149ff. At the end of the 'Autumn floods' dialogue we tentatively attach three fragments on the Great Man:

　　(1) 24/70–73, passage ending 大 人 之 誠, following a story about Confucius in Ch'u but without any obvious connection.

(2) 11/63–66, fragment starting 大人之教, of a series (11/57–74) for which the *Shih-wen* notes no comments earlier than Kuo Hsiang; Takeuchi Yoshio (154) drew the conclusion that Kuo Hsiang incorporated them from discarded chapters when he made his abridgement.

(3) 17/24–28, fragment starting 是故大人之行 stuck in the middle of the 'Autumn floods' but recognized by Ch'en Ku-ying as out of place.

The neatly contrasting key phrases, 'integrity/teaching/conduct of the Great Man,' suggest that the three belong together. Moreover 3 ends with a summing-up: "I have heard: the man of the Way is not heard of, utmost Power does not win gains, the Great Man has no self." The first and last of these three points connect not with 3 but with 1 ("Therefore alive he has no dignities, dead no posthumous title, his deeds are unrecorded, his name unestablished") and 2 ("In ultimate sameness he has no self. Having no self, how could he get to have anything?").

The grounds for suspecting that they are the *disjecta membra* of the end of the 'Autumn floods' dialogue are as follows:

(1) The opening sentence "Therefore the sea which accepts all that flows east is the utmost in greatness" (24/70) sounds like the sea god Jo talking to the lord of the Yellow River. Cf. His "Of the waters of the world none is greater than the sea, the myriad streams end up in it…" (17/7).

(2) This is a fragment of dialogue, for someone is being addressed as 'you' (汝):

11/65 挈汝適復之撓撓，以遊無端，出入無旁，與日無始。

"Be finished with the restlessness of your journeying and returning, and roam out into the infinite; have no banks between which you go in and out, and every day renew your beginnings." (Taking 挈 as 契 in the sense of 絕 'snap off,' Morohashi, 5917 def. 1/5, with Wu Ju-lun; and 旁 as in 水旁 'riverside,' found for example in *Kuan Tzu* (chapter 57) BSS 3/18/8 cf. –2.)

This would be appropriate to the Lord of the River, who goes down the river annually, confined by the banks and the seasons, and never ventures out into the limitless ocean. Also the Lord of the River was formerly an admirer of Confucius and Po Yi (17/4 cf. 13ff.), so is suitably described as 'yesterday's gentleman' (昔 之 君 子) who is now the 'friend of heaven and earth' (天 地 之 友).

(3) This does stand in the 'Autumn floods,' although misplaced, and echoes its relativism: "He knows that the right and the wrong cannot be treated as portions or the minute and the great as standards" (17/27...細 大 之 不 可 爲 倪), cf. 17/19ff. "How do I know that the tip of a hair is enough to fix the standard for the most minute?" (至 細 之 倪).

149 17/52 無 以 人 滅 天 ，無 以 故 滅 命 ，[無 以 得 殉 名]，謹 守 而 勿 失 ，是 謂 反 其 眞 。
This is a rhymed quatrain with an AABA rhyme scheme: 天 *T'IĔN 命 *MIĔN (rather than its alternative *MIǍNG) 眞 *TIEN. The deleted phrase is unsymmetrical also in that Heaven and Destiny are good things while reputation (*ming* 名) is not.

151 25/61 立 'stand.' For evidence that *li* 'stand' and *wei* 位 'seat' were used of levels of counting in disputation, cf. G3: 363, 431ff.

25/61 丘 山 積 卑 而 爲 高 ，江 河 合 (水) *小 而 爲 大 ，大 人 合 (幷) *私 而 爲 公 。

The first emendation was proposed by Yü Yüeh on grounds of parallelism, which also demands the second.

25/63 文 武 <殊 能> Wang Shu-min.

25/67, 68, 75 讀 I have failed to find examples of *tu* 'read' which throw light on its usage here. *Tu*/*D'UK is phonologically and graphically related to *hsü*/*DZIUK 續 'continue,' with which it is known to interchange (Morohashi, 36088 def. 1/5). Its implication seems to be of reading *off*, punctuating phrase by phrase, and in the present context may be reasonably taken as the process of counting up the 10,000 things or measuring up towards the infinite or back to the origin of things.

25/68 斯 Not the demonstrative *ssu* 'this' (never found in *Chuang Tzu*) but the verb *ssu* 'chop,' found in the same dialogue (25/75).

25/69 狗 馬 In disputation horse is the typical common name, dog the typical thing with two names (犬, 狗). Cf. G3: 217–219.

25/75 意 <測> Wang Shu-min.

153 25/80 有 (=又) 不可無

25/80 假 For *chia* used of loan-naming (metaphorical naming) cf. G3: 358.

25/23 (十) *七 Yü Yüeh.

154 25/30 蠻 The name of the other state (觸) must have dropped out here.

25/31 [客出] 惠子見 Wang Hsien-ch'ien.

25/32 *Hsiao* 嚆 'scream.' The supposed meaning 'sound of flute' (Moro-hashi, 4041 def. 4/3) has the *Shih-wen* note on this passage as its sole authority.

155 17/70 還<視>, with *T'ai-p'ing yü-lan* SPTK 189/4A/7, supported by sub-commentary paraphrase (Ma Hsü-lun).

156 12/37ff. 太初有無，無有無名 "In the ultimate beginning there is Nothing, without anything, without a name." The identification of the Tao with Nothing is a commonplace of the Neo-Taoism of about A.D. 300, but the general position in *Chuang Tzu*, not excluding the 'Great Man' passages (cf. 25/73–82), is that the dichotomy of 'something' and 'nothing' does not apply to the Tao. Several scholars therefore prefer to punctuate one place later: "In the ultimate beginning there is that which is without nothing, that which is without a name" (Ch'ien Mu, Liu Wen-tien). Li Mien agrees, but emends to 太初有無 *形，有無名。 "In the ultimate beginning there is the shapeless, there is the nameless." However, that the Tao is not Nothing but beyond the dichotomy of Something and Nothing is an idea so abstract that one would not be surprised if even a Taoist who maintained it might fail to hold on to it consistently. Here the fundamental test is in the punctuation. Rhythm and parallelism are elements within classical Chinese syntax; it is safest to go by the rule-of-thumb that if an eight-word unit which is ambiguous *can* be read as falling into two four-word sub-units, then, irrespective of what one would like the sentence to mean, it should be.

CTIC Part 3, Chapter 5 (Irrationalizing the Way: 'Knowledge Wanders North')

161   22/28 食 不 知 所 (味) *以 Emended from the parallel in *Lieh Tzu* chapter 1 (Yang 21/2).

22/46 正 獲 之 問 於 監 市 履 豨 也 ，每 下 愈 況 。

"When Director Huo asks the Superintendent of the Market about trampling the pigs (to test how fat they are), each time he tramples lower, the more he will *k'uang* (generalize from part to whole, or from minor to major instance)."

22/46 汝 唯 莫 必

"You deal only in 'in no case' and 'necessarily'." Cf. *Analects* 4/10 君 子 之 於 天 地 也 ，無 適 也 ，無 莫 也 。 "In his dealings with the world the gentleman is not invariably for or against anything." (Lau p. 73) 9/4 毋 意 ，毋 必 ，毋 固 ，毋 我 。 "He refused to entertain conjectures or insist on certainty; he refused to be inflexible or to be egotistical." (Lau, 96) In the Later Mohist disputation *pi* is the term for the logically necessary, while *mo* 'none/in no case' is the basic quantifier in relation to which 'all' and 'some' are defined (G3:299–301, 294); although they are never directly contrasted in the Mohist dialectical writings, they are suitable words to represent affirmed and denied alternatives.

164   22/74 冉 求 未 對 。仲 尼 曰 ，已 矣 ，未 應 矣 。

"Jan Ch'iu failed to reply. 'Enough,' said Confucius, 'You failed to answer.'"

A verb followed by the perfective particle *yi* 矣 may be negated by *pu* 不 (*pu...yi* cf. colloquial *pu...le* 了 'no longer'), but not normally by *wei* 未 'not yet' (cf. colloquial 沒 有...呢, in which *le* would not be expected in place of the *ne*). But this is a highly philosophical context. Confucius is waiting for the *failure* to reply, for the passing of the point when it becomes significant to say "Jan Ch'iu has *not yet* replied."

22/51 (殺) *隆 with Ma Hsü-lun.

14/16ff. 夫 至 樂 者...太 和 萬 物 These 35 characters have long been recognized as a piece of Kuo Hsiang's commentary which has intruded into the text. Cf. Ch'en Ku-ying, 404 ff.

14/17 光 = 廣 Ch'ien Mu.

165   14/20 塗 = 杜 Ch'en Ku-ying.

14/21 I take *ming* 名 'name' to be the titles of the items in the performance, for want of a better suggestion. Cf. Ch'en Ku-ying 406.

14/24 混逐 (= 遯) Ma Hsü-lun.

14/24 林樂 With an unidentified binome (as this surely is) one can only guess from the context.

168   21/21 規= 闚 Ma Hsü-lun, as in 5/44.

21/21 徂 = 且 'be about to be,' cf. page 22 above.

21/22 著 'attract attention,' cf. page 32 The function of post-verbal *hu* is as usual continuative, as throughout this passage (21/51, 17 twice, 21, 22, 23).

169   21/23 不忘者 'the unforgetting' (not 'the unforgotten'). *Wang* 'forget' is in Cikoski's terminology not an ergative but a neutral verb, as indeed is illustrated above in the same line (甚忘 'forget absolutely,' not 'be forgotten absolutely').

CTIC Part 3, Chapter 6
(Utopia and The Decline of Government)

71   16/1 [俗] 俗 *Ch'üeh-wu* variant.

16/3 (容) *和, on grounds of parallelism.

16/3 As noticed by Ma Hsü-lun, the structure of the definition requires a missing definition of *hsin* 信 'good faith' (deriving it from *jen* 仁 'benevolence'). It also implies 中 = 忠 (the 忠 in the preceding sentence similarly had its radical missing in a *Ch'üeh-wu* variant).

16/4 (遍) *偏 *Ch'üeh-wu*, supported by Kuo commentary.

16/4 Without much confidence, I take 彼正 as 'the other straightens' in contrast with the 正己 'straighten oneself' of 16/17 (but since *cheng* 正 'straight' is an ergative verb one would expect it to mean 'the other is straight'). Judging by the 蔽蒙 'blinkered and benighted' of 16/1, the 蒙己德 must be understood in an unfavorable sense, 'blinker one's own Power.' This connects with the *mao* 冒 of 16/5, taking it in its basic sense as defined in the *Shuo wen*, 冡 (=蒙) 而 前 也 ， 從 曰 目 "'Go ahead blindly.' Components *mao* ('cover over') and *mu* ('eyes')."

172   16/15 (行) *存 *Shih-te-t' ang* edition.

16/19 The Ch'eng sub-commentary implies 古 for 故, contrasting with the 今 of 16/20; this both clarifies the sense and eliminates the apparent repetition of *ku* 故 'therefore' in the next line. We should presumably fill out to 古 人 (with the sub-commentary) or 古 者.

Editor's Note: There are no textual notes for sections 3/7 and 3/8

CTIC Part 3, Chapter 9 (Stray Ideas)

184   18/41–46 Since the generative chain is intended to show that "the myriad things all come out from the germs, all go into the germs," one would expect it to be complete. It may be restored from the quotation in *T'ai-p'ing yü-lan* SPTK 887/7B/3–5 and from the parallel in *Lieh Tzu* in chapter 1, Yang 9/1–4:

line 44 斯 彌 爲 食 醯 <頤 輅 。 食 醯>[a] 頤 輅 生 乎 食 醯 <黃 軦 。 食 醯>[b] 黃 軦 生 乎 九 猷 ，<九 猷 生 乎 瞀 芮>[c] 瞀 芮 生 乎 腐 蠸 。 <腐 蠸 生 乎 羊 奚>[d]
(a. *Lieh Tzu*; b. *Lieh Tzu* and TPYL ; c. *Lieh Tzu* and TPYL; d. TPYL)

187   12/67ff. 識 其 一 ， 不 知 其 二 "Perceives the oneness of it, does not know about the duality in it" (*Not* "perceives one side of it, does not know about the other"). The interpretation of this ambiguous sentence becomes plain in the context in which it reappears in *Huai-nan Tzu* chapter 7 (Liu 7/7A/2).

188   25/44 (強) *僵 Ma Hsü-lun.

25/48 (愚) *過 Yü Yüeh.

CTIC Part 3, Chapter 10 (Miscellaneous)

189   18/39 彼 必 相 與 異 ， 其 好 惡 故(= 固) 異 也 。

190   18/39 福 = 輻 Ch'ien Mu.

23/70 欽 = 厰 defined in *Shuo wen* as: 陳 與 服 於 庭 'laying out carriages and kit in the yard' (Yü Yüeh).

23/71 謨 = 摹 Ch'ien Mu. Cf. G3: 196.

PART 4
ESSAYS OF THE PRIMITIVIST AND EPISODES RELATED TO THEM

CTIC Part 4, Chapter 1 (*Chuang Tzu* 8)

201   8/1–8 Here there are three complementary pairs of words:

(1) *P'ien* 駢 'web' (of webbed toes) and *chih* 枝 'branch out' (of a sixth finger),

(2) *To* 多 'have too much' and a word written three times as *fang* 方 and once as *p'ang* 旁 (both used of Confucian morality),

(3) *Yin* 淫 'go to excess' and *p'i* 僻 'go out of the way' (cf. Also 11/1, 2 淫 'take to excess' 遷 'displace').

The obscure word should probably be taken as *p'ang* 旁 'go to the side, branch off' (Morohashi, 13637 def. 6, 8–10). The usage is not very well attested, but we find *pang* combined with *p'i* 辟 (= 僻) 'go out of the way' in *Hsün Tzu* chapter 15 (Liang 205/4):

旁 辟 曲 私 之 屬 爲 之 化 而 公 "The sort who are one-sided, aberrant, crooked and selfish are transformed by it to impartiality," on which the T'ang commentator Yang Liang notes: 旁 , 偏 頗 也 "*P'ang* is one-sided."

There is also a doubtful case in *Chuang Tzu* of *p'ang* in the sense of 'branch off':

4/65 十 仞 而 後 有 枝 ， 其 可 以 爲 舟 者 旁 十 數 。 (of a great tree) "It was 80 feet up before there was a branch; those big enough to make a boat jutted out (?) in dozens" (*Shih-wen*, Ts'ui 旁 , 旁 枝 也 "*P'ang* is side-branch")

The Primitivist's case is that morality is an excrescence like toes being webbed or a sixth finger branching out from the hand; it both adds to (*to*) and diverges from (*p'ang*) the natural course of development (which is *cheng* 正 'straight, correct'), is both excess (*yin*) and aberration (*p'i*).

The distribution of the first two pairs shows that in 8/6 the *p'ien* is a mistake for *p'ang*:

8/1 駢...枝...多 方

8/3 多方駢枝

8/4–6 駢...多...枝...(駢) *旁

8/7 多駢旁枝

8/6 竅 句 <極 辭> restored from the T'ang MS of the *Shih-wen*. (Wang Shu-min).

8/8 (正) *至 正 emended from the preceding sentence (Yü Yüeh).

8/8 而 (枝) *歧 者 不 爲 (跂) *枝 The latter reading is that of the Ts'ui text; and a reading 歧 (but for 跂) is reported in *Ch'üeh-wu*.

202 8/26 The Primitivist fragment 12/95–102 seems best located here. For the stylistic grounds for classing it as Primitivist, see G6: 476ff.

12/96 <桀> 跖 restored from Ch'eng sub-commentary (Liu Shih-p'ei). The two names are paired also in 11/22, 28 (both Primitivist).

203 8/26–31 The elaborate parallelism of the two four-sentence sequences shows that in 8/29 the clause 非 所 謂 仁 義 之 謂 也 has replaced (by assimilation to the preceding sentence) an original 非 五 味 之 謂 也.

8/30, 31 自 聞 / 見 / 得 'hear/see/grasp for oneself.' Cf. 23/18, 19 盲 / 聾 / 狂 者 不 能 自 見 / 聞 / 得 "The blind/deaf/mad cannot see/hear/grasp for themselves."

CTIC Part 4, Chapter 2 (*Chuang Tzu* 9)

205 9/15ff. The readings chosen are 扼 = 軛, 倪 = 輗, 曼 = 輓 and some emendations of Ma Hsü-lun: (月) *軏, (題) *輗, (介) *抚, (驚) *摰

CTIC Part 4, Chapter 2 (*Chuang Tzu* 10)

207 10/8–10 This passage appears to consist of two displaced fragments:

> (A) "Let's try to sort it out. Are there any whom conventional opinion calls supremely wise who are not piling up a store for the greater robber? Or any whom it calls supreme sages who are not guarding the store for the great robber? How would we know that this is so?"

> (B) "Formerly Lung Feng was chopped in two, Pi-kan ripped open, Chang Hung disemboweled, Tzu-hsü left to rot; so for all their worth they did not escape execution."

A is a repetition of 10/3ff., but with 知 'wise' and 聖 'sage' strengthened to 至 知, 至 聖. The repetition would be intelligible if the argument were now being extended to the greatest sages, but there is no such development.

B does not follow on to A; the four victims are credited with 'worth' (賢) but not sagehood, and their deaths elsewhere illustrate quite a different theme, the fickleness of rulers and mutability of fortune (cf. 26/1ff., 29/46). There seems no choice but to discard the whole passage, either as rendered unintelligible by a lacuna between A and B, or more probably as a doublet of 10/3ff. Followed by a misplaced fragment (possibly belonging with the fragments collected in 26/1–6).

208 10/14, 21ff., 26; 11/28 These four aphorisms introduced by 故 曰 'therefore it is said…' (three of them from *Lao Tzu*) are nearly all difficult to relate to their context and should probably be discarded as glosses.

> (1) 10/14 "Hence it is said:

> > (A) 'When the lips are off the teeth are cold'

> > (B) 'When the wine of Lu was too thin Hantan was besieged.'"

A is familiar as a metaphor for being weakened by the loss of a buffer state, as in *Han Fei Tzu* chapter 2 (Ch'en 43/8).

B appears in *Huai-nan Tzu* chapter 10 (Liu 10/13A/2) as an illustration of events having obscure beginnings which only the sage can discern. Neither seems to have any relevance here.

> (2) 10/21ff. "Hence it is said: 'The fish cannot be let out of the deep, the state's sharp tools cannot be shown to men.'" (*Lao Tzu* 36) This does connect with the next sentence: "The sage is the world's sharpest

tool, he is not a means of enlightening the world." However the Primitivist's point is that the sage's morality (which is a mere tool in politics) is to be rejected, while the quotation, if relevant, would imply that it ought to be treasured as a state secret. Probably a reader was simply reminded of the *Lao Tzu* sentence and wrote it into the margin.

(3) 10/26 "Hence it is said: 'The greatest skill seems awkward,'" (*Lao Tzu* 45). This is relevant to the preceding sentence, which is indeed about skill, but again it may be suspected that a reader has simply been reminded of *Lao Tzu*. The sentence it follows is the third of four that are strictly parallel (10/24–27), and since none of the others has a similar illustration it destroys their balance. It is omitted as a gloss in Ch'en Ku-ying's recent edition.

(4) 11/28 "Hence it is said: 'Get rid of the sages, abandon knowledge, and the empire will be in perfect order.'" The first clause is from *Lao Tzu* 19; it appears also in 10/23, but not as an explicit quotation. This aphorism stands at the very end of the last Primitivist essay, and although suitable to the context may be dismissed as a gloss if we reject the rest.

It is notable that all four aphorisms share a crucial word or words with the context in which they are found: 10/15 竭 22 利器, 26 巧; 11/27 聖知. It may be suspected that in each case it is the words rather than the thought which have reminded the glossator of a popular maxim or an aphorism from *Lao Tzu*.

208 10/20 (豕) *遂 於 大 盜 "is successful in becoming a great robber" (?). The text as it stands is unacceptable since *chu* 逐 is an ergative verb, 'be chased': *chu X* 'chase X' but *chu yü X* 'be chased from X.' Cf. 19/65 逐 於 州 部 "chased out from the town"; 20/37 吾 再 逐 於 魯 "I was twice chased from Lu."

10/27 鑠 Morohashi, 41019 def. 6, 'glitter' Li Mien.

209 10/35 機(變) *辟 Wu Yen-hsü. The pair as emended occur in 1/45; 20/13. Wu Yen-hsü ingeniously suggests that the original corruption was to 辮.

10/36 Cf. The note on 24/111 (treated at CTIC 63 above).

CTIC Part 4, Chapter 4 (*Chuang Tzu* 11/1–28)

211 11/1 在 宥(= 囿) Cf. CTIC 57, 2/55 above. We take *tsai* 'keep in place'
     and *yu* 'keep in bounds' as the first pair in the Eight Powers (八 德)
     of *The sorting which evens things out*. The second pair, 'sorting and
     assessing' (論 議) appear in 10/24. In the Primitivist essays and the
     related story of Tzu-kung and Old Tan (14/60–74) all eight words ap-
     pear; the first two pairs are assumed to be good, but the words in the
     last two pairs always have a bad sense: 分 (9/12), 辯 (8/6; 10/37), 競
     (14/69), 爭 (9/18; 10/24).

212 11/14 故 貴 以 身 於 爲 天 下...愛 以 身 於 爲 天 下。The
     parallel in *Lao Tzu* 13 is 故 貴 以 身 爲 天 下 者...愛 以 身 爲
     天 下 者。But for the first clause the two Ma-wang-tui MSS have
     故 貴 爲 身 於 爲 天 下。"Therefore if you value governing
     your own person more than governing the world." In the *Chuang Tzu*
     version the phrase 以 身 should presumably be equated with 爲 身
     'govern one's person.'

     11/17 Since *ch'iu* 囚 is an ergative verb ('be imprisoned') but *sha* 殺 a
     neutral one ('kill'), I take the elliptical phrase 上 下 囚 殺 as "when
     down it is the prisoner, when up it is the executioner."

     11/18 廉 劌 彫 琢 *Kuei* 劌 is neutral ('jab'), so the first pair of words
     are to be taken as 'have corners and jab' (cf. *Lao Tzu* 58 廉 而 不 劌
     'has corners but does not jab'). The latter pair on the other hand are er-
     gative verbs, 'be carved and polished.'

CTIC Part 4, Chapter 5 (Episodes Related to the Primitivist Essays)

214 14/62 翻 = 養 Liu Shih-p'ei.

215 14/64ff. 三 王 (*Shih-wen* variant 皇) 五 帝. 67 三 皇 (Shih-te-t'ang
     edition, 王) 五 帝; 72 三 皇 五 帝; 72 三 皇. The chronological
     sequence seems at first sight to guarantee that the correct reading is
     San huang 皇. However the monarchs discussed are in fact from the
     Five Emperors and Three Kings, and Old Tan starts the decline of
     government from the Yellow Emperor, who in the scheme followed in
     the *Shih chi* is the first of the Five Emperors. Moreover this passage is

close in thought to the essays of the Primitivist (if not actually his work); and the Primitivist not only agrees in starting the decline from the Yellow Emperor (11/19), but conceives the primeval Utopia as lasting until Fu-hsi and Shen-nung (10/31), who belong to the *San huang*. One can only suppose that the original reading was *Wu ti san wang* 五 帝 三 王, and that an accidental reversal of the two elements in one instance (perhaps the first) caused a scribe to emend *wang* to *huang* and assimilate the other instances to it.

14/66 堯 授 舜 ，舜 授 禹 Read 堯 與 而 舜 受 with the Tun-huang MS.

14/70 (變) *辯 There is the same confusion in 1/21 (Cf. above note to line 10/35). The successive stages of the decline are from unity (一) to preference for one's kin (親), contention (競), and finally disputation under Yü, the sage admired by the Mohists, here credited with the Later Mohist thesis "Killing robbers is not killing people" (G3: 487–489).

14/71 自 爲 種 而 天 下 耳 (= 爾) The sentence is almost certainly radically corrupt; but for lack of a better suggestion I follow Fuku-naga's proposal.

14/71ff. 而 今 乎 婦 女 ，何 言 哉 "But now they use their daughters as their wives, unspeakable!" This has been the traditional interpretation since Kuo Hsiang, and I follow it in the absence of a convincing emendation. I take 今 乎 as a formation like 於 是 乎, but it is unattested in any concordanced pre-Han text.

14/73 規 = 闚 Wu Ju-lun.

12/84ff. 而 未 知 此 其 必 然 邪 "…but do they not yet know that it is necessarily so in the instance here (i.e. their own case)?" This is a formula used in the Mohist logic in inferring by analogy. Cf. G3: 346–351. *Canons* A 97 彼 舉 然 者 以 爲 此 其 然 也 "If the other man referring to a respect in which it is so, deems it so in the instance here…." B 1 彼 以 此 其 然 也 ，説 是 其 然 也 "The other, on the grounds that it is so of the instance here, argues that it is so of the thing it is." B 2 此 然 是 必 然 ，則 俱 爲 麋 "If what is so of the instance here were necessarily so of the thing it is, all would be milu deer."

12/85 故 = 固 Wu Ju-lun.

12/91 祈 = 旂 'signal flag' (Ma Hsü-lun).

12/92 以=(缶) *垂 鍾 惑 with Ssu-ma Piao's text. That the first two words can mean 'crossroads' is argued from slightly different angles by Ma Ch'i-ch'iang and by Liu Shih-p'ei. 鍾 = 重 'redouble' (?).

12/94ff. The incident of the leper seems isolated, but becomes intelligible if we take 11/57–63 as the continuation of 12/83–95 (cf. G6: 476ff.).

11/59 因 眾 以 寧 所 聞，不 如 眾 技 眾 矣 "To have the support of the many to confirm the doctrine you were taught is not as good as the many arts of ruling (眾 技 cf. 33/12 猶 百 家 眾 技 也 'like the many arts of the Hundred Schools') being as many as possible."

PART 5

THE YANGIST MISCELLANY

CTIC Part 5, Chapter 1 (*Chuang Tzu* 28)

226   28/25 恐 聽 [者] 謬 with the parallel in *Lü-shih ch'un-ch'iu* chapter 2/2 (Hsü 2/5B/1).

227   28/26 (眞) *非 惡 富 貴 也 with *Lü-shih ch'un-ch'iu* op. cit. 2/6A/2. The error probably comes from confusion with the 眞 9 characters later.

28/27 道 之 眞 以 (治) *持 身 with *Lü-shih ch'un-ch'iu* op. cit. 2/6A/5.

228   28/45 弦 <歌> *Ch'üeh-wu* variant.

28/46 華 Morohashi, 31214 def. 1/26, 'split down the middle' (T'ao Hung-ch'ing).

28/47 學 <道> Wang Shu-min.

28/48 厲 Morohashi, 11100 def. 1/6, 'be polluted.'

230   28/65 (天) *大 寒 Yü Yüeh.

28/67 德 = 得 Yü Yüeh.

232   28/81 喜 = 禧 Yü Yüeh 政 = 正 Yü Yüeh.

28/83 [下] 行 貨 Wang Nien-sun.

CTIC Part 5, Chapter 2 (*Chuang Tzu* 29)

234–253 Note on chapters 29–31:

> Ma Hsü-lun noticed (in the preface to his commentary) that Kuo Hsiang has only three comments on these chapters, two headed 此 篇... summing up the first episode of *Robber Chih* (chapter 29) and the whole of *The old fisherman* (chapter 31) respectively, and another headed 此 章... summing up the remaining episodes of *Robber Chih*. He concluded that, in Kuo Hsiang's abridgement, the parts of *Robber Chih* were separate chapters numbered 29 and 30. With the loss of the title of the second, chapter 30 was assumed to be missing, and someone substituted the present chapter 30 (*Discourse on swords*) from the unabridged text of Ssu-ma Piao (the only commentator quoted for more than phonetic glosses in Lu Te-ming's *Shih-wen* on this chapter). Thus in *Discourse on swords* we have an actual specimen of those chapters which Kuo Hsiang thought inferior and excised from the book. There is no reason to doubt that in the unabridged text it belonged to the block of chapters we call the *Yangist miscellany* (the present chapter 28–31, already recognized as distinctive and unlike the work of Chuang Tzu by Su Shih in the Sung dynasty). The restorer of what he took to be the missing chapter between *Robber Chih* and *The old fisherman* would, assuming that the order of chapters had remained unchanged, have found it in the same position in the unabridged text. In any case the form of the title, taken from the theme of the chapter, groups it with the rest of chapter 28–31 against all the other "outer" and "mixed" chapters.

235　29/8 (敵) *謫

238　29/39 [文王拘羑里] Deleted by Li Mien because (1) The number of rulers in this series, from the Yellow Emperor to King Wen, is seven but is said to be six; (2) King Wen should precede Wu, not follow him; (3) King Wen's imprisonment is hardly comparable with the other events in the series, which can all be understood as moral faults.

　　29/41 <莫若> 伯夷叔齊 Restored from the parallels in 29/38, 45 (Wang Shu-min).

239　29/56–100 In the last two *Robber Chih* dialogues, we find a technical use of falling-tone *wei* 爲 'be *for*' characteristic of Mohist and Yangist disputation. In the Later Mohist disputation the basic concepts in ethics are the pair *yü* 欲 'desire' and *wu* 惡 'dislike,' both of which may either be 'direct, immediate' (*cheng* 正) or follow the 'weighing' (*ch'uan* 權) of the heavier against the lighter (G3: 252–255, 332). Ethical argument starts from what one is 'for,' one's ends in life; the term is defined in *Canons* A 75, "To be 'for' is, having taken account of all that one knows, to give most weight in relation to the desires" (爲，窮知㒵而於欲也). The term is central also to a Yangist chapter in the *Lü-shih ch'un-ch'iu*, chapter 21/4 'Be aware of what you are *for*' (審爲). This *wei* occurs 12 times in the present two dialogues, which we class also as Yangist. In the first dialogue, Tzu-chang advocates moral 'conduct' (行) and speaks of being *for* it (爲行); his opponent prefers 'trustworthiness' (信) in the service of superiors without regard for morality. Both claims are supported by appeals to both reputation and profit. But as the debate proceeds it becomes clear that, as Tzu-chang's opponent observes, "your end is in the last resort (*cheng* 'directly, immediately') reputation, mine in the last resort is profit." (且子正爲名，我正爲利)

29/58 [不] 可 一 日 不 爲 乎 The deletion seems necessary if we are to take the sentence as a genuine question, like its parallel in 29/60 抱 其 天 乎.

240   29/70 吾 (日) *嘗 與 子 訟 於 無 約。<無 約> 曰 …"Let us both try referring the matter to the arbitration of Wu-Yüeh. Wu-Yüeh said…" Cf. 2/76 吾 嘗 爲 女 妄 言 之 "Let me try saying it for you in extravagant words," 21/58 嘗 與 汝 登 高 山 "Let us both try climbing a high mountain…" Previous editors have understood the passage as Burton Watson does: "The other day, when we referred the matter to Wu Yüeh for arbitration, he gave this answer…" (op. cit. 334). This follows Yü Yüeh in understanding *jih* as 'on a former day.' In this sense however one would expect *jih* before—instead of after—the subject (in which position it would be expected to mean 'daily'). Further, the whole dialogue is unsymmetrical if the arbitration *precedes* the debate and is simply quoted at the end by one of the two parties. (As for the restoration of the second 'Wu-Yüeh,' it was already seen to be necessary by T'ao Hung-ch'ing).

240   29/71 殉 = 徇

241   29/73 轉 = 專 Wang Nien-sun.

29/75 [不] 自 (理) *埋 *Shih-wen* variant.

29/79 主正 The 'master' (主) within which assimilates what one learns from outside and makes it one's own; and the 'director' (正) which guides one's words so that they will be acceptable outside. Cf. The note to CTIC 129, 14/49 above.

242　29/83 俠 = 夾 Ma Hsü-lun.

29/86 Punctuate 知者之爲故，動以百姓。

243　29/90 (雍) *推 Sun Yi-jang.

29/95 慰 = 蔚 'illness' Kuo Ch'ing-fan.

29/96 服 膺 'grip to chest and not let go' Morohashi, 14345/139.

29/99 觀之名...求之利 'observe *it* through reputation...seek *it* through profitability.' The reference is to what is "truly the right (way to live)" (眞是), referring back to 29/57, 59.

CTIC Part 5, Chapter 3 (*Chuang Tzu* 30)

246　30/17 (魏) *衛 Wang Shu-min.

30/20 紀 = 基? Ma Hsü-lun.

247　30/29 (服) *伏 斃其處 (也) *矣 with Kōzanji MS.

CSIS Part 5, Chapter 4 (*Chuang Tzu* 31)

249　31/14 (憂) *處, with Kōzanji MS (Yü Hsing-wu).

31/23 煩 = 夾 T'ao Hung-ch'ing.

251　31/28 數 = 速 Li Mien.

252　31/39 祿 = 嫁 Hsi T'ung.

31/44 戚 = 畏 Kao Heng.

253　31/46 (言) *再拜 31/48 至人 (= 仁) These emendations are both introduced into the text of Ch'ien Mu's edition, without annotation. The latter is supported by Li Mien.

PART 6
THE SYNCRETIST WRITINGS

CTIC Part 6, Chapter 1 (*Chuang Tzu* 13/1–45)

260 13/16 其 (鬼) *魄 不 (崇) *疵 Ma Hsü-lun.

261 13/21 (彫) *周 Chang Ping-lin.

13/25 形 名 (比) *之 詳 Li Mien. The parallelism with the surrounding sentences confirms this emendation, which has also to be made in 13/40.

13/29 萌 區 I follow Li Mien in taking this disputed phrase as 'sprouting straight or bent' (區 = 鉤).

13/30ff. 宗 廟...大 道 之 序 也 This sentence of 21 characters is parenthetic and I reject it as a gloss. In the next sentence the phrase 其 序 'their sequence' 其 道 'their way' (13/31) refer back to the 天 地 'heaven and earth' of the sentence before (13/30).

262 13/35 [仁] 賢 不 肖 Wu Yen-hsü.

263 13/43 (出) *土 Sun Yi-jang.

CTIC Part 6, Chapter 2 (*Chuang Tzu* 15)

265 15/8 故 [曰] 聖人...T'ao Hung-ch'ing, with the near parallel in 13/5.

15/9 聖 人 休 [休 焉] <焉。 休> 則 平 易 矣 Yü Yüeh, with a *Ch'üeh-wu* variant and the near parallel in 13/5.

266 15/14 (德) *心 之 失 Wang Shu-min.

15/16 則 [勞 勞 則] 竭 Wang Shu-min.

15/18 不 敢 <輕> 用 也 Wang Shu-min.

CTIC Part 6, Chapter 3 (Syncretist Fragments, from *Chuang Tzu* 11, 12, and 14)

268 11/67 (匡) *縳 Ma Hsü-lun.

269 12/2 天 下 之 (君) *名 正 Ch'ien Mu.

12/3ff. 故 通 於 天 <者 ，道 也 。 順 於> 地 者 ， 德 也 。 行 於 萬 物 者 ， (道) *義 也 。 Restored from the *Ch'üeh-wu* variant, which is confirmed by the sentence (12/4ff.) which resumes the steps between skills (技) and Heaven (天).

14/3 (隆) *降 Yu Yüeh.

270 14/4 六 極 五 常 (= 祥), the Six Calamities (六 極) and Five Felicities (五 福) enumerated in the last sentence of the *Hung fan* 洪 範 (Yü Yüeh).

CTIC Part 6, Chapter 4 (Three Rhapsodies on the Way, from *Chuang Tzu* 12 and 13)

271 12/10 (藏) *沈 珠 於 淵 *Ch'üeh-wu* variant.

12/12 [顯 則 明] Ch'ien Mu.

272 12/18 (脩 遠) *各 *有 *其 *具 with the parallel in *Huai-nan Tzu* chapter 1 (Liu 1/6B/11).

CTIC Part 6, Chapter 5 (*Chuang Tzu* 33)

274 Chapter 33: Throughout this chapter there is a consistent contrast between the ancient and now disintegrated 'tradition of the Way' (道 術: 33/1, 15, 35, 42, 55, 63) and the one-sided 'formula' (方: 33/14) or 'tradition of a formula' (方 術: 33/1) of each of the Hundred Schools except for the Sophists, who have 'many formulae' (多 方 33/69) but no 'tradition' (術 33/81).

33/4 (兆) *逃 with *Shih-wen* variant.

33/7 醇= 準 Chang Ping-lin.

275   33/9ff. 詩 以 道 志…名 分 This parenthesis, in which the four classics already named have grown to six, is probably a gloss (Ma Hsü-lun).

276   33/18 [不 異]. 不 與 先 王 同 I take the deleted words as a corrupt doublet of the next two words.

     33/26 名(山) *川 Yü Yüeh.

278   33/34 (苟) *苛 Chang Ping-lin.

     33/36, 38 請 欲 Cf. 33/41 情 欲 'essential desires' (without which one would not be human), cf. G3: 181ff.

     33/39 (圖) *喬 Ma Hsü-lun.

279   33/46 (後) *復 Sun Yi-jang (鄰) *磷 Liang Ch'i-ch'ao.

281   33/54 積 Since in the introductory formula of each episode the Syncretist is using his own terminology, not that of the school described, we must understand *chi* 'accumulate' as in other Syncretist contexts (11/68, 70; 13/1, three times), as referring to the accumulation of a residue of precedents from past experience.

282   33/59ff. 歸 然 而 有 餘 Probable gloss (Liu Wen-tien).

     33/61ff. 可 謂 至 極 The Kōzanji MS and the *Ch'üeh-wu* read 雖 未 至 極, preferable as *lectio difficilior*. (The latter notes the now standard reading as a variant). The Kuo Hsiang commentary and Ch'eng Hsüan-ying sub-commentary both ignore this clause, which suggests that they knew it in the reading which would embarrass them.

283   33/68 (稠) *調 *Shih-wen* variant.

     33/68ff. 雖 然, 其 應 於 化 而 解 於 物 也, 其 理 不 竭, 其 來 不 蛻。芒 乎 昧 乎, 未 之 盡 者。 "However, when one assents to transformation and is released from things, the body has not exhausted its pattern, having come it cannot be shaken off (i.e. the man who escapes beyond life and death remains a living body with the practical problems of life). Abstruse! Obscure! A man who did not succeed in getting it all."

Commentators have been reluctant to admit that this passage can be criticizing Chuang Tzu. But the opening 雖 然 'However' ought to mark a change of attitude towards him, and Li Mien goes as far as to delete the words. Burton Watson's translation of the conclusion,

"Veiled and arcane, he is one who has never yet been completely comprehended" represents a tradition of interpretation going back to Ch'eng Hsüan-ying, but it is surely unwarranted by the text.

283 33/71 Measurement of *ta* 大 'size' is by circumference. Cf. 43, 1/1 above and G3: 379.

284 33/74 *T'i* 體 in disputation is a unit in counting G3: 265ff.

33/76 On the evidence of *Canons* A 88, *chüeh* 絕 should probably be understood in the sense of 'detach' (from interrelations with other things), cf. G3: 460.

33/80 與人 [之] 辯 Li Mien

Originally published as item no. 7 in appended Bibliography

Chapter 2

How Much of *Chuang Tzu* Did Chuang Tzu Write?

A. C. GRAHAM

TESTS OF CHUANG TZU'S AUTHORSHIP

It is now widely recognized that *Chuang Tzu* 莊子 is a collection of writings of the fourth, third, and second centuries B.C., in which only the "inner chapters" 內篇 (chapters 1–7) can be confidently ascribed to Chuang Tzu himself. They are not necessarily all Taoist, and even among those which are, only the last six of the "outer chapters" 外篇 (chapters 17–22) need be accepted as belonging consistently to Chuang Tzu's own branch of Taoism.[1]

Two basic questions may be asked about the limits of Chuang Tzu's authorship:

1. Can we take for granted the common authorship of the "inner chapters"? There have been attempts to deny Chuang Tzu some of them, notably Fu Ssu-nien's ascription of *Equalizing things* 齊物論 (chapter 2) to Shen Tao 慎到[2]—a proposal as unsettling as it would be to credit Bacon with *Hamlet* while leaving the rest of the plays to Shakespeare.

2. Six of the "mixed chapters" 雜 篇 (chapters 23–27, 32) consist of miscellaneous and often fragmentary pieces, which may be from any or all of the authors in the book. Can we identify Chuang Tzu's hand in them? The "inner chapters" are at some places badly mutilated; it is probable that we could fill some of the gaps with neglected scraps from the "mixed chapters," if we knew where to look.

Let us start by tabulating positive and negative criteria, usages either characteristic of the "inner chapters" or missing from them (the negative we distinguish by parentheses). The positive criteria will be especially interesting when examples outside the "inner chapters" tend to congregate in chapters 23–27, 32. It will be seen that the tests we propose are heterogeneous and of very unequal value, and will have to be used with discrimination. Indeed, a mere listing of favorite words and patterns, although adequate to distinguish such writers as the one we call the "Primitivist," in the case of Chuang Tzu himself comes up against the difficulty that his language is exceptionally rich and varied and also served as a model for other writers in the book, especially in chapters 17–22. It is to be hoped that future scholarship will develop a more sophisticated technique for dealing with him. However, the present table will serve to show up the profound differences between the "inner" and the "outer chapters," to confirm that chapter 2 cannot be denied to Chuang Tzu, and to provide some tests for deciding whether a "mixed chapters" fragment is to be classed rather with the "inner" or with the "outer" chapters. After some comments on the table illustrating its uses for supporting or rejecting claims to Chuang Tzu's authorship, we shall try to show how some scraps from the "mixed chapters" can be used to restore the mutilated introduction to chapter 3.

Table 2

1. Idioms	"inner chapters" (chapter 1–7)	Certain "mixed chapters" (chapters 23–27, 32)	Elsewhere in book (chapters 8–22, 28–31, 33)
1/1 Life and death			
1/1/1 死 生 存 亡	5/43; 6/46; 7/16		

(continued)

1. Idioms	"inner chapters" (chapter 1–7)	Certain "mixed chapters" (chapters 23–27, 32)	Elsewhere in book (chapters 8–22, 28–31, 33)
1/1/2 (未/不) 終其天年 而(不)中道 夭	4/70, 80; 6/2		
1/1/3 悅生 || 惡死	2/79; 4/44; 6/8		
1/2 Perfection			
1/2/1 至矣 (as full phrase)	2/40, 60; 4/53; 6/1	23/45, 58; 24/69, 107	22/67
1/2/2 盡矣	2/40; 4/29	23/58	
1/2/3 進於/ 乎X	2/64; 3/5; 6/76		
1/2/4 X之盛	2/44; 4/42; 5/46; 6/2		12/83
1/3 "How do I know?"			
1/3/1 惡乎知	2/64, 65x2, 78, 79, 80		9/10
1/3/2 惡知 惡識	4/73; 6/65, 68, 78, 79; 2/94x2		17/10
1/3/3 庸詎知	2/66x2; 6/3, 80, 81		
1/3/4 奚以知	1/10		
(1/3/5) 何以知			(8/18; 10/4, 9, 19, 35; 17/19, 20 19/61)
(1/3/6) 焉知			(11/28; 20/59, 60)
(1/3/7) 安知	(5/27)		(17/88, 89, 90)
(1/3/8) 豈識			(13/68)
1/4 Miscellaneous			
1/4/1 古之眞 人	6/4, 6, 7, 14	24/97, 98	21/66

1. Idioms	"inner chapters" (chapter 1–7)	Certain "mixed chapters" (chapters 23–27, 32)	Elsewhere in book (chapters 8–22, 28–31, 33)
1/4/2 若然者	2/72; 4/19, 22, 55; 5/4, 7; 6/4, 5, 10, 68	23/65; 24/97; 25/37	12/10, 51; 21/67
(1/4/3) (若是者) (as subject)		(23/41; 24/6)	(18/31; 19/12; 22/64)
1/4/4 不亦悲乎	1/13; 2/19	24/104; 32/52	12/91
(1/4/5) (悲夫)		(24/38)	(11/61, 72; 13/67; 19/3; 20/9; 22/82; 28/7; 33/14, 87)
1/4/6 形骸	1/31; 5/23x2; 6/66		12/59
(1/4/7) (形軀)			(11/65; 19/58, 68)
(1/4/8) (形體)			(11/54; 12/39; 19/57; 21/25)
1/4/9 惡惡可	4/15, 23; 6/37		
1/4/10 因以	6/50, 51, 52; 7/29x2	23/28, 64x3, 77; 26/47; 27/5; 32/40	
因之以	2/92		
1/4/11 已乎已乎	2/14; 4/88	25/53; 27/14	
1/4/12 薪	1/32; 2/81; 3/14, 17; 4/19; 5/29		14/36; 21/9x2
1/4/13 未定	2/24; 4/5; 6/3; 7/27		
1/4/14 以爲事	1/32, 34, 38; 5/13	25/16	11/8

(continued)

1. Idioms	"inner chapters" (chapter 1–7)	Certain "mixed chapters" (chapters 23–27, 32)	Elsewhere in book (chapters 8–22, 28–31, 33)
1/4/15 爲人使	4/30		
爲天使	4/31		
爲之使		32/51	
所爲使	2/15		
1/4/16 敢問其方	2/4; 4/24; 6/72		17/68
1/4/17 可不...乎/邪/與	1/19, 20; 4/52, 64	24/110; 25/53	21/18, 22
1/4/18 有德者	4/37; 5/20	32/15	

2. Grammar	"inner chapters" (chapter 1–7)	Certain "mixed chapters" (chapters 23–27, 32)	Elsewhere in book (chapters 8–22, 28–31, 33)
2/1 "Never yet"			
未始	2/40, 41x2, 49x3, 50x3, 55x2; 4/28, 29; 6/27, 79; 7/2, 3, 28, 30	23/58; 24/44, 45, 46, 47, 89, 102; 25/17x4	12/25; 21/34, 70x2
2/2 "Only now"			
乃今	1/7, 8, 12; 4/71; 7/1	23/43	
(乃今也)			(11/57)
(乃今於是乎)			(14/61)
2/3 "It is this that is called 'X'"			
是之謂 X	2/40; 4/19, 21, 22, 32, 41; 5/46; 6/9x2, 20	27/4	12/45; 18/39

2. Grammar	"inner chapters" (chapter 1–7)	Certain "mixed chapters" (chapters 23–27, 32)	Elsewhere in book (chapters 8–22, 28–31, 33)
(是謂X)		(23/40, 54, 57; 27/10)	(9/7, 10; 11/63x2; 12/40, 66; 17/42x2, 44, 51, 52, 53; 19/7, 67)
2/4 "Only"			
特	1/12; 2/15, 23; 6/3, 21, 22, 26, 79, 80	32/3	28/30; 33/80
2/5 "Or rather…" with explicit alternatives			
其	1/4x2 (?); 2/16, 17x2, 20, 24x3, 51x2, 86x2; 3/13x2, 16; 5/16; 6/81x2	24/15x2	12/79; 21/25; 22/65
(亡其)		(26/21)	
2/6 Interrogative adverbs			
2/6/1 惡乎	1/21; 2/24, 25x3, 33, 34, 40, 64, 65x2, 78, 79, 80; 3/12; 4/69; 6/43, 60	23/16; 24/24x2, 52; 27/7x3, 8, 19x2, 20; 32/1	9/10; 11/66; 14/45, 46; 22/44; 33/1
2/6/2 惡	2/70, 87, 88x2, 94x2; 4/9, 73; 5/52x2, 53x3, 56, 57; 6/65, 68, 70, 78, 79	23/42; 24/63, 64; 25/69	8/26; 17/38x2, 40; 19/25, 40, 66, 76
2/6/3 庸詎	2/66x2; 4/17; 6/3, 80, 87		

(continued)

2. Grammar	"inner chapters" (chapter 1–7)	Certain "mixed chapters" (chapters 23–27, 32)	Elsewhere in book (chapters 8–22, 28–31, 33)
2/6/4 (安)	(5/27, 31)	(23/27; 25/50; 26/49)	(9/12, 13; 11/17; 13/32, 39, 71; 14/81; 17/56, 88, 89, 90; 18/29; 20/19, 70; 29/26)
(安所)	(1/47)		(30/6)
2/6/5 (焉)		(23/51; 32/9)	(11/28; 19/10; 20/59x2)
2/7 "Since"			
(既…矣)	2/53x2, 84, 87, 88x2, 89; 4/38; 5/19, 25; 6/83	25/23; 27/15; 32/13	12/46
2/8 "Much more / less"			
況…乎	Passim x17	Passim x10	Passim x11
(況於…乎)		(32/4)	
(況乎…乎)		(24/13; 27/24)	(20/56; 22/70)
2/9 "Now"			
2/9/1 今	Passim	Passim	Passim
(今也)		(24/81; 27/22x4)	(11/57; 12/90, 92; 20/24x2; 21/9)
2/9/2 Initial 向, 鄉	3/16; 7/21, 23, 25	23/28	
曩	2/93x2		
(向也)		(27/22x4)	(20/23, 24)
2/10 "Then"			
於是	4/50	24/42; 25/70x2	Passim x18
(於是乎)		(24/83; 26/4, 6, 42)	(11/6, 19, 22, 24; 14/61)
(於是焉)			(17/1, 2; 21/54)

3. Philosophical terms	"inner chapters" (chapter 1–7)	Certain "mixed chapters" (chapters 23–27, 32)	Elsewhere in book (chapters 8–22, 28–31, 33)
3/1 "That which fashions…"			
造物者	6/48, 49, 67, 87; 7/9	32/13	33/67 (of Chuang Tzu)
造化者	6/59		
造化	6/55, 60		
3/2 "Hugest of clumps of soil"			
大塊	2/4; 6/24, 57		
3/3 Receive endowment			
受 (receive endowment)	2/18; 3/17; 5/10, 53; 6/9; 7/32	27/12; 32/28	12/22; 21/20; 31/38
3/4 Combinations with *shih*			
3/4/1 因是	2/28, 29x2, 37, 39, 55	25/55	
3/4/2 爲是	2/35, 36, 47, 55	23/63; 27/3	
3/4/3 移是		23/61, 62, 63x2, 65	
3/4/4 公是		24/39	
3/5 Other terms from chapter 2			
3/5/1 天倪	2/90, 92	27/1, 5, 9, 10	
3/5/2 天鈞	2/40	23/45; 27/10x2	
3/5/3 曼衍	2/92	27/5	33/65 (of Chuang Tzu)
3/5/4 寓	2/36, 47, 92; 4/30; 5/12		
寓言		27/1x2	33/65 (of Chuang Tzu)

(continued)

3. Philosophical terms	"inner chapters" (chapter 1–7)	Certain "mixed chapters" (chapters 23–27, 32)	Elsewhere in book (chapters 8–22, 28–31, 33)
3/6 Stillness			
(靜)		(23/69x2; 98; 26/43)	(11/18, 36x2; 12/6; ch. 13x18; 15/10, 15, 17; 16/6; 19/56; 20/12; 22/48; 29/95; 31/29, 30; 33/49, 50, 57)
(水靜)	"water is still"		(13/3, 4)
止水	"still water" 5/10; 7/26		
止止	"stills the still" 4/32; 5/10		
3/7 Way and Power			
(道德)		(23/32)	(8/2, 17, 33; 9/12, 14; 13/5, 17, 32x2; 15/8; 20/6, 9, 46; 28/67; 33/11)
3/8 (Human) Nature			
(性)		(23/29, 70x2; 24/38; 25/9, 12, 14, 41, 42x3; 32/27)	ch. 8x16; 9/1, 5, 7, 11; 10/39; 11/1, 2, 3x2; ch. 12x9; 13/48, 49, 53; 14/79; 15/16; ch. 16x7; 17/37; ch. 19x5; 20/61; ch. 29x5; 31/5)

3. Philosophical terms	"inner chapters" (chapter 1–7)	Certain "mixed chapters" (chapters 23–27, 32)	Elsewhere in book (chapters 8–22, 28–31, 33)
3/9 Attachment			
累		(23/67, 69; 26/14; 32/21).	(10/28; 11/70, 73; 13/15, 62; 15/12; 17/81; 18/26; ch. 19x5; ch. 20x7; 21/7; 28/14, 54; 31/31; 33/33, 49)

4. Persons and themes	"inner chapters" (chapter 1–7)	Certain "mixed chapters" (chapters 23–27, 32)	Elsewhere in book (chapters 8–22, 28–31, 33)
4/1 Confucius criticized or preached to face to face			
4/1/1 by Lao Tzu			(12/41–44; 13/45–53; 14/44–56, 57–60, 74–82; 21/24–38; 22/28–43)
4/1/2 by others		(26/18–24)	(20/37–44; 29/1–56; ch. 31)
4/2 Lao Tzu as teacher			
4/2/1 to Confucius: (cf. 4/1/1)			
4/2/2 to others	(7/11–15)	(23/23–42; 25/43, 44; 27/25–30)	(11/16–19; 13/53–60; 14/60–74)

(continued)

4. Persons and themes	"inner chapters" (chapter 1–7)	Certain "mixed chapters" (chapters 23–27, 32)	Elsewhere in book (chapters 8–22, 28–31, 33)
4/2/3 (Verbal parallels with Lao Tzu listed *Ku shih pien* 古史辨 vol. 4/357–359)		(23/33–36; 25/63; 27/29)	(10/22, 23, 26, 31, 32; 11/14, 28, 55; 12/5, 81; 13/68; 18/11, 13; 19/67; 20/15, 33; 21/68; 22/7–10, 66)
4/3 Other distinctive characters			
4/3/1 (Yellow Emperor Stories)		(24/25–33)	(11/28–44; 12/18–20; 14/13–30; 22/1–16)
4/3/2 The mad-man of Ch'u	1/27; 4/86–91; 7/4–7		
4/4 Physical deformities			
Physical deformities	4/83; 5/59, 60		
of cripple	6/48–52		18/20
of dying	1/3 (n. 10)		
chopped foot	5/13, 13–24, 24–31, 40		
leper	2/35		12/94
freak (?) (介)	3/12	23/76	
ugly man	5/31–49		
hunchback			19/17–21
4/5 A deformed life conceived as crippling or punishment			
fettering	5/30		
branding and chopped nose	6/84		
天刑之	5/31		
內刑		32/30, 31	
天之戮民	6/71		14/54
遁天之形	3/18	32/16	

4. Persons and themes	"inner chapters" (chapter 1–7)	Certain "mixed chapters" (chapters 23–27, 32)	Elsewhere in book (chapters 8–22, 28–31, 33)
Salvation as release from hanging in bonds (縣解)	3/19; 6/53		
4/6 Use and talent			
Preferring the useless (無用)	1/35–42, 42–47; 4/64–75, 86–91	26/31–33	
Preferring not utilizing (不用) to utilizing		23/65	22/68–70
Preferring untalented (不材) to talented	4/64–75, 75–79		
(Compromising between talented and untalented)			(20/1–9)
(Rejecting as useless)			(8/2, 3, 7; 29/96)
4/7 Irreverence about death			
Irreverence about death and funerals	3/14–19; 6/45–60, 60–74	32/47–50 (Stories about Chuang Tzu himself)	18/15–19 (Stories about Chuang Tzu himself)
4/8 Waking / dreaming			
Waking experience as no more real than dream	2/81–83, 94–96; 6/79–81		

NB: In the tables "x" stands for "times."

Comments

Section 1/1/2. Outside the "inner chapters," the two phrases of the clause appear, but separately (chapter 19/68; 20/2, 4. Cf. also 4/86).

Section 1/4/15. That this passive construction ("is caused/employed by man," "is caused by Heaven," "is caused by it," "that by which it is caused") is not a contraction of the semantically similar construction (爲—subject—所—verb) is especially obvious in these phrases, where the substituted pronouns show that the noun is object: the grammatical analysis remains controversial.

Section 2/5. This is not the familiar exclamatory or rhetorical question pattern exemplified in the opening sentences of chapter 14 (天 其 運 乎，地 其 處 乎) ("Does not heaven turn round? Does not earth stand still?"), which do not present alternatives. The second alternative may be declarative: chapter 2/6,17: 汝 皆 説 之 乎。其 有 私 焉。…其 有 眞 君 存。

> "Are you pleased with them all? Rather, you have a favorite among them…Rather, there is a true ruler present among them." More often it is interrogative: chapter 3/12 天 與，其 人 與 "Is it Heaven? Or rather is it man?"[3]

Sections 2/8; 2/9. These two criteria may be used to decide the relationship between the two versions of the story of the penumbra and the shadow (chapters 2/92–94; 27/21–25). The latter looks at first sight like other parallels with *Equalizing things* in the "mixed chapters" discussed under Section 3/4, but differs from the others in being poetic rather than philosophical. Since the longer version of chapter 27 uses 況 乎…乎, and also 向 也…今 也 where the former uses 曩…今…, we may conclude that it is a later literary embellishment of Chuang Tzu's story.

Section 3/4 *Yin shih* appears first as a verbal phrase in chapter 2/28 因 是 因 非 "If basing yourself on something you judge 'That's it,' then basing yourself on something you judge 'That's not'"; in all subsequent cases it may be taken as the phrase nominalized as a technical term, "the adaptive *shih.*" You may call a thing "X," but must be ready to judge it "not X" in another situation; the error is to assume that it unalterably *is* what you call it, which is *wei shih*, "the constitutive *shih.*" The latter phrase is once used verbally: chapter 27/2: 同 於 己 爲 是 之 ，異 於 己 爲 非 之 "Of what agrees with their own judgment they judge 'That's it' constitutively, of what disagrees they judge 'That's not' constitutively." We may take the two phrases as technical terms expandable to 因 而 是 "to *shih* taking it as one's basis" and 以 爲 X 而 是 "to *shih* deeming it to be 'X'."[4] Cf. Chapter 13/33, also *Han Fei tzu* 43/1/15; 50/5/18 (*Han Fei tzu so-yin* 韓 非 子 索 引, Peking 1982) 因 任 "giving responsibility going by qualifications," *Han Fei tzu* 5/1/51; 8/3/10 因 而 任 之 "going by qualifications he gave them responsibility."

This terminology is confined to *Equalizing things* and to certain sections of the "mixed chapters" which with one exception (chapter 25/54–59) treat the same themes, often with close verbal parallels (chapter 23/52–66; 24/38–48; 27/1–9). These and other "mixed chapters" sections related to *Equalizing things* (chapter 24/61–65, 65–69; 25/15–18, 51–54; 27/10–16; 32/11–16) belong with the "inner chapters" wherever the criteria we have tabulated apply, except for several cases of the pattern 是 謂 X (section 2/3). In several of them Chuang Tzu is debating with the sophist Hui Shih 惠 施 (chapters 24/38–48; 27/10–16. Cf. Also 26/31–33; 24/48–51). The terminology must come from a time of reaction against the sophists in which Chuang Tzu had to devise concepts of his own with which to clarify his rejection of disputation. The need for them would hardly have outlasted his lifetime, and there is no trace of them in the "outer chapters." In general one has the impression that Chuang Tzu was an enemy of logic who knew what logic is, while his successors did not. In the "outer chapters" one may notice that, just as in *Utmost joy* the eloquence about death is concentrated in stories about Chuang Tzu himself, so in *Autumn waters* the little bit of logic-chopping is found in the conversation between Chuang Tzu and Hui Shih about whether the fish are happy. Consequently we need not be worried by the fact that certain "mixed chapters" sections look more like commentary on *Equalizing things* than Chuang Tzu's own writing (for example, chapter 27/1–9). They may well be jottings by disciples to whom Chuang Tzu has been explaining his obscurer thoughts, but must in any case come from very early in the history of the school.

Section 3/5/4. *Yü* 寓 "lodge" is used of assuming temporary instead of permanent standpoints (or, in chapter 5/12, of accepting life as temporary). *Yü yen* 寓 言 "saying from a lodging-point" has established itself in Chinese usage as a word for "parable," but judging by its context refers to borrowing the other man's standpoint for purposes of discussion (using names according to his own definitions, which for Chuang Tzu will be no better or worse than any other).

Section 4/1. The Confucius of the "inner chapters" has an abstract knowledge of the Way but cannot live by it, because it is his nature to live by
rules. This is not his fault, he can't help it; as one of the mutilated
criminals tells Lao Tzu, "Heaven has punished him" (chapter 5/31 天
刑 之). He knows himself that there can be no communion between
those who "roam outside the rules" (遊 方 之 外) and those who
roam within them, and that he belongs irremediably to the latter, as one
of "Heaven's convicts" (chapter 6/67, 71. 天 之 戮 民 . For the imagery, cf. Section 4/5 and comment). When a disciple does achieve the
Way Confucius recognizes him as superior to himself (chapter 6/93).
The madman of Ch'u sings outside his gate (chapter 4/86–91), but no
one ever criticizes or preaches to him face to face. There would be no
point; he knows it all already but it does him no good. Chuang Tzu's
attitude to Confucius has neither the condescension of the dialogues of
Lao Tzu and Confucius in the "outer chapters" nor the scorn of *Robber
Chih* 盜 跖 and *The old fisherman* 漁 父, and only as much mockery
in it as he extends to the whole of life.

Section 4/2. Lao Tzu is a very minor sage in the "inner chapters." In two
stories he appears incidentally (chapters 3/14; 5/29, 30), but only once
does he teach, in the dialogue with Yang Tzu-chü 陽 子 居 (chapter
7/11–15). As a spokesman for Chuang Tzu he cuts a very poor figure
compared with the madman of Ch'u (chapters 1/27–30; 4/86–91; 7/4–
7), who is never mentioned outside the "inner chapters." Any verbal parallel with *Lao Tzu* can be taken as evidence that a passage was not
written by Chuang Tzu. Cf. CTIC 208, 10/14, 21ff. above, for example.

Section 4/4. The "inner chapters" have as fantastic a menagerie of invalids
as the Gospels, but the viewpoint is quite different; they are seen quite
without pity and with the same interest and respect as princes and sages.
Besides illustrating the advantages of uselessness and the irrelevance of
all scales of human importance, they remind us that the supreme test of
possessing the Way is to be reconciled to the least tolerable of disasters,
on the one hand death, on the other physical deformity in life (in particular, the mutilation which exposes you to the public eye as a con-
victed criminal). The concrete detail about deformity and dying, at once
vivid and quite unmorbid, is characteristic of the "inner chapters"; later
writers in the book have no stomach for it. In the "outer chapters" the
humped back of the cicada-catcher (chapter 19/17–21) is incidental to
the story, and the dialogue of Uncle Cripple (支 離 叔) and Uncle
Scatterbrain (滑 介 叔), when at the graveyard a willow sprouts from

the latter's shoulder, is symbolic and not realistic (chapter 18/19–22). The more vivid evocations of death in *Utmost joy* 至 樂, mild as they are compared with *The teacher who is the ultimate ancestor* 大 宗 師, are in stories about Chuang Tzu himself. When Lieh Tzu finds a skull he merely points his stick at it; Chuang Tzu uses it as a pillow and dreams about it (chapter 18/22–29, 40).

Section 4/5. The deformed life of the moralist and conformist is for Chuang Tzu one kind of crippling, a punishment from Heaven which he cannot help. (For Confucius as the most eminent example, cf. Section 4/1). The most explicit account is in the story of the Confucian Huan 緩 (chapter 32/11–16), attributable to Chuang Tzu on this and other grounds (cf. The criteria under sections 1/4/18; 2/7; 3/1). In reaction to Huan's rigor his younger brother became a Mohist; their father took the side of "Ti" 翟 (Mo Tzu insultingly called by his personal name, as Confucius is often called "Ch'iu" 丘), and Huan committed suicide. This was the "punishment for retreating from Heaven (遁 天 之 刑)," for renouncing spontaneity to conceive and choose between the alternatives, Confucianism and Mohism. It had nothing to do with intentions: "the Maker of Things when he recompenses a man recompenses not the man but what is from Heaven in the man. (夫 造 物 者 之 報 人 也 ， 不 報 其 人 而 報 其 人 之 天)" The passage seems to contrast alternatives as *shih* "It" and *pi* "the other," a usage otherwise limited to *Equalizing things*; his fault was to "judge himself *shih*" (自 是), "He 'othered,' therefore caused others to 'other'" (彼 故 使 彼).

Section 4/6. The opening episode of *Mountain trees* (chapter 20/1–9), where Chuang Tzu is represented as balancing judiciously between the talented and the untalented, is a retreat from the unqualified praise of uselessness in the "inner chapters." Elsewhere uselessness is preferred only in a brief exchange between Chuang Tzu and Hui Shih, the first of a string of fragments concluding *Outside things* (chapter 26/31–38). The abruptness of the opening 惠 子 謂 莊 子 曰 。 「 子 言 無 用 」 。 莊 子 曰 "Hui Tzu said to Chuang Tzu: 'Your words are useless.' Chuang Tzu said:...)" suggests that it was added by an editor. He had some remaining scraps at his disposal, noticed the names of Hui Shih and Chuang Tzu in one of them, wrote in an introductory sentence and put it first, then added a "Chuang Tzu said" (chapter 26/33 莊 子 曰) as a heading for the rest. Probably the scrap comes from one of the dialogues on uselessness at the end of chapter 1 (perhaps from after the second stop in chapter 1/46).

A RECONSTRUCTION OF THE INTRODUCTION TO CHAPTER 3

The most obviously mutilated of the "inner chapters" is the shortest, *What matters in nurturing life* (chapter 3). It opens with what looks like the start of an introductory essay similar to that of chapter 6, but breaks off at line 2. The rest consists of three stories, with a little fragment about the pheasant of the marshes between the second and third (line 14). We must assume considerable losses, involving in particular most of an introductory essay.

At the end of chapter 24 (lines 105–111) there is a fragment in which the phrases 無 崖 (= 涯) "unbounded" and (有 崖) "bounded" are contrasted as in the first sentence of chapter 3 (chapter 24/109, 110). This is the last of a string of fragments, thrown together apparently for no better reason than that all start with *ku* 故 "therefore." The editor presumably excised unintelligible material before each *ku*, so that we cannot hope to establish the lengths of the strips (some of which would in any case be broken) by counting the graphs. The immediately preceding fragment (chapter 24/103–105) must come from a later position in the same document, for its phrase "It is because they do not know how to put their questions to this" (不 知 問 是 也), refers back to line 110 "May it not be said that there is a grand total of all? Why not after all put your questions to this?" (可 不 謂 有 大 揚 榷 乎。 闔 不 亦 問 是 已). This shorter piece is rounded off like the conclusion of an essay, and its repetitions of the word *tai* (殆) "dangerous" again recall the start of chapter 3.

Let us attempt a reconstruction of the introductory essay, supplying for good measure two more "mixed chapters" fragments. By the tests which we have tabulated in Table 2 all four are cognate with the "inner" and not with the "outer chapters":

Table 3

CT Fragments	Table 2 Idioms
25/51–54	1/4/17; 1/4/11
24/105–111	1/2/1; 1/4/17
32/50–52	1/4/4; 1/4/15
24/103–105	1/4/4

The sequence turns out to provide a bridge between the first sentences of Chapter 3 and the story of Cook Ting which follows. When the cook "resolves, takes apart" (解) the ox he illustrates how a problem is "resolved, unravelled" (解) by trusting to the "daemonic" (神), without depending on knowledge and the senses.

TRANSLATION

CHAPTER 3/1, 2

吾生也有涯。而知也無涯。以有涯隨無
涯。殆已。已而爲知者。殆而已矣。爲善
無近名。爲惡无近刑。緣督以爲經。可以
保身。可以全生。可以養親。可以盡年。

My life flows between confines, but knowing has no confines. If we use the confined to follow after the unconfined, there is danger of falling short; and to exercise knowledge when it falls short is purest danger.

Doer of good, stay clear of reputation.
Doer of ill, stay clear of punishment.
Trace the vein which is central and take it for your standard.
You can protect your body,
keep your life whole,
nurture your parents,
last out your years.

CHAPTER 25/51–54

蘧伯玉行年六十而六十化。未嘗不殆於
是之。而卒詘之以非也。未知今之所謂莫其
是之。非五十九非也。萬物有乎生而尊其
見其根。有乎出而莫見其門。人皆尊其
知之所知。而莫知恃其知之所不知而後
知。可不謂大疑乎。已乎已乎。且無所
逃。此所謂然與然乎。

Ch'ü Po-yu by the age of 60 changed his mind 60 times; over and over again what he began by affirming as the right alternative he ended by rejecting as the wrong. We do not yet know of what we now affirm that we shall not reject it 59 times over. The myriad

things have something from which they draw life but no one sees
the root, they issue from somewhere but no one sees the door. Men
all respect what their wits know, but no one knows how to know by
depending on that which his wits do not know; may that not be
called the ultimate uncertainty? Enough, enough! Even so they
have nowhere to escape from it; is it what one might call "both the
alternative which is *so*, and the alternative which is *so*"?

CHAPTER 24/105–111

故 足 之 於 地 也 踐。雖 踐。恃 其 所 不 蹍。而
後 善 博 也。人 之 於 知 也 少。雖 少。恃 其 所
不 知。而 後 知 天 之 所 謂 也。知 大 一。知 大
陰。知 大 目。知 大 均。知 大 方。知 大 信。
知 大 定。至 矣。大 一 通 之。大 陰 解 之。
大 目 視 之。大 均 緣 之。大 方 體 之。大 信 稽
之。大 定 持 之。盡 有 天。循 有 照。冥 有
樞。始 有 彼。則 其 解 之 也。似 不 解 之 者。
其 知 之 也。似 不 知 之 也。不 知 而 後 知 之。
其 問 之 也。不 可 以 有 崖。而 不 可 以 無 崖。
頡 滑 有 實。古 今 不 代。而 不 可 以 虧。則
可 不 謂 有 大 揚 搉 乎。闔 不 亦 問 是 已。奚
惑 然 爲。以 不 惑 解 惑。復 於 不 惑。是 尚 大
不 惑。

Therefore though the foot needs ground only to step on, even as it
steps it depends on the untrodden ground to have scope to range;
and though the knowledge a man needs is little, little as it is he depends on what he does not know to know what is meant by
"Heaven." If you know the ultimate One, the ultimate Yin, the ul-
timate eye, the ultimate adjuster, the ultimate in scope, the ultimately dependable, the ultimately fixed, you have arrived. Have
the ultimate One to recognize things as interchangeable, the pas-
sivity of the ultimate Yin to let them unravel, have the ultimate eye
to observe them, the ultimate adjuster to set your route by them, the
ultimate in scope to identify with them, the ultimately dependable
to verify them, the ultimately fixed to support them.

If to exhaust them we have Heaven and to stay on course have its
light, if in obscurity we have the axis on which everything turns
and to start from have that which is other than ourselves, then our
unravelling will resemble leaving unravelled, our knowing will re-

semble ignorance. The questions which we put to that which we know only by being ignorant cannot have confines yet cannot be without confines. If when we wrench everything apart there are objects, each in its own position past or present, and we cannot afford to leave any of them out of account, then can it be denied that there is a grand total of all? Why not after all put your questions to *it*?

What does doubt matter? If you use the undoubted to unravel the doubted and transfer it to the undoubted, this is to have too much respect for the undoubted.

CHAPTER 32/50–52

以不平平。其平也不平。以不徵徵。其徵
也不徵。<u>明</u>者唯為之使。<u>神</u>者徵之。夫
明之不勝神也久矣‹ 而愚者<u>恃其所見</u>。
入於人。其功外也。不亦悲乎。

If you use the unlevel to level, what you level will not be levelled; if you use the untested to test, what you test will not be tested. The sight of the eye is only something it employs; the daemonic in us tests it. It is no new thing that the sight of the eye does not prevail over the daemonic; and is it not sad that fools should depend on what they see and confine themselves to what is of man, so that their achievements are external?

CHAPTER 24/103–105

故<u>且</u>之於<u>明</u>也<u>殆</u>。耳之於聰也殆。心之
於殉也殆。凡能其於府也殆。殆之成也
不給改。禍之長也茲萃。其反也緣功。其
果也待久。而人以為已寶。不亦悲乎。故
有亡國戮民無已。<u>不知問是也</u>。

Therefore the capacity of the eye to see presents dangers, the capacity of the ear to hear presents dangers, the capacity of the heart to understand presents dangers. All ability in what concerns the organs presents dangers, and when the dangers become actual it is too late to mend one's ways. As disaster grows complications multiply, and recovery depends on successful action, which takes a long time to be effective; and is it not sad that men should think of the organs as their greatest treasures? Therefore that there is no end

to ruined states and massacred people is because we do not know
how to put our questions to *it*.

CHAPTER 3/2–12

庖丁爲文惠君解牛。手之所觸。肩之所
倚。足之所履。膝之所踦。砉然嚮然。奏
刀騞然。莫不中音。合於桑林之舞。乃中
經首之會。文惠君曰。譆。善哉。技蓋至
此乎。庖丁釋刀對曰。臣之所好者道也。
進乎技矣。始臣之解牛之時。所見無非
牛者。三年之後。未嘗見全牛也。方今之
時。臣以神遇。而不以目視。官知止而神
欲行。依乎天理。批大郤。導大窾。因其
固然。技經肯綮之未嘗。而況大軱乎。良
庖歲更刀。割也。族庖月更刀。折也。今
臣之刀十九年矣。所解數千牛矣。而刀
刃若新發於硎。彼節者有閒。而刀刃者
無厚。以無厚入有閒。恢恢乎其於遊刃
必有餘地矣。是以十九年而刀刃若新
發於硎。雖然。每至於族。吾見其難爲。怵
然爲戒。視爲止。行爲遲。動刀甚微。謋
然已解。如土委地。提刀而立。爲之四
顧。爲之躊躇滿志。善刀而藏之。文惠君
曰。善哉。吾聞庖丁之言。得養生焉。

Cook Ting was carving an ox for Lord Wen-hui. Wherever his
hand slapped and shoulder lunged, foot stamped and knee crooked,
with a hiss! With a thud! The brandished blade as it sliced never
missed the rhythm, now in time with the Mulberry Forest dance,
now with an orchestra playing the Ching-shou.

"Ah, good!" said Lord Wen-hui, "Has the craft reached such
heights?"

"What your servant cares for is the Way, I have left the craft behind me. When I first began to carve oxen, wherever I looked I saw
nothing but oxen. Three years more, and I never saw an ox as a
whole. And by now I come on it through the daemonic in me, do
not look with the eye. With the senses I know when to stop, but the
daemonic I want to run its course. I rely on Heaven's structuring,
cleave along the main seams, let myself be guided by the main
cavities, adapt to whatever is inherently so. A ligament or tendon I
never touch, not to mention solid bone. A good cook changes his

knife once a year, because he hacks. A common cook changes it once a month, because he smashes. Now I have had this knife for nineteen years, and have carved several thousand oxen, but the edge is as though it were fresh from the grindstone. At that joint there is an interval, and the edge of a knife has no thickness; if you insert what has no thickness where there is an interval, then, what more could you ask, of course there is ample room to move the edge about. That's why after nineteen years the edge of my knife is as though fresh from the grindstone.

However, each time I come to something intricate, I see where it will be hard to handle and gravely prepare myself, my gaze settles on it, action slows down for it, I move the knife very gently—and at one stroke the tangle has been unravelled, as a clod crumbles to the ground. I stand knife in hand, look round proudly at everyone, dawdle to enjoy the triumph until I'm quite satisfied, then clean the knife and put it away."

"Good!" said Lord Wen-hui. "Listening to the words of Cook Ting, I have learned from them how to nurture life."

Comments

We have underlined the words and phrases which link the fragments with each other and with their context in Chapter 3. It must be assumed of course that even if the fragments are correctly identified and placed some of the essay is still missing.

Chapter 3/1. The *yi* (已) resumed by the *yi erh* 已 而 starting the next sentence, and therefore not a final particle but the full verb ("come to an end"), appears also in chapter 2/37. 因 是 已。已 而 不 知 其 然 謂 之 道 "The 'adaptive *shih*' comes to an end; and when it comes to an end, that of which we do not know what is so of it we call the 'Way.'"

Chapter 3/2 督: the vein down the center of the back.

Chapter 25/53. On the present interpretation; 然 與 然 "the so and the so." Even the man who insists on distinguishing alternatives cannot escape from the all-encompassing whole by conceiving an alternative to what is "so" of it; instead of "so" and "not so," his alternatives would be "so" and "so" (cf. chapter 2/90 然 不 然 "Treat what is not so as so").

Chapter 24/111 頡 滑. The only firm evidence for the meaning of this compound is chapter 10/36: 頡 滑 堅 白 解 垢 同 異 "wrench apart (?) the hard and the white, jumble together (?) the same and the different," a stronger variation on the formula 合 同 異 ， 離 堅 白 (chapter 17/66) "combine the same and the different, separate the hard and the white."

Chapter 24/111, For examples of 揚 榷 "total number, sum of all," cf. *Tz'u t'ung* 司 通 2298.

Chapter 24/103. 殉 = 恂

THE PRIMITIVIST DOCUMENTS

The first three of the "outer chapters," *Webbed toes* 駢 拇, *Horses' hooves* 馬 蹄 and *Rifling trunks* 胠 篋 (chapters 8–10), and the essay introducing *Keep it in place and within bounds* 在 宥 (chapter 11/1–28), constitute what is perhaps the most obviously homogeneous body of writings in *Chuang Tzu*. They consist exclusively of essays, in which the two brief dialogues (of Robber Chih and his band, of Lao Tzu and an inquirer, chapters 10/10–13; 11/16–19) serve merely as illustrations imbedded in the argument. The remainder of *Keep it in place and within bounds* consists of stories and essay fragments which with one exception (chapter 11/57–63) have nothing in common with the chapters I shall call "Primitivist"; the last of them (chapter 11/66–74), as Kuan Feng recognizes, is in the manner of the *Heaven and earth* chapter which follows (chapter 12). We may take them as miscellaneous materials used to fill up the scroll.[5] On the other hand the last two passages in the *Heaven and earth* chapter itself do suggest the hand of the Primitivist:

1. Chapter 12/83–95. The odd conclusion ("A leper, when in the middle of the night a child is born to him, hurries torch in hand to look at it, for there is nothing that in his suspense he fears more than that it will resemble himself") becomes intelligible if read as the introduction of chapter 11/57–63, which we have just noticed as a possible Primitivist fragment.

2. Chapter 12/95–102. This fragment would fit in conveniently at chapter 8/26.

There are other passages which expound a philosophy resembling the Primitivist's, in particular the whole of *Mending nature* 繕性 (chapter 16), and a story of Lao Tzu and Tzu-kung (chapter 14/60–74), which uses the Primitivist's slogan "our true nature and destiny" (性命之情) and several times echoes phrases of the Primitivist (chapter 14/63, 72, 73 cf. 11/15; 10/39). But as the tests of his actual authorship we must take expressions characteristic of his very distinctive style:

Table 4

Chapter	8	9	10	11/1–28	12/83–95 11/57–63	12/95– 102	Rest of book
# of lines	(33)	(19)	(41)	(28)	(19)	(8)	
曾史	2		2	3		1	
楊墨	1		2			1	
五色	2	1				1	
五聲	2	1				1	
五味	1					1	
五臭						1	
五藏	2			2			
性命之情	3			4			14/73 (Lao Tzu Story), 24/2
好知		1	4	1			
何以知其然邪	1		4				
曷	(曷嘗…哉)		(10/5)	(曷常[嚐]…哉)	(11/58)		
其於 X 也	2					1	
X 乃始		1		3		1	19/73
聖人之過也		2	1				

(continued)

Chapter	8	9	10	11/1–28	12/83–95 11/57–63	12/95–102	Rest of book
# of lines	(33)	(19)	(41)	(28)	(19)	(8)	
X 之 過 也		1	1				11/52
世俗 謂之/ 所 謂			3		2 (12/84, 85)		
嘗 試 論 之	1		2				
自 三 代 以 下 者	2		1	1			
跖	4		5	3		1	29/1–56

It will be seen that only one of these expressions appears in the miscellaneous material of chapter 11 which we have rejected. In the case of the two joined fragments the evidence is meager, but the general flavor of the Primitivist's crotchety, pugnacious style in them makes me more confident of his authorship than in the case of the story of Lao Tzu and Tzu-kung. Clearly we can leave *Mending nature* out of consideration altogether. We may take the Primitivist as the author of chapters 8–11/28, with the addition certainly of chapter 12/95–102, and probably of chapter 12/83–95 joined with chapter 11/57–63.

The Primitivist's philosophy is as distinctive as his vivid, idiosyncratic, combative manner of writing. It starts from the concepts of *hsing* (性), the specific "nature" of a man, or a crane, or a duck, in accordance with which it is generated and lives out its term, and of *te* (德), the "power" specific to it, its capacity to "achieve" *te* (得), which is to hit spontaneously on the course which is the Way. The difference is explained at the start of *Webbed toes*: webbed toes or a sixth finger grow out of a man's *hsing* but are extraneous to his *te* (they grow naturally but add nothing to the body's powers); on the other hand a wart or a wen is extraneous even to his *hsing*. Unfortunately in civilized society the simple living out of man's term and the simple exercise of eyesight, hearing, and the other capacities of his *te*, are complicated by additions as superfluous as a sixth finger, such as visual adornments, music, moral rules, and logical disputation. The effect is to over-stimulate natural inclinations (淫 其 性

"indulge his nature to excess") and divert capacities to the wrong objects (遷其德 "displace his powers").

The Primitivist looks back to a tribal Utopia in which men lived as spontaneously as the animals, there was no distinction of gentleman and knave, and leaders had names followed by *shih* (氏) implying that their position was that of head of a clan or family. Ever since the Yellow Emperor the original, spontaneous harmony has progressively deteriorated, hastened first by the invention of moral rules, later by disputation to settle disagreements over moral rules. The two great bugbears of the Primitivist are the moralism of the schools of Confucius and Mo Tzu and the disputation of the schools of Mo Tzu and Yang Chu.

The Primitivist's concerns are exclusively social and political, and he hardly mentions the pursuit of the Way as a personal and mystical quest. In the present degenerate times, "if a gentleman has no choice but to preside over the empire" (故君子不得已而臨莅天下 chapter 11/13) he should refrain from governing but take care to "keep in place and within bounds" (*tsai yu* 在宥), allow the people to act according to their nature and power but deny them opportunities to overindulge and be diverted to the wrong objects. The obscure term *tsai yu* seems to be taken from *Equalizing things* in the "inner chapters," where there is a phrase which in one text cited in the *Shih-wen* (釋文) read 左宥, surely *tsai yu* with one accidentally added stroke; the standard text reads 左右 "left and right," unintelligible in the context:

CHAPTER 2/55–57

請言其畛。有在有宥，有倫(＝論)有義(＝議)，有分有辯，有競有爭。此之謂八德。六合之外，聖人存(＝在)而不論，六合之內，聖人論而不議，春秋經世，先王之志，聖人議而不辯。

Let me speak of the marking of its boundaries. One may recognize as there and enclose by a line, sort out and assess, divide up and argue over alternatives, compete over and fight over; these I call the Eight *Te*. What is outside the cosmos the sage recognizes as there but does not sort out, what is inside the cosmos the sage sorts out but does not assess, the successive ages of the annals and the records of the former kings the sage assesses but does not argue over.

There are then eight degrees of aptitude, the least of which are the capacities for competing and fighting; the sage with the highest *te* has the capability simply to put things in their places and enclose them with a boundary.

When did the Primitivist write? The episode of Robber Chih discoursing on the morality of robbers (chapter 10/10–13) appears also in chapter 11 (part 4) of the *Lü-shih ch'un-ch'iu* (c. 240 B.C.); the parallelism is of the type in which there is little identity of phrasing except in the more pungent sayings, suggesting different written versions of a story in oral circulation. The practice of pairing "Tseng and Shih" as models of morality is shared only by *Han Fei tzu* (chapters 26, 27, 49, 51), which in chapter 26 also agrees with the Primitivist in contrasting them with Robber Chih as the model of crime.[6] The crucial evidence of date, as Kuan Feng and others recognize, is in a reference to the state of Ch'i:

CHAPTER 10/6–8

然而田成子一旦殺齊君而盜其國...十二世有齊國。

However T'ien Ch'eng-tzu in one morning killed the lord of Ch'i and stole his state...and possessed the state of Ch'i for twelve generations.

The *Shih chi* records only ten generations of the T'ien family ruling Ch'i down to the fall of the state in 221 B.C.; but the T'ang commentator already noticed that it missed two names in the *Bamboo books*, and quoted this Chuang Tzu passage as confirmation.[7] Now Ch'i was the very last state to fall to Ch'in, so that the Primitivist must have written after the reunification of the Empire. At first sight this is puzzling, for the Primitivist documents assume a background both of political disunity and of fierce competition between the pre-Ch'in schools. But we can find a clue in a historical sketch in *Keep it in place and within bounds*. "Formerly the Yellow Emperor used Kindness and Duty for the first time to tamper with men's hearts" (昔者黃帝始以仁義攖人之心 chapter 11/19). By the time of the Three Dynasties the use of moral rules had led to utter disorder, and "all the Confucians and Mohists arose" (line 22 儒墨畢起), to make things worse by disagreeing over the moral rules. "Therefore men of worth hid away down among the great mountains and craggy cliffs and the lords of 10,000 chariots trembled with anxiety up in their ancestral shrines. In the present age men condemned to death lie back to back, the shackled in cangues and fetters are elbow to elbow, the mutilated are never out of each other's sight, yet it is just now that the Confucians and Mohists start putting on airs and flipping back their sleeves among the fettered and manacled" (lines 25, 26: 故賢者伏處大山嵁巖之下，而萬乘之君憂慄乎廟堂之上。今世殊死者相枕也，桁楊者相推也，刑戮者相望也。而儒墨乃始離跂攘臂乎桎梏之間).

Why does the Primitivist say that the Confucians and Mohists, whose origin he has already recorded, are "only now" (乃始) starting to preach? There is a similar expression in the best attested of the Primitivist fragments: "Yet Yang and Mo are starting to put on airs and think they are getting somewhere" (chapter 12/98: 而楊墨乃始離跂自以爲得).

The reference must surely be to a revival of the schools during the break-down of Ch'in. The schools were suppressed in 213 B.C.; the period of civil war lasted from the revolt of Ch'en Sheng 陳勝 in 209 B.C. to the defeat of Hsiang Chi 項籍 in 202 B.C., and at the very beginning the Confucians joined up with Ch'en Sheng, and K'ung Fu 孔鮒, head of the K'ung family, was appointed a *po shih* 博士 by him.[8] We know from the five Yangist essays in the *Lü-shih ch'un-ch'iu*[9] and the account of the Mohist sects as still active in *Han Fei Tzu* chapter 50, that the schools of "Yang and Mo" survived until the beginning of Ch'in; after a suppression of only four years they would surely, like the Confucians, emerge from hiding to compete for the favors of the various contenders for the Empire. No doubt they soon withered in the very different climate of the Han; but down to 202 B.C. it would seem to a philosopher that he was still living in the age of the Warring Kingdoms, interrupted by only a decade of political unity. Consequently such passages as the following are evidence only that the Primitivist is pre-Han, not that he is pre-Ch'in:

> "Once the sages have died out great robbers will not arise, the Empire will be at peace and have no more troubles" (聖人已死則大盜不起，天下平而無故矣。 chapter 10/16).

> "The stealer of a buckle is executed, the stealer of a state becomes a feudal lord, and at a feudal lord's gate you will find the 'kind' and the 'dutiful'" (彼竊鉤者誅竊國者爲諸侯，諸侯之門，而仁義存焉。 chapter 10/19. The

Confucians looking for Ch'en Sheng's patronage would be a very
good example.).

"At present it has come to the point that the people crane
their necks and stand on tiptoe saying 'At such–and–such place
there's a worthy one,' and pack their bags to head for him, so that
within the family they abandon their own parents and outside the
family leave the service of their own lords; their footprints cross
at the borders of the feudal lords, their carriage ruts meet a thousand miles away." (今遂至使民延頸舉踵曰，某
所有賢者，贏糧而趣之，則內棄其親，而
外去其主之事，足跡接乎諸侯之境，車軌
結乎千里之外。 chapter 10/32–34).

We can therefore date the Primitivist with surprising precision, within
a few years on either side of 205 B.C.

Does the Primitivist belong to the tradition of Chuang Tzu, or rather
to that of Lao Tzu? Certainly the verbal parallels with *Lao Tzu*, which
were noticed in Table 2; 4/2/3, are much more obvious than the echoes of
the "inner chapters" (chapter 8/32 cf. 6/14, and the term *tsai yu* if we are
right in deriving it from chapter 2/55). The Primitivist is indeed one of the
earliest datable witnesses (with Han Fei tzu) to the sudden and extraordinary impact of *Lao Tzu* when it began to circulate in the late third century
B.C. In particular the picture of an idealized village life has an extended
parallel with *Lao Tzu* 80 (chapter 10/31, 32). Probably we should think of
the Primitivist as an exponent of Lao Tzu's ideal of government, only incidentally interested in Chuang Tzu.

THE YANGIST DOCUMENTS

There are three chapters which Kuan Feng ascribes to late representatives of the school of Yang Chu, *Yielding the throne* 讓王 (chapter 28),
Robber Chih 盜跖 (chapter 29), and *The old fisherman* 漁父 (chapter
31). Like the Primitivist essays these are highly combative, attacking moralism on the one hand and worldly ambition on the other from a viewpoint
which Kuan Feng is surely right in identifying not as Taoist but as Yangist. I wish to show that they are examples of that very disputation of
"Yang and Mo" which the Primitivist was attacking about 205 B.C.

These chapters lack the clear evidence of common authorship which we noticed in the Primitivist documents. *Yielding the throne* is a miscellany of older stories (mostly paralleled in the *Lü-shih ch'un-ch'iu* and elsewhere), starting with two versions of the same story about Shun; the compiler may or may not have been the author of one or more of the other chapters. *The old fisherman* and the first episode of *Robber Chih* are alike in being the two stories in *Chuang Tzu* which are most irreverent to Confucius and also the two with the most developed narrative art. (*The old fisherman* indeed is a landmark in Chinese literature, perhaps the earliest story told not by summarizing events but by presenting a changing scene to the inner eye and ear, and coaxing the reader's curiosity about an unnamed and mysterious central character.) But they are not much alike in mood, style, or vocabulary; for example, as the interrogative equivalent of final *yeh* 也 *Robber Chih* uses *yeh* 邪 nine times and *yü* 與 never, *The old fisherman yü* three times and *yeh* never.

It would appear that the *Lü-shih ch'un-ch'iu* is one of the sources of *Yielding the throne*, which is therefore later than 240 B.C. (In the *Lü-shih ch'un-ch'iu* the stories are followed by comments integrating them into the arguments of the chapters, and *Yielding the throne* shares some of the comments.) The title *tsai-hsiang* 宰相 'Prime minister,' first attested in *Han Fei Tzu* and the *Lü-shih ch'un-ch'iu*[10] occurs in *Robber Chih* (chapter 29/62). The same chapter implies the end of Chou in 256 B.C. and the extinction of its descendants (chapter 29/27 "T'ang and Wu stood up as Emperor, but their lines were cut off and extinguished [後世絕滅]"). The great robber is described as a tall man 8 *ch'ih* 2 *ts'un* high (chapter 29/19), which would make him a mere 5 foot 4 inches by the Chou measure (in *Mencius* 6B/2 a visitor who annoys Mencius by boasting of his height is 9 *ch'ih* 4 *ts'un*); evidently the Ch'in and Han measure is assumed, making him 7 foot 5 inches.

Of especial interest are the striking resemblances to the Primitivist essays, which suggest that the two sets of documents must be very close in date. The Primitivist too uses Robber Chih as the exemplary criminal, but nowhere else in *Chuang Tzu* is he mentioned. Themes which *Robber Chih* shares with the Primitivist are the tribal Utopia of long ago and the progressive degeneration under the sage Emperors, the equal harmfulness of moralist and criminal, the usurpation of the state as a crime which makes it moral to serve a criminal (chapter 29/63, 64: "A petty robber goes to gaol, a great robber becomes a feudal lord, and at the gate of a feudal lord you will find the dutiful knights [小盜者拘, 大盜者爲諸

侯，諸侯之門，義士存焉]" is a variant of the dictum in chapter 10/19 which we have already quoted).

During the Ch'in and Han the interregnum of 209–202 B.C. in which we place the Primitivist is the only time when this kind of cynicism about morality and government might be expected to flourish in the open. The story of Confucius courting the robber might even be a direct satire on the head of the K'ung family serving the peasant rebel Ch'en Sheng 陳勝 in 209–208 B.C., an incident which must surely have raised eyebrows at the time. *The old fisherman* on the other hand implies contentment with a stable political order in which "the Son of Heaven's authorities" (天子有司) stand above the feudal lords (chapter 31/13–20); apparently the Han dynasty has already consolidated its power, but the date need not be more than a decade or so after 202 B.C. In any case neither *The old fisherman* nor *Robber Chih* is later than the second century B.C., since Ssu-ma Ch'ien mentions both in his biographical note on Chuang Tzu.[11]

Before proceeding to the thought of the three chapters we must ask a preliminary question: how does one tell a Yangist from a Taoist? According to *Huai-nan Tzu* chapter 13 Yang Chu preached the doctrines of "keeping one's life/nature intact" (全性, a phrase often written 全生; in either case it refers to caring for the body's potentiality to last out man's natural term of life in good health); "protecting one's genuineness" (保真); and "not involving the body in ties for the sake of other things" (不以物累形), not risking life and health for the sake of material possessions.[12] It is because they expound these themes that Fung Yu-lan in his *History of Chinese Philosophy* classed five essays in the *Lü-shih ch'un-ch'iu* as Yangist (chapter 1, parts 2, 3, *Treating life as basic* 本生 and *Giving weight to self* 重己, chapter 2, parts 2, 3, *Valuing life* 貴生 and *The essential desires* 情欲 chapter 21, part 4 *Being aware of what one is for* 審為). However, since Taoists to some extent share these concepts, and Yangists of course identify their doctrine with the Way, it may not always be easy to tell a Taoist, for whom life and genuineness are marginal considerations, from a Yangist for whom they are central. But a crucial difference is implied in the Primitivist's objection to both Yang and Mo, that they engage in *pien* 辯 "disputation," in distinguishing and arguing about alternatives. A Yangist, who is as unmystical as a Mohist, deliberately weighs relative benefits and harm to his person, and defends his philosophy of life by giving his reasons. A Taoist on the other hand denies that one should distinguish between alternatives and premeditated action;

he believes that to aim purposely at the beneficial, the right alternative, destroys the capacity in one's *te* to hit on it spontaneously.

Judged by this criterion, there is an obvious difference between the last two of the three dialogues in *Robber Chih* and those of the rest of *Chuang Tzu*, in which either a question is little more than a stimulus to another burst of Taoist rhapsody, or Hui Shih is arguing logically while Chuang Tzu is mocking logic. They are serious debates in which both parties argue on the same terms, and the spokesman of moralism or worldly success is allowed his say. They are definitely examples of *pien* 辯, not indeed of the sophistical sort, but of the sort which got Mencius his unwelcomed reputation for being "fond of *pien.*"[13] This is hardly true of the first episode, the satirical dialogue between Confucius and the robber, but one notices that the adjectival *pien* "subtle (in distinguishing and arguing)" is used twice of Confucius and twice of the robber (chapter 29/7, 8, 18, 33). In *The old fisherman* Confucius is hardly allowed to get in a word, but the fisherman himself develops at length a coherent case against moralism, solemnly enumerating the eight defects of moralists and the four nuisances which they commit.

If we think of the three chapters as the *pien* of the Yang school we have in the first place a clue to the very puzzling organization of *Yielding the throne*. The stories fall into two sequences, each in chronological order:

(a) Chapter 28/1–68 (from Yao to Confucius): stories about men content with a humble position in life. A number are from the Yangist essays in the *Lü-shih ch'un-ch'iu*, and preserve its Yangist comments. Yet the stories of Confucius and his disciples in adversity are plainly Confucian, and several have parallels in the *Han-shih wai-chuan*.

(b) Chapter 28/68–87 (from Shun to the foundation of Chou): stories of men who sacrificed their lives on minute points of honor. This series is shorter and since it breaks off so early in history probably mutilated. Where the *Lü-shih ch'un-ch'iu* parallel has an approving comment this is excised, as would be natural for an editor who regards "keeping life intact" as the supreme value.

The Shun story in the B series is formally structured like the last Shun story in the A series (chapter 28/8–9, 68–70). On referring to the *Lü-shih ch'un-ch'iu* (chapter 19, part 1), it turns out that they are successive episodes in one story, followed at once by the next story in the B series, of T'ang's attempts to abdicate (chapter 28/70–78), and rounded off by an approving comment which *Yielding the throne* omits.[14] The editor approved of only one of the acts of renunciation (not involving loss of life), and therefore detached it from the rest and placed it in the A series. But why does he fail to tell us that the B series are examples which we are supposed to *avoid*?

We find the answer when we look at the rhetorical devices employed in *Robber Chih*. The debaters constantly appeal, in the traditional fashion, to examples in history or legend. To illustrate the importance of refusing even the greatest of material possessions if it endangers life, one refers to the refusal of a throne by Hsü Yu 許由 or Shan Chüan 善卷 (chapter 29/90); both are among the stories in the A series (chapter 28/1; 5/8). As examples of the absurdity of vainly sacrificing life one appeals to the cases of Po Yi 伯夷 and Shu Ch'i 叔齊, Pao Chiao 鮑焦, Shen-t'u Ti 申徒狄, Chieh Tzu-t'ui 介子推, and Wei Sheng 尾生 (chapter 29/41–45); the first two are the last of the B series, which since it is probably mutilated may have continued with the rest, all chronologically later. It would be useful for a debater of the Yang school to have a miscellany of such examples at his elbow, copied from standard sources such as the *Lü-shih ch'un-ch'iu*. In such a document comments would be unnecessary, although there would be no point in cutting out comments in the sources which agree with the Yangist point of view. Nor would it matter that a story is obviously Confucian; it would be up to the debater to use it for his own purposes. It appears then that *Yielding the throne* is a reference book for debaters of the Yang school.

Proceeding to *Robber Chih*, we must think of the Yangist debater as contending with two enemies, the moralist who insists that it is his moral duty to take office and benefit the people even if it endangers his life, and the worldly people who deride him as a failure. *Robber Chih* begins by attacking the former, in the splendid story of Confucius and the great robber. Its lesson is that moralism in politics can only be a disguise for self-seeking: the Confucian who professes to be seeking office only to benefit the people must fawn on whichever criminal has been strong enough to seize the throne, reduce his moral requirement to a mere respect for the forms (Confucius does not even try to reform the robber, merely to turn him from a *defacto* into a *dejure* ruler), and be despised as a hypocrite by the man to whom he preaches. As Kuan Feng notices, the robber in his replies always appeals to the Yangist concepts, nature, genuineness, long life. Since the robber is not necessarily a direct spokesman for the writer, and his replies are very much in character, this may not convince everyone that the viewpoint of the story is Yangist. In the next dialogue however the representatives of moralism and worldly success refer to an arbiter called Wu Yüeh (無 約 "nowhere committed"), who must speak for the author.[15] He answers with three quatrains of verse (chapter 29/71–73) which sound more Taoist than anything else in the three chapters, at any rate in the concluding line, "Meander with the Way" (與 道 徘 徊). However, didactic verse of all schools tends to have a Taoist ring; it is in his prose that a writer shows how much or little of a Taoist he is, as one often notices in *Han Fei Tzu*. When he speaks in prose, it becomes clear that to "meander with the Way" is simply to adapt opportunistically to circumstances, refusing to get into trouble by being too loyal, trustworthy, honest, or dutiful. Both the moralist and the ambitious man "alter the essential in them, substitute something for their nature" (chapter 29/70 變 其 情 ， 易 其 性). In the third and last dialogue the author's spokesman is an advocate of the quiet life who answers a worldly man from an explicitly Yangist viewpoint. If like Hsü Yu and Shan Chüan one refuses a throne it is not out of high-mindedness but because one "estimates the trouble it will cost, anticipates reversals of fortune, judges it harmful to one's nature (計 其 患 ， 盧 其 反 ， 以 為 害 於 性)" because one "will not for the sake of glory injure life" (不 以 美 害 生 也; chapter 29/89, 90).

In the remaining Yangist chapter the fisherman refuses to take Confucius as his companion on his quest for the "profoundest Way" (chapter 31/41 妙 道 This may sound Taoist, but of course what a philosopher means by the profoundest Way depends on what his philosophy is. The key term in this chapter is *chen* (眞) "genuineness," used thirteen times. This is in fact the fullest account we have of what was understood by Yang Chu's "protecting one's genuineness." In answer to Confucius's inquiry about the term the fisherman says that "forced tears, however woeful, do not sadden; forced anger, however formidable, does not strike awe; forced affection, however much you smile, will not be reciprocated. Genuine woe saddens without uttering a sound, genuine anger strikes awe before it is expressed, genuine affection is reciprocated before you smile. (故 強 哭 者 雖 悲 不 哀 ， 強 怒 者 雖 嚴 不 威 ， 強 親 者 雖 笑 不 和 。 眞 悲 無 聲 而 哀 ， 眞 怒 未 發 而 威 ， 眞 親 未 笑 而 和 。" chapter 31/33, 34). The trouble with moralists, apart from their meddling with other people's affairs, is that they sacrifice genuineness for the artifice of the rites. Although the Taoist attitude to the emotions is not a simple question, it seems safe to affirm that no Taoist would discuss them exclusively in terms of their genuineness.

If these chapters belong to the Yang school, why do they never mention Yang Chu himself? The same problem is raised by the five Yangist chapters of the *Lü-shih ch'un-ch'iu*, which totally ignore him (the philosopher they do mention is Tzu Hua Tzu 子華子),[16] although elsewhere in the book a list of ten philosophers does include him as the representative of *kuei chi* 貴己 "valuing self" (*Lü-shih ch'un-ch'iu* chapter 17, part 7).[17] The answer, paradoxical as it may seem, is probably that the school commonly identified by the name "Yang" had very little interest in Yang Chu. He is not known to have left any writings; no book appears under his name in the Han bibliography, and *Below in the Empire* (*Chuang Tzu* chapter 33), which as far as we can judge by the surviving texts is based throughout on the writings of the philosophers, does not include him. The Yangists were not, like Confucians and Mohists, a school committed to a founder and a book. No doubt they honored Yang Chu as the first, or with Tzu Hua Tzu and others one of the first, advocates of Nurture of Life (養生) in the fourth century B.C.; but his notoriety as an egoist may well have discouraged them from calling attention to him unnecessarily. It would be the outsider who needed the name of a supposed founder to identify the school. If, for example, you are listing the ten major philosophical schools, you need the name of a representative "Nurture of Life" man to put beside Confucius, Mo Tzu, and the rest. If like the Primitivist you are denouncing the disputation of Mohists on the one side and the "Nurture of Life" school on the other, you need a name to pair with Mo Tzu ("Yang and Mo").

Kuan Feng does not include *Explaining Swords* 説劍 (chapter 30) among the Yangist documents. It does indeed seem at first sight to be the one chapter in *Chuang Tzu* without any philosophical message at all. It tells how a certain Chuang Chou, who may be the philosopher but shares nothing identifiable with him except his name, dissuades a king from making his swordsmen fight to the death for his own amusement. But for an advocate of "keeping life intact" the story would have a message, that one ought not to sacrifice life pointlessly. We may therefore treat chapters 28–31 as a block, a Yangist library including stories from outside the school assembled for use in disputation. This explains why the titles of chapters 28–31 all sum up the contents of the chapters, breaking with the otherwise consistent practice in the "outer" and "mixed" chapters (resumed in chapters 32, 33) of taking the title from the chapter's opening words. The name of "Chuang Tzu" in *Explaining swords*, the irreverence to Confucius in *Robber Chih* and *The old fisherman*, the obscuring of the Yangist point by the citing of miscellaneous stories, might well help the reader of a casually assembled bunch of Yangist documents to spring to the conclusion: "Of course, these must be from Chuang Tzu!"

THE SYNCRETIST DOCUMENTS

The Primitivist chapters are followed by a block of three chapters (chapters 12–14) with similar titles *Heaven and earth* (天 地), *The Way of Heaven* (天 道), and *The cycles of Heaven* (天 運), expounding a political philosophy in which the Way of Heaven and of earth is the model for government, and then by *Finicky notions* (刻 意; chapter 15), a single essay with extensive verbal parallels with *The Way of Heaven*. The traditional practice, followed by Kuan Feng, has been to take the first three together, discard some passages, but otherwise assume their unity. But this is to be deceived by their proximity and similar titles into two oversights:

1. The philosophy, which we shall call "Syncretist," is plainly expressed only in the essays introducing the chapters, all but one quite short (chapters 12/1–6; 13/1–45; 14/1–5), and perhaps also in three rhapsodies on the Way headed "The Master said" (夫 子 曰), (chapter 12/7–18; chapter 13/60–64). It is in fact only *Finicky notions* which is a single essay Syncretist throughout. As for the rest of the contents of the chapters, it would seem that like chapter 11, they have been filled out with miscellaneous stories and essay fragments. The displacement of one of the rhapsodies to chapter 13, and the presence, as we noticed earlier, of another Syncretist fragment at the end of chapter 11 (chapter 11/66–74), and of two Primitivist fragments at the end of chapter 12, confirm that it is dangerous to treat the chapters as wholes.

2. At the end of the book there is another Syncretist chapter with a similar title, *T'ien hsia* 天 下 "Below Heaven" (chapter 33). The term means of course "the world," but if we consider why the author uses it so persistently (no less than 30 times in the course of the chapter), it becomes plain, as we shall see shortly, that he is talking about the theorizing over the Way which goes on *below* the administrative hierarchy to which it properly belongs. *Below in the Empire* is perhaps the most convenient

translation of the title. Since the chapter is a historical summing-up of the pre-Han schools placing Chuang Tzu in perspective, it may well have been split off from the rest to serve as conclusion to the book.

We may check these proposals by a linguistic test. Readers of *Chuang Tzu* will be aware of the frequency of the particle *hu* 乎 which follows the verb or its object and is traditionally taken as synonymous with the preposition *yü* 於, in some parts almost as common as *yü* 於 itself; but in the Syncretist writings it is nearly absent. There are no examples in *Finicky notions*, nor in the essays in chapters 11/66–74; 12/1–6; 13/1–45; 14/1–5. In *Below in the Empire* we find the phrase 無 乎 不 在 "There is nowhere it is not" (chapter 33/2, 8), in which *hu* operates like the pronoun *so* 所, but only one doubtful example of the particle (chapter 33/9, the obscure sentence 圖 傲 乎 救 世 之 士 哉). The rhapsodies on the Way do use it (chapter 12/16 twice; 13/63, 64 twice); this may have something to do with their poetic style, but leaves one in some doubt whether to class them with the rest. In the material which fills out the chapters post-verbal *hu* is common (8 times in chapter 12/18–102; twice in chapter 13/45–60, although not in 64–74; 6 times in chapter 14/5–82).

The reluctance to use *hu* shows up in the four phrases which we put at the head of the following table, of expressions characteristic of the Syncretist documents:

Table 5

				Rhapso-dies?	
Chapter	11/66–74 12/1–6 13/1–45 14/1–5	15	33	12/6–18 13/60–64	Rest of book
Number of lines	(73)	(22)	(87)	(18)	
通 於	11/72; 12/3, 6; 13/2, 16			12/13, 14	28/64 (*hu* 13/64; 18/19; 19/12)
明 於	11/72x2 13/2		33/7		17/48x2 (*hu* 11/62; 21/8, 11; 23/49x2)

Chapter	11/66–74 12/1–6 13/1–45 14/1–5	15	33	Rhapso- dies? 12/6–18 13/60–64	Rest of book
Number of lines	(73)	(22)	(87)	(18)	
成 於	11/69; 12/1				(*hu* 2/22; 19/52, 53)
原 於	12/1		33/2	12/9	
天 道	11/72, 93x3; 13/1				23/6 (variant)
天 地 之 道		15/7	33/84		
天 德	12/2 13/43	15/14, 17			
帝 王 之 道	13/2, 8, 17, 23				12/48
天 地 || 神 明	13/29		33/7, 13, 62		
宗 || 本	13/11		33/3, 68		
主 || 臣	11/73; 13/19, 24				
王 天 下	13/15, 21, 45			12/11	
畜 下, 畜 天 下	12/5; 13/17 35, 41				
育 萬 物	13/22; 13/8x2	15/19	33/7; 33/5		
以 此	9x2; 34x4		22x2, 34, 37, 74, 78, 85		4/79 (9/17 = 已 此)

The extent to which *Below in the Empire* shares the Syncretist vocabulary is striking, especially since for most of its length the author is describing other philosophies, not his own; this is no doubt the reason why
its connection with the other chapters which have "Heaven" in their titles

has been overlooked. The table also goes some way to confirm that the three rhapsodies belong with the Syncretist writings. It may be noticed, however, that in spite of the common terminology there is a pronounced difference between the stately, parallistic style and bare vocabulary with which *The Way of Heaven* and cognate essays present the political philosophy, and the liveliness and verbal richness of discussions of rival schools in *Finicky notions* and *Below in the Empire*. This may have something to do with the content, since nothing livens up one's style as much as being roused to combat, but it seems safer to think of a Syncretist school rather than a single author like the Primitivist.

Kuan Feng notices a strong general resemblance between the philosophy and that of four chapters of *Kuan Tzu*, *The lore of the heart* A and B and *Exposing the heart* (心 術 上 ， 下 and 白 心; chapters 36–38) and *Inward training* (內 業 chapter 49)—the sage king modeling himself on heaven and earth, cultivating his "quintessence" (*ching* 精) in order that daemonic power (*shen* 神) may enter him from outside, practicing inaction himself but requiring both morality and law of his ministers. The Syncretist documents indeed use the phrases "lore of the heart" (chapter 13/26) and "expose the heart" (chapter 33/34), the latter in the formula introducing the school of Sung Hsing and Yin Wen, to which Kuo Mo-jo, followed by Kuan Feng, ascribes the four *Kuan Tzu* chapters on very dubious grounds.[18] (The reference to "exposing the heart" is one of the strongest pieces of evidence. But in the introductory formulae of *Below in the Empire* the author describes in his own words the limited aspect of the Way appreciated by the school; he does not, judging by the examples of Mo Tzu, Lao Tzu and Chuang Tzu, use its specific terminology.) Kuan Feng puts the Syncretist documents in the early Han, on general considerations to which we may add Ch'ien Mu's observations that the term *su wang* 素 王 "untitled king" (chapter 13/9) and the enumeration of the classics as six (chapter 33/9, 10), are not attested before the Han.[19] Certainly the general impression made by them is of a settled Empire and of a Taoist-based eclecticism of the sort officially favored in the second century B.C., although a reference to the Mohist school as still alive (chapter 33/31) suggests that we cannot put them too long after 202 B.C.

We may suspect that it was the Syncretists who edited the book *Chuang Tzu*, placed *Below in the Empire* at the end in order to show that irresponsible genius Chuang Tzu in a proper perspective, and even supplied the titles of the seven "inner chapters." These strange three-word titles resemble those of the Han apocryphal books, and Jen Chi-yu even took them as proof that the seven chapters are Han forgeries.[20] If we pick out paired words in the titles which appear in the text of *Chuang Tzu*, and discard two taken from the chapters themselves (逍遙 chapter 1/47 and 養生 chapter 3/12) and one which belongs to ordinary rather than philosophical vocabulary (人間), we find that the rest belongs to the Syncretist documents:

Table 6

Syncretist	Elsewhere in *Chuang Tzu*
齊物 33/43	
大宗 13/11	
帝王 13/2, 5, 8, 17, 22, 23; 14/4	13/48; 17/39; 28/27

It may be objected that in the title *Ta tsung shih* (大宗師) the paired words are 宗師 "ancestral teacher." But the context in the *Way of Heaven* essay suggests that we should understand the title as "The teacher who is the ultimate ancestor," that is, Heaven (cf. chapter 33/3 以天爲宗 "He takes Heaven as his ancestor," and outside the Syncretist documents, chapter 25/10 以天爲師 "He takes Heaven as his teacher"):

CHAPTER 13/11, 12

此之謂大本大宗與天和者也，…莊子
曰，「吾師乎，吾師乎。虀萬物而不爲
戾，澤及萬世而不爲仁…」

It is this that is meant by being from the ultimate root and the *ultimate ancestor* in harmony with Heaven…Chuang Tzu said: 'My *teacher*, O my *teacher*! He chops to shreds the myriad things but is not deemed cruel, his bounty extends to a myriad ages but he is not deemed kind...'

The quotation from Chuang Tzu (the only acknowledged quotation from the "inner chapters" anywhere in the book) is actually from the *Ta tsung shih* chapter (chapter 6/88).

In the Syncretist philosophy Heaven is the superior member of the pair "Heaven and earth," and the Way is the "Way of Heaven" or "Way of

heaven and earth." The sage king who mirrors events and responds without premeditation shares in the spontaneous motions by which heaven and
earth proceed on their courses. The power by which heaven, earth, and
Emperor hit on their undeviating paths is *shen* (神), the "daemonic," the
numinous, the marvellous. "Nothing is more daemonic than Heaven" (莫
神於天 chapter 13/22), "Heaven and earth are perfectly daemonic" (夫
天地至神 chapter 13/30), and the spirits throughout heaven and earth
called *shen ming* (神 明), "daemonic and illuminated" (chapter 13/29;
33/7, 13, 55, 62) embody this pervasive and mysterious power. The sage
"lives in tranquility alone with the *shen ming*" (詹然獨與神明居
chapter 33/55); and the question to which the Syncretist philosophy is the
answer is stated at the beginning of *Below in the Empire* as "From where
does the daemonic descend, from where does illumination come forth?"
(chapter 33/2 神何由降， 明何由出). The "Way to nurture the
daemonic" 養神之道 (chapter 15/18) is to preserve one's *ching*
"quintessence" in unadulterated purity. It is by his *ching shen* (精 神),
the "quintessential and daemonic" in him, that the sage in the stillness of
his heart mirrors the myriad things (chapter 13/4); war, reward and punishment, rites, music, mourning, all follow the motions of his *ching shen*
(chapter 13/26).

However it is only the emperor who practices the Way of Heaven and
"does nothing"; below him are the ministers who follow the "Way of
man" and "do something" (無 / 有爲 chapters 11/72–74; 13/17–21). In
fact there is room for only one Taoist in the world, except in private life;
and even the private Taoist is conceived as a potential ruler, an "obscure
sage and untitled king" (chapter 13/9 玄聖素王). Below the Emperor
himself administration requires both Confucian morality and the Legalist
techniques of reward and punishment and comparison of "title and performance" (形 名).[21] The "comprehensive Way" (大 道) has nine levels;
the first place belongs to Heaven, the second to the Way and the Power of
Taoism, the third to the Kindness and Duty (仁 義) of Confucianism, the
rest to the various administrative techniques (chapter 13/32–34). The
author strongly emphasizes that "title and performance" comes only fifth
on the list, and that reward and punishment has the ninth and lowest place
(chapter 13/37), thus taking a definite stand on the early Han issue of how
much to retain of the Legalist methods of the Ch'in. He warns us against
the rhetoricians (辯 士) who mistake these tools of government for the
Way itself (chapter 13/40).

Finicky notions and *Below in the Empire* both criticize various limited philosophies of life from the viewpoint of the more comprehensive "Way of heaven and earth." (天地之道) The former starts by attacking five kinds of persons who refuse office or take it for the wrong reasons—moralists who disapprove of the regime, other moralists who prefer teaching and self-improvement, politicians concerned only with personal ambition and organizational issues, hermits who sit fishing by the river (Chuang Tzu himself would be a good example), and the cultivators of longevity. Only one of the types criticized does take office; public life is if anything even more important for the Syncretist than for a Confucian, who can at least withdraw from it on moral grounds. These five fail to see that their aims are all encompassed by "the Way of heaven and earth, the Power of the sage" (天地之道，聖人之德 chapter 15/7, 8), which the author proceeds to describe by summarizing, with many close verbal parallels, a passage in *The Way of Heaven* (chapter 15/8–13, cf. 13/5–16). Although Kuan Feng recognizes this relationship he seems to me to confuse the issue by grouping *Finicky notions* with the next chapter, *Mending nature* 繕性 (chapter 16). *Mending nature* is Primitivist in tone, treating all government as a deviation from the original tribal Utopia, and defending private life. *Finicky notions* assumes the importance of taking office and is Syncretist throughout, including the final passage on "nurturing the daemonic" by keeping one's quintessence pure. The post-verbal *hu*, the absence of which we noticed in *Finicky notions*, appears eight times in *Mending nature*.

The great value of *Below in the Empire* for the historian of Chinese philosophy makes it important to recognize the Syncretist assumptions behind its judgments. It begins by contrasting the comprehensive "tradition of the Way" (道術) with the one-sided "tradition of a formula" (方術) possessed by a philosophical school. The philosophers, like the rhetoricians in *The Way of Heaven*, are described as "men each with his own little corner" (chapters 13/40; 33/12, 13 一曲之人 / 士). The "tradition of the Way," which centers on "the Way to be inwardly a sage and outwardly a king" (chapter 33/14 內聖外王之道), comprises first the Taoist arts for becoming a sage, conceived in Syncretist terms (chapter 33/3 不離於精，謂之神人 "One not parted from his quintessence is called the 'daemonic man'"); second, the morality of the Confucian gentleman; and third, the laws, comparisons of title and performance, and other techniques of the officials (chapter 33/3–6). Originally all this lore was a unity, now it survives fragmented at two social levels:

1. Much of administrative technique is preserved by "the scribes (*shih* 史), by whom the old models are passed down through the generations," much of the morality by the Confucian teachers of Tsou 鄒 and Lu 魯 (chapter 33/8–10). The Yin and Yang are also mentioned, under the Confucian teaching of the *Changes* (chapter 33/10).

2. The rest has become scattered *below* in the Empire, among the hundred competing schools. "If scholars of later generations unhappily do not perceive the pure doctrine of heaven and earth and the grand corpus of the ancients, the tradition of the Way will be ripped to pieces down below in the Empire" (後世之學者，不幸不見天地之純，古人之大體，道術將爲天下裂 chapter 33/15).

This division explains why the author does not discuss the Confucians, Legalists, or theoreticians of Yin and Yang among the schools competing below; their lore survives where it belongs, among teachers and officials with acknowledged functions in the governing apparatus.

The Syncretist next lays down which aspect of the Way is recognized by each of five major schools, introducing all of them with the same formula: "A, B, C, anything in the ancient tradition of the Way which resides in these, X got wind of and delighted in." (A, B, C, 古之道術有在於是者，X 聞風而說之) Thus Mo Tzu inherited the tradition of thrift, stern self-discipline, and practicality, which unlike Chuang Tzu the Syncretist values. Since we are in the habit of assuming that this writer would think of himself as a Taoist and of Lao Tzu and Chuang Tzu as his authorities, it is easy not to notice that he fits them both into the same frame as Mo Tzu. It is true that he is much more polite to Lao Tzu and his stablemate Kuan-yin 關尹, and in the standard text even says that "they can be said to have attained the ultimate" (chapter 33/61 可謂至極). However we must accept as the *lectio difficilior* the variant "although they did not succeed in attaining the ultimate" (雖未至於極);[22] evidently some pious Taoist altered the text. Chuang Tzu himself is presented less as a philosopher than as a poet of the Way, who because of the extravagance of his language must be approached with caution; the concluding phrase 未之盡者, although commentators have explained it otherwise, surely pronounces him "a man who did not succeed in exhausting it." The explicit quotation from Chuang Tzu which we noticed in *The Way of Heaven* (chapter 13/12) has the comment, "It is this that is meant by the joy from Heaven, (此之謂天樂)" suggesting that it is cited as an eloquent expression of that joy. If writers as square as the Syncretists respected a writer as hip as Chuang Tzu, it would have to be primarily for literary reasons.

Below in the Empire concludes by disposing of Hui Shih and the sophists. This section is out of chronological sequence and lacks the formula introducing the previous five schools; Kuan Feng shares the common opinion that it was tacked on from some other source.[23] But on closer inspection one sees that the sophists are treated separately because, unlike the rest, they do *not* have a *fang shu* (方術), tradition of a formula. "Hui Shih had many formulae" (惠施多方) and said, "I keep to the male role (discover things for myself), I have no tradition behind me" (施存雄而無術 chapter 33/69, 81). The Syncretist is especially scornful of the triviality of his approach to the greatest of all themes, heaven and earth; he tried to explain why heaven does not fall down and earth does not give way, and the causes of wind, rain, and thunder. "If you consider Hui Shih's abilities from the viewpoint of the Way of heaven and earth, yes, it's like the labors of a gnat or a mosquito" (由天地之道觀惠施之能，其猶一蚊一虻之勞者也 chapter 33/84). The teaching of Hui Shih differs from the rest in being quite worthless; there is none of the ancient tradition of the Way in it, nothing at all except original thinking, logic, scientific curiosity.

Notes

Originally published as item no. 42 in appended Bibliography

[1] Cf. Kuan Feng 關鋒, in *Chuang Tzu che-hsüeh t'ao-lun chi* 莊子哲學討論集 (Peking, 1962), 61–98.

[2] Fu Ssu-nien 傅斯年, "On the authorship of *Ts'i-wu-lun* in *Chuang Tzu*," *Bulletin of Academia Sinica* 6/4 (1936): 557–567.

[3] Ma Hsü-lun 馬敘倫, *Chuang-tzu yi-cheng* 莊子義證 (Commercial Press, 1930), 3/5B.

[4] Cf. my "Chuang Tzu's Essay on treating things as equal," *History of Religions* 9/2, 3 (1969): 143, 144, where however I took *wei* in the sense of acting with contrivance. For the relativism of Chuang Tzu there is no *kung shih* "common shih-ing" (universal agreement that something is "X"). "A constitutive *shih* refers to a shifting *shih*" (chapter 23/56 爲是舉移是); the example given is that those we now call "the living" were formerly "nothing" and in future will be "the dead" (chapter 23/58–66).

[5] It is probable that Chapter 11 was built up in three stages: (1) The Primitivist essay (lines 1–28). (2) The addition of the stories of Kuang-ch'eng and of the Cloud General (lines 28–57). The former is one of only two stories in *Chuang Tzu* advocating the immortality cult (the other is chapter 12/26–33). The Primitivist slogan "one's true nature and destiny" (性 命 之 情) surely implies acceptance of the destined term of life, like the phrase "fathoming one's true destiny" (達 命 之 情) expounded at the beginning of chapter 19. (3) For the remaining episodes (lines 57–74) the *Shih-wen* records no items from commentators earlier than Kuo Hsiang, suggesting that when Kuo Hsiang abridged *Chuang Tzu* he incorporated them from the chapters which he discarded (an observation of Takeuchi Yoshio 武 内 義 雄 in *Roshi genshi* 老子 原 始 [Tokyo, 1967], 154).

[6] *Han Fei Tzu chi-shih* 韓 非 子 集 釋 edited by Ch'en Ch'i-yu 陳 奇 猷 (Peking, 1958), 491, 492, 868, 950, 952, 974.

[7] *Shih chi* 史 記 (Peking, 1969). Chapter 46, *So-yin* 索 隱 (1886).

[8] Ibid., chapter 47 (1947).

[9] The parallels are noted throughout in Ch'ien Mu 錢 穆 *Chuang Tzu tsuan-chien* 莊 子 纂 箋 (Hong Kong, 1951), 233–242.

[10] *Han Fei Tzu*, chapter 50 (Ch'en 1093). *Lü-shih ch'un-ch'iu chi-shih* 呂 氏 春 秋 集 釋 edited by Hsü Wei-yu 許 維 遹 (Peking, 1955), chapter 6 part 3, 6/14A.

[11] *Shih chi* (chapter 63), 2143.

[12] *Huai-nan Tzu chu-shih* 淮 南 子 注 釋 (Taipei: Hua-lien 華 聯 Publishing Company, 1973), chapter 13, 218.

[13] *Mencius* 3B/9.

[14] *Lü-shih ch'un-ch'iu chi-shih* 19/1B-3A.

[15] The bridging passage seems to be corrupt: chapter 29/70 吾 (曰) 嘗 與 子 訟 無 約 。〈無 約〉 曰 "'Suppose I go with you to put our case to Wu Yüeh?'. Wu Yüeh said:…" (For the syntax cf. chapters 2/76 予 嘗 為 汝 妄 言 之 "Suppose I say it for you in wild words?": 21/58 嘗 與 汝 登 高 山 "Suppose I climb a high mountain with you?")

[16] *Lü-shih ch'un-ch'iu chi-shih* (chapter 2, part 2, 21 part 4) 2/7A, 21/9B, 10A.

[17] Op. cit. 17/30B.

[18] Kuo Mo-jo 郭 沫 若, *Sung Hsing Yin Wen yi-chu k'ao* 宋 鈃 尹 文 遺 著 考, in *Ch'ing-t'ung shih-tai* 青 銅 時 代 (Chungking, 1945).

[19] Ch'ien Mu, op. cit., 104, 270.

[20] *Chuang Tzu che-hsüeh t'ao-lun chi* op. cit., 184, 185n.

[21] Following Creel's interpretation of *hsing ming* in H. C. Creel, *What is Taoism?* (Chicago, 1970), 85.

[22] This is the reading of the Kōzanji 高 山 寺 manuscript and of the *Chuang Tzu ch'üeh-wu* 莊 子 舉 誤 of Ch'en Ching-yüan 陳 景 元 (died 1084),

which mentions the now current reading as a variant; since the pre-T'ang and T'ang commentators ignore the sentence, the latter is the earliest witness to the text.

[23] Takeuchi (op. cit., 156) points out that *Shih-wen* quotations from the commentary of Ts'ui Chuan 崔 譔 (died A.D. 290) are plentiful earlier in the chapter but missing in the Hui Shih episode. He infers that Kuo Hsiang incorporated the passage from a discarded chapter, which he identifies as the *Chuang Tzu Hui Shih p'ien* mentioned in *Pei Ch'i shu* 北 齊 書 (Peking, 1972), chapter 24, 353. But the Ts'ui Chuan comments break off much too early, at the first sentence of the P'eng Meng section, missing the whole of the Lao Tzu and Chuang Tzu as well as the Hui Shih sections. We cannot ignore this discrepancy, for in all the "inner chapters" and in all other chapters annotated by Ts'ui Chuan which are consecutive essays (chapters 8, 9, 10, 16) his comments continue to the end. Whatever the explanation (the commentary may have been mutilated or never finished) it has nothing to do with the textual history of *Below in the Empire*.

Chapter 3

Chuang Tzu's Essay on Seeing Things as Equal

A. C. GRAHAM

INTRODUCTION

The *Ch'i wu lun* ("Essay on Seeing Things as Equal") is the second chapter of *Chuang Tzu*, one of the seven "inner chapters" which Chuang Tzu (ca. 300 B.C.) is generally believed to have written himself.[1] There is a wide consensus that it is the most important chapter in the book, which amounts to saying that it is the most important document of early Taoism outside the *Tao Te ching* itself. It contains many of the most famous examples of Chuang Tzu's poetic lyricism, parable, humor, mystical insights and subtle, elliptical reasoning. There is a further quality which is not easy to define but perhaps the principal reason why a student of Taoism returns so often to this chapter. It is the sensation of a man thinking aloud, jotting the living thought at the moment of its inception, of thought which is not yet systematic but "existential" if you like the word, a sensation quite unique for the reader of early Chinese philosophy and uncommon at any period except the most recent in the intellectual history of any civilization. In this respect there is an interesting contrast with the *Ch'iu shui* ("Autumn floods") in the "outer chapters," where we also find a crystallization of Chuang Tzu's ideas, but this time a mature systematization, very probably by a later member of his school. It goes without saying

104

that a document which affects us in this way is likely to present great difficulties in addition to the ordinary textual and linguistic problems of an ancient text; we cannot be sure that Chuang Tzu, struggling with his own developing thoughts, was immediately concerned with making himself intelligible even to readers of his own time. In the following notes I shall discuss some of the problems of the chapter, and conclude with a new translation of the whole.[2]

1. Throughout the chapter we frequently find Chuang Tzu formulating an idea and then revising or attacking it. Sometimes perhaps he is criticizing a provisional formulation of his own; often certainly he is attacking an idea already current. The recurrence of this pattern seems to have been generally overlooked. Thus it is common to credit Chuang Tzu with the statement that "heaven and earth were born together with me and the myriad things and I are one" (§12). Yet Chuang Tzu immediately proceeds to argue that the claim that everything is one is self-contradictory. In sections 3, 6, 11, and 15 we find other statements immediately followed by "This is somewhere near it," "However....," "These five are not so far from the right direction." All will be marked in the translation by inverted commas, although we need not assume that all of them are actual quotations. Wen Yi-to has noticed that in section 2 it is necessary to distinguish between a text which he takes to be Chuang Tzu's and a commentary which he supposes to be later;[3] in the light of the other examples it seems more likely that Chuang Tzu is himself commenting on a text which he quotes.

2. The main targets of Chuang Tzu's attack are his contemporaries—the sophists Hui Shih and Kung-sun Lung.[4] The chapter once mentions Hui Shih by name (§10) and twice mentions paradoxes quoted as his in the *T'ien-hsia* ("The World") chapter: "I go to Yüeh today but arrived yesterday" (§4) and "A thing at birth is simultaneously dying" (§6). It also quotes two sophisms of Kung-sun Lung defended in the second and third chapters of the extant *Kung-sun Lung Tzu*,[5] "A white horse is not a horse" and "The meaning is not the meaning" (§7). Throughout he uses the technical vocabulary which we find in the main surviving document of Chinese dialectics, the *Canons* (a point which previous commentators and translators do not seem to have fully appreciated):[6]

Pien [辯] "disputation" (passim), literally "distinguishing, discriminating" (between proposed alternatives).

Liang [兩] "on both sides" (§9), referring to the alternatives between which disputants must decide.

Ch'ü [取] "choose, prefer" (§§1, 3, 4) one alternative rather than the other.

Sheng [勝] "win" (§§2, 13), one alternative prevailing.

Ming shih [名 實] "names and objects" (§9).

Chü [舉] "pick out" (§8) one object from others by means of its name.

Lei [類] "kind," as a verb "(be) of the same kind" (§11).

Chien pai [堅 白] "as hardness to whiteness" (§10), inseparables which sophists try to prove separate, also used as a term for sophistical hair-splitting in general.[7]

K'o [可] "admissible, valid" (passim), of a proposition.

Shih [是] "(is) the one in question" and *fei* [非] "is not" (passim), the alternatives in disputation, for example whether a thing is or is not an ox.

Jan [然] "so" (passim), what is so of a thing rather than what it is. For example in "Seeing Things as Equal," concrete examples of *shih/fei* are being or not being a horse (§7) and being a stalk or a pillar (§8), of *jan* it being so that a man who climbs a tree is frightened while an ape is not (§17), and that a shadow moves or is still (§19).

Chuang Tzu contains many anecdotes of meetings between Hui Shih and Chuang Tzu, in most of which the Taoist laughs at the sophist's logic. But in chapter 24, in the story of his visit to Hui Shih's tomb, he recognizes that he has learned from these encounters:[8] "Since the Master died I have had no one to sharpen my wits on, no one with whom to discuss things." In spite of the absolute contrast in temperament and point of view between the rational Hui Shih and the mystical, intuitive Chuang Tzu there is, as Fung Yu-lan recognizes,[9] considerable common ground between them, and in this essay we actually see Chuang Tzu in the process of sharpening his wits on Hui Shih. It is remarkable that the last of the theses of Hui Shih quoted in the *T'ien-hsia* chapter[10] is "Love the myriad things without exception, heaven and earth are one body," and that although Hui Shih's explanations no longer survive, the whole list can be read, like Zeno's paradoxes, as a series of proofs that it is impossible to divide space and time without contradiction:

(a) "The absolutely great has nothing outside it; it is called the Greatest One. The absolutely small has nothing inside it; it is called the Smallest One."

(b) "What is without thickness cannot be accumulated, yet its size is a thousand miles." (If we divide, the smallest division will be the one not further divisible, the "Smallest One," which is a point. A thousand miles is therefore an accumulation of points, yet no number of points is larger than one point.)[11]

(c) "The sky is as low as the earth, mountains are level with marshes." (If we count divisions we have the concept of the infinite, the "Greatest One": then two positions, however high or low, will have infinite and therefore equal distances both above and below, and so will be level.)

(d) "The sun at noon is simultaneously declining, a thing at birth is simultaneously dying." (If we divide time, the smallest division is the moment, which also presents a contradiction; the moment when the sun begins to decline and a creature to die is the moment of noon and birth.)

(e) "The largely similar [? is the same as the slightly different?] but different from the slightly similar; it is this that we call 'Treating both similarities and differences as slight.'[12] The myriad things are all similar and all different; it is this that we call 'Treating both similarities and differences as large.'" (If we divide, we find the things which we distinguish both similar and different, which involves two pairs of contradictions: [1] Things are both less similar than they are different and less different than they are similar. The point, which is obscured by textual corruption, is perhaps that we may describe them as simply more or less similar, recognizing no difference except between degrees of similarity, or as simply more or less different, recognizing no similarity except that all alike are different. [2] The converse is that things are both more similar than they are different and more different than they are similar.)

(f) "The south has a limit yet has no limit." (The familiar paradox of infinite or finite space.)

(g) "I go to Yüeh today and arrive yesterday." (This can be taken as an illustration of the problems of dividing both space and time; either claim is true if I cross the frontier at the moment between one day and the next.)

(h) "Linked rings can be detached." (If the infinitely small exists we can have rings of infinite thinness, pure geometrical lines which can be passed through each other.)

(i) "I know the center of the world; it is north of Yen in the far north, south of Yüeh in the far south." (Any position in space is the center because from any position space extends infinitely, and therefore there are equal distances in every direction.)

(j) "Love the myriad things without exception, heaven and earth are one body."

In each case, on the present interpretation, the paradox arises from dividing space or time and counting or comparing divisions; the conclusion is that division leads to self-contradiction and therefore "heaven and earth are one body," with the practical corollary that we should "love the myriad things without exception" (the doctrine of universal love which Hui Shih inherited from the Mohist school of the fifth century). It is clear that in taking this position Hui Shih comes dangerously close to discrediting his own tool, analytic reason. He wishes to discredit only spatial and temporal divisions, but it will take only one more step to observe that all reasoning depends on making distinctions and to reach the conclusion that we should abandon reason for the immediate experience of an undifferentiated world, transforming "heaven and earth are one body" from a moral into a mystical affirmation. Chuang Tzu takes this step in a passage which refers directly to Hui Shih's fourth thesis ("A thing at birth is simultaneously dying") and to the claim to "make admissible even the inadmissible" ascribed to Kung-sun Lung in the "Autumn floods" chapter.[13] Here he declares that the possibility of proving contradictory theses which so delights sophists arises as soon as we make the distinction which is basic to analytic thought, that between the "it" which a thing is and the "other" which it is not. We should therefore avoid contradiction by refusing to make this distinction:

> Therefore it is said: "Other comes out from it, It too adapts to Other," the opinion that It and Other are born simultaneously. However, "at birth we are simultaneously dying" and at death we are simultaneously living, the admissible is simultaneously inadmissible and the inadmissible is simultaneously admissible, if adapting to the one "that's it" then adapting to the other "that's

not" and if adapting to the one it is not then adapting to the other it is. Therefore the sage does not take this course but illuminates all in the light of heaven (§6).

3. Chuang Tzu's basic objection to dialectics, the arbitrariness of all naming, first appears in section 5: "Saying is not blowing breath, saying says something; the only trouble is that what it says is never fixed." As he observes in section 7, there is no need of Kung-sun Lung's sophistical proofs that "A white horse is not a horse" and "The meaning is not the meaning"; I have only to take some other thing and name it "horse," and the animal commonly called a horse will no longer be a horse in my terminology. Recognition that all naming is conventional had become a commonplace by the third century, when the Confucian Hsün Tzu can be observed taking the fact quite calmly in his *Cheng ming* ("Correction of Names").[14] But throughout "Seeing Things as Equal" we feel the exhilarating shock of the discovery when it was still new, the apparent overthrow of all received ideas when it is first seen that in principle anything might be called anything. There is some difficulty in finding English equivalents of the key terms *shih* and *fei* which will not obscure this part of the argument. Ordinarily we translate them by "right" and "wrong," and are not worried by the fact that *shih* is basically a demonstrative ("this, it, the one in question") used verbally ("is the one in question"). Another key term in judgments, *jan* ("so, thus, as the one in question") also has a demonstrative basis, but in this case not disguised by the English equivalent "so." This grammatical point is quite crucial to the understanding of Chuang Tzu and to the whole conception of disputation as we find it in the *Canons*. There the typical disputation is over such issues as whether X is or is not an ox, horse, or dog, in which one side says *shih* ("It is the thing in question"), the other *fei* ("It is not").

Canon A 74: "One man says it is an ox *wei chih niu* 謂 之 牛 one says it is not an ox *wei chih fei niu*...In this case the claims do not both fit, and if they do not both fit, necessarily one does not fit."

Canon B 35: "In disputation one man says it is the thing in question *wei chih shih*, one says it is not *wei chih fei*, and the one whose claim fits is the winner."

Chuang Tzu's familiarity with the stock illustrations in disputation can be seen in chapter 25: "If we use this (the Tao) for disputation, and compare it to a dog or a horse, we shall fall a long way short of it." It also explains a curious remark which he ascribes to Lao Tzu in chapter 13: "Formerly, when you declared me an ox I 'said it was an ox' *wei chih niu*, when you declared me a horse I 'said it was a horse.' If there is the object, to refuse the name which someone gives to it is to make twice as much trouble for yourself."[15] (See also ch. 7 "At one time he deemed himself a horse, at another deemed himself an ox."[16])

Disputation therefore assumes agreement as to what is *shih*, "this, the one in question," in contrast to what is *pi*, "that, other." For Chuang Tzu it is highly significant that judgments are made with demonstratives, which are obviously relative to the speaker's standpoint; just as if you and I stand at different places my "here" will be your "there," so if we start from different systems of naming (for example the different moral terminologies of Confucians and Mohists) what is *shih* for me will be *fei* for you. Previous translators have generally abandoned all hope of making this part of the argument intelligible in English by such inconsistencies as translating *shih* and *pi* by "this" and "that" but *shih* and *fei* by "right" and "wrong." It is admittedly difficult to achieve a consistent set of equivalents without resorting to very forced English. I have used "it" and "other" for *shih* and *pi*, and such phrases as "that's it, that's not" for *shih* and *fei* (in their transitive uses "accept" and "reject"), always avoiding "right" and "wrong" even when they would allow much smoother English.

An important question is raised by two unobtrusive phrases, *yin-shih* 因是 and *wei-shih* 爲是, which seem to me to be contrasted technical terms previously overlooked, the "adaptive *shih*" and the "contrived *shih*." The former appears six times in the chapter, the latter four times. *Yin* and *wei* in isolation are familiar Taoist terms, sometimes contrasted, as in the *Chih-tu* ("Knowing Measures") chapter of the philosophical encyclopedia *Lü-shih ch'un-ch'iu* (ca. 240 B.C.): "Therefore the prince who has the Way adapts and does not contrive (*yin erh pu wei* 因 而 不 爲)." *Yin* is to base one's actions on the changing situation, to adapt to circumstances without imposing fixed principles; *wei* is to act on inflexible principles, forcing one's will against the spontaneous course of things (as in the Taoist formula *wu-wei*, for which a translation equivalent, no worse than most others proposed, would be "without contrivance"). It may therefore be suggested that the two phrases refer to opposite kinds of *shih* "approval, recognition as 'it'": *yin-shih* is "to approve adapting to the situation," to make relative judgments according to changing conditions like the Taoist sage; *wei-shih* is "to approve according to contrived principles," to judge between alternatives according to one's fixed preconceptions, like Confucians and Mohists. It is noticeable that the first appearance of *yin-shih* is shortly after the quotation *shih yi yin pi* 是 亦 因 彼 ("*Shih* too adapts to *pi*") in section 6. Criticizing the quoted phrase, Chuang Tzu writes *yin shih yin fei* 因 是 因 非 "If adapting you *shih* then adapting you *fei*."

Such technical compounds with *shih*, odd as they may seem, have parallels in the *kung* 公 *shih* "universally recognized *shih*" and *yi* 移 *shih* "shifting *shih*" of other chapters.[17] We may compare "when a contrived 'that's it' picks out a stalk from a pillar" 為 是 舉 莛 與 楹 in section 8 with the obscure phrase which we may provisionally translate "A contrived 'that's it' picks out a shifting 'it'" 為 是 舉 移 是 in chapter 23.[18] Sinologists can make up their minds about the present hypothesis from the handling of the ten examples in the present translation; if accepted, it greatly clarifies a number of the most difficult passages. But there are also examples in other chapters. In chapter 25, Confucius asks three historiographers why a notoriously dissolute duke has been given an auspicious posthumous name: the first answers simply 是 因 是 也 "It was a case of doing what we thought acceptable in the circumstances."[19] At the beginning of chapter 27, which has much in common with "Seeing Things as Equal," we find the sentence 同 於 己 為 是 之 ， 異 於 己 為 非 之. "Those who agree with themselves they contrive to approve, those who differ from themselves they contrive to reject."[20]

For Chuang Tzu, then, competing thinkers do not really disagree; they simply divide up the world into It and Other from different standpoints. When a philosopher clings to his assertions although the situation is changing and insists on their absolute validity against the conflicting assertions of others, he is guilty of the error of *wei-shih*. But if he changes his judgments with the changing situation and understands that rival philosophies are all equally valid or invalid, he is practicing *yin-shih*. The latter is the proper attitude of the Taoist in action who does not distinguish alternatives, take one or other as goal, reason how to attain it, but who reacts with his whole being to the situation from one moment to the next, as the shadow to the form or the echo to the sound; he takes one course rather than another but without having envisaged and chosen between alternatives, as a swimmer or angler spontaneously moves without having considered and rejected the other courses which he might have taken. However, as we are twice told (§§8, 12) even *yin-shih* comes to an end in the state (presumably of withdrawal from action into contemplation) in which any distinction between It and Other is seen to be illusory and all language dissolves in the immediate experience of an undifferentiated world.

4. Chuang Tzu several times mentions sophisms but never discusses them; he takes it for granted that the sophists do prove contradictory claims and do not see that in doing so they discredit logical proof. But at one place (§§11, 12) he surprises us by himself arguing very subtly in the manner of the sophists. The reason for this betrayal of his own antira- tionalism is that he wishes to dispose of two apparent exceptions to his claim that every statement identifies an "it" and excludes an "other," so that no statement can be independent of the speaker's standpoint. The second is Hui Shih's "heaven and earth are one body," which might seem to be a proposition independent of standpoint to which Chuang Tzu is himself committed. But in section 12 he presents it in the form "heaven and earth were born together with me and the myriad things and I are one" (the incantatory splendor of the whole passage suggests that the phrasing is his own) and rejects it on the grounds that as soon as I say it there are two things, the world and my statement about it. His point resembles the difficulty about the One and its name raised by Plato in the *Sophist*.[21] Chuang Tzu's position is that we should cease to distinguish between one thing and another, but this does not entitle us to affirm that "everything is one," a proposition which imme- diately distinguishes itself from the world which is other than it. That he is attacking Hui Shih is confirmed by section 9, where he derides the er- ror of "wearing out one's wits treating things as one without knowing that they are the same," a phrase close in wording to his mockery of Hui Shih for overstraining his intellect at the end of chapter 5.[22] We may notice also that he does not recommend the principle of universal love, which for Hui Shih is the practical corollary of "heaven and earth are one body." For him love originates with division, when we begin to prefer one thing to another (§10).

Section 11, immediately preceding the criticism of "the myriad things and I are one," has not previously been interpreted as the answer to an- other objection of this type.[23] It is a basic assumption of disputation as we find it in the *Canons* that we can state alternatives which exhaust all pos- sibilities, so that one claim must be right and the other wrong. This im- plies what we call the law of the excluded middle, that anything is either X or not X (see *Canons* A 74, B 35 quoted in item 3 above) and that what is not not X is X (see *Canon* B 67: 牛 不 非 牛 ， 馬 不 非 馬 "an ox is not not an ox and a horse is not not a horse"). It would seem to follow that as a description of everything "oxen and non-oxen" is independent of standpoint, valid whatever I choose to call by the name "ox." Chuang Tzu begins by stating this objection, that there is no "other" left out if both alternatives are presented together:

> Now suppose that I speak of something, and do not know whether
> it is of a kind with the "it" in question or not of a kind. If what is of
> a kind and what is not are grouped together as of a kind with one
> another there is no longer any difference from an "other."

But Chuang Tzu believes that to distinguish alternatives is always to miss something out (§10: "The displaying of It and Other is the reason why something is missing from the Way"). To show this he takes as example "beginning."

> However, let us try an example. There is "having begun," there is
> "not yet having begun."

The description or its negation does apply to every concrete thing, which has either already begun or not yet begun. But if we negate the negation we do not return to the affirmation, but arrive at a third possibility: "There is 'not yet having not yet begun.'" This brings us nearer to what the two alternatives left out, the Tao which at no time in the past has not yet begun. But the "not yet" still implies a beginning in the future, and we are caught in an infinite regress which never quite brings us to what neither had nor will have a beginning.

> Next he tries *yu* "there being" and *wu* "there not being."

> There is "there being," there is "there not being."

But these alternatives assume that we are distinguishing things of which we can say "there is" or "there is not." Prior to making distinctions we can say neither, only say "There is 'there not yet being "there not being"'." But with this we are caught in the same infinite regress as before: "There is 'there not yet being "there not yet being 'there not being"'"."

We may notice that elsewhere Chuang Tzu describes the Tao by both *wu yu* "there is no 'there being something'" and *wu wu* "there is no 'there not being something'."[24] He is much more sophisticated than later Taoists who describe the Tao simply by *wu* "there is not anything." Here he rounds off his criticism by pointing out that as soon as we distinguish *yu* and *wu* we find ourselves in the anomaly of saying *yu wu* "there is 'there not being.' "

There is a third point on which Chuang Tzu exercises his logical skill: the impossibility of knowing whether we know. If another man's convictions contradict mine, how do I know which of us knows? The question arises also when I change my mind; in chapter 27 we find Chuang Tzu saying to Hui Shih "Confucius in sixty years of his life changed sixty times; what he approved before he ended by rejecting. We cannot know whether what we approve now we shall not reject fifty-nine times."[25] There can be no answer unless there really is an independent standpoint from which others may be judged. But, as he points out in section 13, there can be no such standpoint; any third person called in to judge between debaters merely offers a third opinion from his own standpoint (he is of course assuming debaters who, like the Confucians and the Mohists, disagree over first principles). Consequently "not I nor you nor he can know which of us has won." One implication of this line of thought would be that even if the whole world agreed on something we could never know that we do know what we all agree on, since the possibility of any further standpoint from which to judge would be excluded by definition. This implication seems to lie behind the first exchange in a remarkable dialogue in section 17:

> Would you know something which all things agreed in accepting?
>
> How (*wu-hu* 惡 乎, literally "from where?") would I know that?
>
> Do you know what you do not know?
>
> How would I know that?
>
> Then does no thing know anything?
>
> How would I know that? However let me try to find words for it:—
> "How do I know that what I call knowing is not ignorance? How
> do I know that what I call ignorance is not knowledge?"

The questioner wishes to show that it is possible to know something for certain. He makes three proposals:

(a) I know what is universally accepted. But then, as we have just seen, there can be no further standpoint from which to know that we know.

(b) If not, at least I know what it is I do not know. But Chuang Tzu like Plato in the *Meno* takes this as obviously self-contradictory. This is one of the claims found in *Chuang Tzu* which are criticized in the *Canons*,[26] where the difficulty is explained in terms of the Mohist distinction between knowing names (which includes all understanding of words) and knowing objects, two of seven kinds of knowing distinguished in the *Canons*:[27]

Canon B 47: Knowing what one does not know. Explanation: "choosing between names."

Explanation If someone mixes things which you know and things which you do not know and asks about them, you will certainly say "This is what I know, this is what I do not know." If you are able to choose the one and disclaim the other, you know both (that is, you know both what you know and what you do not know.)

(c) If not, at least I know that no one knows anything. But this again is self-contradictory, since it implies that I both know nothing and know something (that I know nothing). Chuang Tzu, for whom it is never legitimate to affirm or deny except in relation to the changing situation, will not deny that there is knowledge; he concludes that all that may be allowed is the interrogative form raising a doubt, "How do I know...?"

5. The impression of Chuang Tzu struggling to clarify ideas as they develop is perhaps strongest in sections 2, 3, where he considers the *hsin* "heart." This word presents a basic translation problem. It is common and convenient to translate it by "mind," and at a much later stage in the history of Chinese philosophy, for example in the Neo-Confucianism of the Sung dynasty (A.D. 960-1279), the *hsin* "mind" certainly is clearly distinguished from the *hsin* "heart." But Chuang Tzu's whole argument is about the physical organ, which for Chinese thought is the seat of intelligence and occupies the place of the brain in our own scheme of concepts. We must therefore translate it "heart," in spite of the misleading associations of the English word, which suggests the center of feeling rather than of thought. Chuang Tzu attacks the assumption that the heart directs the body by its judgments of *shih* and *fei*, an assumption which we find, for example, in the *Chieh-pi* ("Getting Rid of Prejudices") of Hsün Tzu.[28] In this section, which begins with what seem to be notes on a quotation concerning the heart from some older source, two lines of thought are of especial interest. Chuang Tzu insists that the heart, being only one of the organs, is no more "me" than any other. We suppose that it controls the rest, but in fact the various members are interdependent and "take turns as each other's ruler and subjects." Nevertheless they do have an order among them, which shows that they have a "true ruler" which is not the heart, namely the Tao. The implication is that if we dislocate the spontaneous ordering of the whole organism to impose control by the intellect, we are diverging from the

Way. A second line of thought, one which leads to the criticism of knowledge later in the chapter, is that if we take as authority the heart which develops, deteriorates, and perishes with the body, each man has his own fallible authority which contradicts everyone else's. Yet we cannot suppose that *shih* and *fei* exist apart from the conflicting intelligences which judge between them: "For *shih* and *fei* to exist before the heart's development would be 'going to Yüeh today and arriving yesterday.' This would be crediting with existence what does not exist."

6. Chuang Tzu uses logic only to attack logicians; to convey his positive vision he uses poetic metaphor. At several places in the chapter he jumps from prose to verse, with a sudden change of key which makes it important to keep the distinction in English; continuous prose translation gives the impression that instead of rising to poetry he is simply relapsing into incoherence. It may be mentioned that there can be no greater misrepresentation of Chuang Tzu than to suggest that there is anything naïve about him (except for the kind of naïveté which is in fact the capacity to look straight at things which for lesser intelligences are obscured by our tangles of preconceptions), or that his thought is muddled even when it is most difficult or, from other points of view, most wrong. It is the astonishing freedom and breadth of Chuang Tzu's intelligence, ranging between subtle intellectuality, humorous anecdote, mysterious dreamlike parable, wild incantatory poetry, and vivid evocation of nature (the grasp of a landscape as a whole is a much later achievement of Chinese culture, but he has a passion for birds, animals, fish, insects, trees, and women—anything in which he senses the spontaneity of the living) which make him unique among Chinese philosophers and the despair of all translators.

The chapter begins with one of his most complicated metaphors, the wind which makes different noises according to the shapes of the hollows into which it blows. From the "pipes of man" (the panpipes through which a man blows different notes according to their lengths) and "pipes of earth" (the hollows in mountains and trees through which the wind, rising from the Great Clod, the earth, blows different noises) he proceeds to the "pipes of heaven." These are apparently the holes in the heart through which thought courses and the mouths which utter it, so that the breath blown by heaven through the different inner formations of different men issues in contradictory utterances. Echoes of this metaphor sound throughout the chapter, in "music coming out of emptiness [the voids of pipes]" (§2), "saying is not blowing breath" (§5), the music and the silence of

Chao Wen's lute (§10), the "voices in their transformations" (§13). Another metaphor rounds off the chapter, the dream in which we suppose ourselves to be awake (§§18, 20). This is not, as a Western reader easily supposes, an intimation that life is an illusion from which we wake to the reality behind it, but an illustration of the relativity of all knowledge; it reminds us that what we think we know while dreaming contradicts what we think we know while awake, and suggests that like the opposite opinions of philosophers, these have equal status. The last sentence suggests that the divergence between Chuang Tzu and the butterfly which he becomes in his dream is no different from the divisions and developments which we think we know about in the waking world.

There is an unobtrusive metaphor which recurs throughout the chapter, that of throwing everything open to the light. It is assumed that when we judge between alternatives we turn the light on what we select as "It" and leave everything which is "Other" in darkness; it is in the wordless illumination which discredits all distinctions that the whole world is open to the light. Examples are: "By what is the Way hidden?" (§5), the sage who "illuminates in the light of heaven" (§6), the "displaying of It and Other" which impairs the Tao, the "bringing to light" (*ming* 明) of one alternative at the cost of the other which leads to the "darkness" of sophistry, the "glitter of glib debate" (§10), the failure of disputation leaving others "in the dark" (§13), the error of "lighting up" the Way (§15), the disputed phrase *pao-kuang* 葆光 here translated "Preserving the Light" (§16). Judging by the example with *ming*, the repeated injunction "The best course is to use *ming* [insight, illumination]" (§7 twice; see also §10, "It is this which I call 'using *ming*'") assumes the same metaphor; it is therefore translated in the present version, "The best course is to throw things open to the light." The metaphor also accounts for a brief episode which may seem irrelevant, the anecdote about the ten suns which rose together and illuminated all things (§16).

TRANSLATION[29]

§1: Nan-kuo Tzu-ch'i sat leaning on his armrest, looked up at the sky and breathed serenely, as though his self had lost its opposite.[30] Standing in attendance before him, Yen-ch'eng Tzu-yu inquired,

"What is this? Can the body really be made to become like a withered tree, the heart like dead ashes? The man who sits here now is not the man who was sitting here before."

"Tzu-yu, it is a good question that you ask! Just now I had lost myself, did you know it? You have heard the pipes of men, it seems, but never the pipes of earth, the pipes of earth but never the pipes of heaven."

"Tell me what you mean."

"The Great Clod blows out breath, its name is 'the wind.' Better if it never begins, for when it begins ten thousand hollow places burst out howling, and have you never heard how the long noise drags on? The bends in mountains and forests, the holes in great trees a hundred spans round, are like nostrils, mouths, ears, sockets, bowls, mortars, pools, puddles. Roaring, hissing, hooting, sucking, shouting, moaning, bellowing, wailing, the winds ahead sing out *aaah*! and the winds behind answer *eeeh*!, a quiet chorus in the breeze, a mighty chorus in the whirlwind. When the fierce wind stops all the hollows become empty, and have you not noticed how the clash resolves as it fails?"[31]

"The pipes of earth, these are the hollows everywhere; the pipes of men, these are rows of tubes; tell me about the pipes of heaven."

"Who is it that blows the ten thousand disputing voices, who when of themselves they stop their talk has sealed them, and puffs out of them the opinions that they choose for themselves?"[32]

§2:   "Great knowledge is free and easy,
        Petty knowledge picks holes.
        Great speech has a mild taste,
        Petty speech is all rant.
        When it sleeps the soul encounters,
        When it wakes the body opens to the world.
        We entangle ourselves with all that we meet
        And daily wrangle over the thoughts in our hearts."[33]

The careless thinkers, the deep thinkers, the complex thinkers.

        "Petty fear is fretful,
        Great fear does not care.
        The heart shoots its thoughts like bolts from a crossbow,"

referring to its judgments, "That's it, that's not."

        "It ties us down as though by oath or treaty,"

referring to the way that it holds fast to the winning alternative.

"It declines as though through autumn and winter,"

referring to its daily deterioration. As it sinks it cannot be made to repeat what it once did.

"Its source is stopped as though it were sealed,"

referring to its degeneration in old age. As the heart nears death nothing can restore its vigor.

Pleasure in things and anger against them, sadness and joy, forethought and regret, change and immobility, excellence and error, like music coming out of emptiness or vapor condensing into mushrooms, alternate before it day and night and no one knows from what soil they spring. Enough! The source from which it has these morning and evening, is it not that from which it was born?

§3: "Without Other there is no Self, without Self no choice between alternatives."

This is somewhere near it, but we do not know by what all this is caused. It seems that there is something genuinely in control, and that the only trouble is that we cannot find a sign of it. That as "Way" it can be walked is true enough, but we do not see its shape; it has identity but no shape. Of the hundred joints, nine openings, six inward organs all present and complete, which should I recognize as more kin to me than another? Are you thinkers pleased with them all? Rather, you have a favorite organ among them. On your assumption, does it have the rest of them as its subjects? Are its subjects incapable of governing each other? Isn't it rather that they take turns as each other's ruler and subjects? Or rather than that, they have a genuine ruler present in them. When we seek to identify it, whether we find it or not neither adds to nor detracts from its genuineness.[34]

§4: Once we have received the developed body we do not lose it all the time that we wait for extinction. Is it not sad how we and other things slash and jostle each other, and our race to extinction is like a gallop which nothing can stop? How can we fail to regret that we labor all our lives without seeing success, wear ourselves out with toil in ignorance where we shall end? What use is it for men to say that we do not die, since when the body dissolves the heart dissolves with it? How can we not call this our supreme regret? Is man's life really as stupid as this? Or is it that I am the only stupid one, and there are others not so stupid? But if you fol-

low the judgments of the heart which develops with the body and take it as
your authority, who is without such an authority? Why should it be only
the man who understands the alternatives and whose heart judges for itself
between them who has such an authority? The fool has one just as he has.
For there to be "That's it, that's not" before the heart's development
would be "going to Yüeh today and arriving yesterday." This would be by
crediting with existence what does not exist; and if you do that even the
divine Yü would not understand you, and how can you expect to be understood by me?[35]

§5: Saying is not blowing breath, saying says something; the only trouble
is that what it says is never fixed. Do we really say something? Or have
we never said anything? If you think that saying is different from the
twitter of fledglings, can you prove a distinction, or is there no distinction?
By what is the Way hidden that there is a genuine or a false? By what is
saying obscured, that sometimes "that's it," sometimes "that's not"?
Wherever we walk how can the Way be absent? How can what is said be
present yet inadmissible? The Way is hidden by development of the lesser,
saying is obscured by its foliage and flowers. And so we have the "That's
it, that's not" of Confucians and Mohists, by which what is *it* for the one is
not for the other, and what is not for the one for the other is. If you wish to
accept what they reject and reject what they accept, the best course is to
throw things open to the light.

§6: Any thing is "other," any thing is "it." What is unseen from the other's
standpoint, from his own standpoint the knower knows. Therefore it is
said "Other comes out from It, It too adapts to Other," the opinion that It
and Other are born simultaneously. However, "at birth we are simultaneously dying" and at death we are simultaneously living, the admissible is
simultaneously inadmissible and the inadmissible is simultaneously admissible, if adapting to the one "that's it" then adapting to the other "that's
not," and if adapting to the one it is not then adapting to the other it is.
Therefore the sage does not take this course but illuminates all by the light
of Heaven; his too is an adaptive "That's it."[36]

§7: What is "it" is also "other," what is "other" is also "it." There they say
"that's it, that's not" from one point of view, here we say "that's it, that's
not" from another point of view. Are there really It and Other? Or really
no It or Other? Where neither It nor Other finds its opposite is called the
axis of the Way. When once the axis is found at the center of the circle
there is no limit to responding with either, on the one hand no limit to

what is *it*, on the other no limit to what is not. That is why I say, "The best course is to throw things open to the light." Rather than use the meaning to show that "the meaning is not the meaning," use what is not the meaning; rather than use the horse to show that "a horse is not a horse," use what is not a horse. Heaven and earth are the one meaning, the myriad things are the one horse.[37]

§8: Admissible deriving from admissible, inadmissible from inadmissible, the Way develops as we walk it, things become so by being called so. Why are they so? They are so from where they are so. Why are they not so? They are not so from where they are not so. If really there are standpoints from which things are so, from which they are admissible, no thing is not so, no thing is inadmissible. Therefore when a contrived "that's it" picks out a stalk from a pillar, a leper from beautiful Hsi Shih, things however unlike and incongruous, the Way interchanges them and treats them as one. Their dividing is their development, their development is their decay; all things developing or decaying are interchanged and treated as one. Only the man who sees right through knows how to interchange and treat as one; the contrived "that's it" he does not use, but finds things their places in the usual. The usual is the useful, the useful is the interchangeable, the interchangeable is the graspable; and once it is grasped we have not far to go. The adaptive "that's it" comes to an end; and when it is at an end, that of which we do not know what is so of it we call the Way.

§9: To wear out one's wits treating things as one without knowing that they are the same I call "three every morning." What do I mean by that? When a monkey keeper handing out nuts said, "Three in the morning and four in the evening," the monkeys were all enraged. When he said, "In that case four in the morning and three in the evening" the monkeys were all pleased. With nothing left out, either in name or in fact, he found by their pleasure or anger which course was useful; his too was an adaptive "that's it." Therefore the sage evens things out with his "that's it, that's not," and finds the place of rest on the potter's wheel of heaven. It is this that is called "going with both alternatives."

§10: There were men in ancient times who arrived at the utmost in knowledge. Where had they arrived? There were some who thought there had never been any things—the utmost, all that can be said, there is no more to add. The next thought that there were things but that there had never been any borders. The next thought that there were borders between things but that no thing had ever been *it* or *not* it. The displaying of It and Other is the reason why something is missing from the Way. The reason why the Way is defective is the reason why love develops. Is anything really developed or defective? Or is nothing really developed or defective? There is both the developed and the defective, if you do not move on from Chao's performance on the lute; there is neither the developed nor the defective, if you get no farther than Chao when his lute was silent.[38] Chao Wen strumming the lute, music master K'uang tapping the time, the sophist Hui Shih leaning on his desk, did not the knowledge of these three have only a short distance to go? They were all men in whom knowledge culminated, and therefore was carried on to the years when it no longer applied. It is simply that what they preferred they differentiated from an Other; what they preferred they wished to bring to light, but they brought it to light without the Other being brought to light, and so they ended in the darkness of hair-splitting sophistries; and Chao Wen's son too ended with only his father's lutestring, and all his life his talent never developed. May men like this be said to have developed? Then so have I. May not men like this be said to have developed? Then neither have I, nor has anything else. Therefore the glitter of glib debate is despised by the sage.[39] The contrived "that's it" he does not use, but finds things their places in the usual. It is this that I call "throwing things open to the light."

§11: "Now suppose that I speak of something, and do not know whether it is of a kind with the 'it' in question or not of a kind. If what is of a kind and what is not are grouped together, as of a kind with one another, there is no longer any difference from an 'other'."

However, let us take an example:

There is "having begun," there is "not yet having begun."

There is "not yet having not yet begun."

There is "there being," there is "there not being."

There is "there not yet being 'there not being'."

There is "there not yet having been 'there not yet being "there not being"'."

Suddenly "there is 'there not being,'" and of "there being" and "there not being" we don't know which there is and which there is not. Now as far as I am concerned I have referred to something, but still do not know whether my reference really referred to something or did not refer to anything.[40]

§12: "Nothing in the world is bigger than the tip of an autumn hair, and
Mount T'ai is small; no one lives longer than one cut off in child-
hood, and P'eng Tsu died young; heaven and earth were born together with me, and the myriad things and I are one."

Now that we are one, can I still say anything? Now that I have called
us one, did I succeed in not saying something? One and the saying make
two, two and one make three. Proceeding from here even an expert calcu-
lator cannot get to the end of it, much less a plain man. Therefore if we
take the step from nothing to something we arrive at three, and how much
worse if we take the step from something to something! Never take this
step, and the adaptive "that's it" comes to an end.

§13: The Way has never had frontiers, saying has never had norms. It is
by a contrived "that's it" that a boundary is marked. Let me speak of the
marking of boundaries. One can have a gift for recognizing as present and
leaving as it is,[41] for discussing and judging, for dividing and disputing
over, for competing and fighting over; these let us call "the eight apti-
tudes." What is outside the universe the sage leaves as it is and does not
discuss. What is inside the universe the sage discusses but does not judge.
The records in the annals of the former kings of successive ages the sage
judges but does not dispute over.[42] Suppose that I dispute with you, and it
is you not I that wins, is it really you who are on to it, I who am not? If it
is I not you that wins, is it really I who am on to it, you who are not? Has
one of us got it and the other not, or both of us or neither? If you and I
cannot know which of us has won others no doubt will be in the dark because of us; whom shall I call in to judge between us? If we call in someone on your side to judge between us, how can he judge between us when
he is on your side? If he is on the side of me or neither or both, how can he
judge between us when he is on the side of me or neither or both? Consequently not I nor you nor he can know which of us has won, and shall we
find another to depend on? It makes no difference whether the voices in
their transformations have each other to depend on or not. Even them out
on the whetstone of heaven,[43] adapt to them following your free course;
this is the way to live out your term. Forget the years, forget duty, stay
where there are no limits, and so find things their places in the limitless.

§14: What do I mean by "even them out on the whetstone of Heaven"?
Treat as *it* even what is not, treat as *so* even what is not. If "it" is finally
"it," and "so" is finally "so," there is no longer a difference for disputation
from what is not. Therefore behind dividing there is something undivided,
behind disputation there is something not argued out. "What?" you ask.

The sage keeps it in his breast, common men dispute over it in order to show it to each other. Therefore I say: "Behind disputation there is something unseen."

§15: "The Great Way is unnamed,
    Great disputation does not speak,
    Great kindness is unkind,
    Great honesty is not ground too sharp,
    Great courage does not offend.
  If the Way is lit it does not guide,
    If speech is disputatious it does not get there,
    If kindness is unvarying it leaves some out,[44]
    If honesty is too pure it is mistrusted,
    If courage offends it does not succeed."

These five are not so far from the right direction.[45] Therefore the man who knows how to stay in the sphere of his ignorance has attained the utmost. Who knows a wordless disputation, an untold Way? It is this, if any is able to know it, which is called the "Treasury of Heaven." Pour into it and it does not fill, bail out from it and it is not drained, and you do not know from whence it comes.

§16: It is this that is called "Preserving the Light." Therefore once when Yao asked Shun, "I wish to attack Tsung, K'uai, and Hsü-ao. Why is it that sitting on the South-facing throne I am not at ease?" Shun answered, "Why be uneasy if these three survive among the weeds? Formerly ten suns rose side by side and the myriad things were all illumined; who can escape the beams of the sage whose virtue is brighter than the sun?"

§17: Nieh Ch'üeh asked Wang Ni:

"Would you know something which all things agreed in accepting?"

    "How would I know that?"

"Do you know what it is that you do not know?"

    "How would I know that?"

"Then does no thing know anything?"

    "How would I know that? However, let me try to find words for it—
    'How do I know that what I call knowing is not ignorance? How do I
    know that what I call ignorance is not knowing?'[46]

    Moreover let me try a question on you. When a man sleeps in the
    damp his waist ails him and he dies paralyzed; is that so of the loach?

When he sits in a tree he shivers and shakes; is that so of the ape? Which of these three knows the proper place to live? Men eat the flesh of grain-fed beasts, deer eat the sweet grass, centipedes relish snakes, owls and crows savor mice; which of the four has a proper sense of taste? Apes mate with monkeys, deer couple with deer, loaches swim with fishes. Lady Li and Lady Mao were beautiful in the eyes of men; but when the fish saw them they plunged deep, when the birds saw them they flew high, when the deer saw them they broke into a run. Which of these four knows what is truly beautiful in the world? In my judgment the principles of kindness and duty, the road of "that's it, that's not," are inextricably confused; how can I know how to prove the distinction between them?"

"If you do not know benefit from harm, is it really that the highest man does not know benefit from harm?"

"The highest man is godlike. When the great marshes blaze they cannot heat him, when the Yellow River and the Han freeze they cannot chill him, when swift thunderbolts smash the mountains and whirlwinds shake the seas they cannot startle him. A man like this yokes the clouds to his chariot, rides the sun and moon and roams beyond the four seas; death and life change nothing for him, and how much less the principles of benefit and harm!"

§18: Ch'ü-ch'üeh-tzu asked Ch'ang-wu-tzu:

"I heard this quoted by my master Confucius: 'The sage does not work for any goal, does not go after benefit or shun harm, does not delight in seeking, does not set his course by the Way, in saying nothing says something and in saying something says nothing, and roams beyond the dust and grime.' My master thought this nonsense but to me it seemed the walking of the most esoteric Way. What do you think of it?"

"This is a saying that would have puzzled the Yellow Emperor, and what would old Confucius know about it? In any case you are getting ahead of yourself; at the sight of an egg you expect the cock, at the sight of the crossbow bolt you expect the roast dove. Suppose that I put it in reckless words, and you listen as recklessly.

Loll on the sun and moon,
Tuck Space and Time under your arm.
Make things fit neatly,
Yet never tidy them up.
Honor others as servants like yourself.

Common men are busy bodies,
The sage is a lazybones.
Through myriads of years in their purity once and for all
All the myriad things are as they are
And it is for this that they go on generating.

How do I know that to delight in life is not a delusion? How do I know that we who hate death are not lost children who have forgotten the way home? Lady Li was the daughter of a frontier officer of Ai; when the kingdom of Chin first took her the tears stained her dress; only when she came to the palace and shared the king's square couch and ate the flesh of grain-fed beasts did she begin to regret her tears. How do I know that the dead do not regret that at first they prayed to live again? We drink wine in our dreams and weep at dawn, we shed tears in our dreams and at dawn go hunting. While we dream we do not know that we are dreaming, and in the middle of a dream interpret a dream within it; not until we wake do we know that we were dreaming. Only at the ultimate awakening shall we know that this is the ultimate dream. Yet fools think they are awake; they know exactly what they are, 'I'm a prince! I'm a herdsman!' So obstinately sure of themselves! You and Confucius are both dreams, and I who call you a dream am also a dream. The saying he quoted is to be named a mystery; if it happens once in a thousand ages that a great sage knows its explanation it will have happened as though between morning and evening."

§19: The penumbra questioned the shadow:

"You moved before, now you stop; you were sitting before, now you stand; why have you no settled principles?"

"Am I so because there is something on which I depend? Is what I depend on so because it too depends on something else? Is it that I depend on snake's scales, cicada's wings? How can I tell why I am so and why I am not so?"

§20: Once Chuang Tzu dreamed that he was a butterfly, a butterfly gaily fluttering (was he showing himself what it would please him to be?), and did not know that he was Chuang Tzu. Suddenly he awoke, and all at once he was Chuang Tzu. He does not know whether he is Chuang Tzu who dreamed that he was a butterfly or a butterfly dreaming that he is Chuang Tzu. Between Chuang Tzu and the butterfly certainly there was a dividing; this is all that is meant by the transformations of things.

Notes

Originally published as item no. 25 in appended Bibliography

[1] The best and most recent full translation of *Chuang Tzu* is Burton Watson's *Complete Works of Chuang Tzu* (New York, 1968). The one outstanding authority on Chinese philosophy to undertake this task is Fung Yu-lan, who translates the seven "inner chapters" in his *Chuang Tzu* (Shanghai, 1933; Paragon Book reprint, New York, 1964). But so much of the text is unintelligible in the present state of scholarship that complete translations inevitably give the false impression of a writer veering from sentence to sentence between sense and nonsense. Arthur Waley in *Three Ways of Thought in Ancient China* (London, 1939) gives what is perhaps the least misleading impression of Chuang Tzu, since he translates only what he is confident of understanding.

[2] The present version often differs widely from that of Burton Watson, but I should like to express my unqualified admiration for his vivid translations of the less controversial chapters.

[3] Wen Yi-to 聞一多, *Ku tien hsin yi* 古典新義 (Peking, 1956), 243.

[4] For the sophists see Fung Yu-lan, *History of Chinese Philosophy* (Princeton, N.J., 1952), 1: 192-220; Kou Pao-koh, *Deux sophistes chinois* (Paris, 1953). The latter contains full translations of the *Kung-sun Lung tzu* and the surviving sophisms of Hui Shih. I have argued elsewhere that of the essays in the *Kung-sun Lung tzu*, only chapters 2 and 3 are genuine pre-Han documents (*Asia Major* n.s. 5, no. 2 [1957]: 147-83).

[5] Translated by Kou, as above. I have translated chapter 3 ("Meanings and Things," the significance of which is highly controversial) in the *Journal of Oriental Studies* 2, no. 2 (1955): 282-301; and chapter 2 ("The White Horse") in *Asia Major* n.s. 11, no. 2 (1965): 128-52.

[6] For the *Canons* (third century B.C.) see Fung, 246-78. At the time when the only complete translation was made (Alfred Forke, *Me Ti des Sozialethikers und seiner Schüler philosophische Werke* [Berlin, 1922]) most of the *Canons* were unintelligible, and in spite of considerable progress since, many of them remain so. I have translated the *Hsiao-ch'ü* chapter in *T'oung Pao* 51, no. 1 (1964): 1-54. References to the *Canons* are to the numbering in *T'an Chieh-fu* 譚戒甫, *Mo-pien fa-wei* 墨辯發微 (Peking, 1958).

[7] *Chien pai* is defined in the *Canons*, A 66, "'As hardness to whiteness' is 'not excluding each other.'" Pre-Han references to sophists who separate the *chien pai* are generally interpreted in the light of chapter 5 ("Hardness and Whiteness") of the *Kung-sun Lung tzu*, which appear to be spurious (cf. n. 4 above). I have argued elsewhere that they refer simply to the separation of inseparables, such as the shape and color of a white horse (*Bulletin of the School of Oriental and African Studies* 30 no. 2 [1967]: 358-68).

[8] Watson, 269.

[9] Fung, 194-97.

[10] Watson, 374-75.

[11] According to another interpretation (Fung, 197) the reference is to a two-dimensional plane, without thickness but a thousand miles wide. But this point seems hardly paradoxical enough to interest Hui Shih. That "thick" (*hou* 厚) and "size" (*ta* 大) refer to the same dimension is confirmed by the definition of the former in the *Canons* A 55 (厚, 有 所 大 也 "'Thick' is 'having size'").

[12] 大 同 <與 小 異 同> 而 與 小 同 異. Corruption must be postulated on grounds of syntax and parallelism, but the proposed restoration is a pure conjecture.

[13] Watson, 185.

[14] Fung, 306; Burton Watson, *Hsün Tzu: Basic Writings* (New York, 1963), 144.

[15] Watson, 150.

[16] Ibid., 92.

[17] Textual citations from the *Chuang Tzu* are taken from the edition in *Chuang Tzu yin-te*. Harvard-Yenching Institute Sinological Index Series no. 20 (Peking, 1947; hereafter: HYCT). They follow the format "page x/chapter y/line z." HYCT 66/24/40; 63/23/62, 63.

[18] Ibid., 63/23/63.

[19] Ibid., 72/25/55.

[20] Ibid., 75/27/3.

[21] Plato, *Sophist*, 244D.

[22] HYCT 15/5/59.

[23] For the explanation of this passage I am partly indebted to a postgraduate class essay by Peter Sergent of Yale University.

[24] HYCT 60/22/65-68.

[25] Ibid., 75/27/10.

[26] See Fung, History, 277.

[27] *Canon* A 80.

[28] Burton Watson, *Hsün Tzu*, pp, 126-31 (where *hsin* is translated "mind").

[29] Among previous scholars who have worked on Chuang Tzu the present translation is especially indebted to Wen Yi-to (see note 3 of Introduction) and to Chu Kuei-yao 朱 桂 曜, *Chuang Tzu nei-p'ien cheng-pu* 莊 子 內 篇 證 補 (Shanghai Commercial Press, 1935).

[30] On the assumption that *ou* 耦 "opposite" is used as in §7 ("Where neither It nor Other finds its opposite," written 偶) we may take this as equivalent to the "I had lost my self" of Tzu-ch'i's first answer, but said the other way around (he has lost the external world).

[31] 勺 for 刀 Chu, 44.

[32] 咸 = 緘 Wen, 242; the latter character appears in §2 ("as though it were sealed"). I take *ch'ü* 取 as "choose (between) proposed alternatives," as in the *Canons* and §§3,4 below.

[33] The verse passage, which seems to be a quotation introduces the theme of the *hsin* "heart" and its judgments between alternatives, continued until §4.

[34] Discussed above, p. 115.

[35] Discussed above, p. 116.

[36] Discussed above, p. 108.

[37] Discussed above, p. 109.

[38] *Ku* "keep as it was," as in chapter 17 終 始 無 故...知 終 始 之 不 可 故 也. "Ending or beginning there is no staying as it was...know that end or beginning cannot be kept as it was."

[39] 圖 = 鄙 Wen, 246.

[40] Discussed above, p. 113.

[41] 左, 右 "left and right" appear to make no sense. I suggest 在, 存, the latter confirmed by the references to four of the eight "degrees of Power" in the following sentences.

[42] From this point there is a major dislocation of the text involving three sections: (*A*) §13 "Suppose that I dispute with you...shall we find another to depend on?" (167 characters) (*B*) §13 from "It makes no difference" (38 characters) (*C*) §14 to "a difference for disputation from what is not" (46 characters). In the standard text the whole stands between §§18 and 19, and *B* and *C* are transposed. The latter transposition is generally recognized, and corrected in Burton Watson's version (p. 48). But having taken this step, it seems necessary to go further; the whole passage deals with disputation, a theme dropped in §17, and it fills a gap in §§13 and 14 where it is otherwise difficult to find a continuing thread of thought. It may be noticed that *A* is almost exactly twice the length of *B* and *C* together, suggesting displacement of writing strips (alternately long and short strips of 38 and 46 characters?).

[43] 倪 = 研 Chu, 81.

[44] Following the variant 周 for 成.

[45] 庶 for 因 而 Chu, 68.

[46] Discussed above, p. 113.

Chapter 4

Two Notes on the Translation of Taoist Classics

A. C. GRAHAM

There are many kinds of translation, one extreme of which is that of the litterateur working at second hand on the drafts or published versions of others. There have been successful examples in Chinese poetry, notably Ezra Pound's *Cathay*, from which every subsequent translator has learned directly or indirectly. Since *Lao Tzu* is a philosophical poem or poem-cycle, is there anything a scholarly translator can learn from such a version as Witter Bynner's *The Way of Life according to Lao Tzu*?[1] The answer I think is "No," but there is something to be learned from considering what is wrong with his approach, which is not simply a matter of the scholarly errors we excuse in Pound. I begin by summarizing some features of the original which one would want to show through in the English.

Certainly a successful rendering of *Lao Tzu* requires more than si-nological expertise; the compulsion it exerts is a matter of style as much as of thought, if indeed one can think of the style as separable from the thought. It is very short, by Chinese standards as well as our own, a loosely strung series of aphorisms grouped in stanzas which are always highly rhythmic and often rhymed. The text which tradition has preferred is pruned to a degree of terseness unusual even in Chinese writing, some-

130

times at the cost of syntactic ambiguity. It is in the essence of the style that the writer presents, asserts and without explanation moves on, juxtaposing aphorisms so that parallels and contrasts explode in the imagination, and then with a crucially placed "Therefore" proceeds to new pronouncements which one perceives to be related but to which there are any number of possible bridges. It appeals to that kind of intelligence which is at the opposite pole from intellect, not simplifying, clarifying, filling in all steps, but plotting the focal points in a complex of thought and leaving it to the reader to make his own jumps across the gaps. One wonders whether anyone in the history of literature has set out to say so much in so few words, to pick that minimum of gnomic utterances which will start the widest variety of readers thinking in the author's direction along their own paths.

The theme of *Lao Tzu* is that of Chinese philosophy generally, the "way" (*Tao*), the way to live and to act, which, since in ancient China one thought less in individual than in social and political terms, is in the first place the proper way to govern the Chinese Empire. Or, looking into ourselves instead of outward at the world, it is the "Power" (*Te*, often translated "Virtue," as in "The virtue of cyanide is to poison" rather than "Virtue is its own reward"), the capacity in a man to act successfully, in spontaneous accord with the Way. Bynner, who defines *Tao* quite reasonably as "the way of all life," misunderstands *Te* as "the fit use of life by men";[2] it is a potentiality, an aptitude, a Power embracing all powers, which some have and some lack, and which can be nurtured and raised to the perfection of the sage.

It was commonly assumed that the Way is a set of rules of conduct formulated in words, such as the moral code of Confucianism. What distinguishes Taoism from other Chinese philosophies is the claim that there are *no* rules, yet in any particular situation there is only one way to act, which we miss if we stick to the rules. It is because Lao Tzu cannot formulate his Way, can use words only to guide us towards it, that there can be no such thing for him as a thought about it which is separable from style. In any situation there is a direction in which activity naturally tends, is spontaneous, "so of itself" (*tzu-jan*), belongs with birth and death to the inevitable processes of heaven and earth. This direction is the Way, and we miss it if we are conscious of self, conceive personal goals and appeal to rules; we find it if we forget self and are content to see clearly and respond from the depths to what we see. Then all activity loses the quality of deliberate action and becomes *wu-wei* "doing nothing": "in doing nothing there is nothing one does not do."[3]

The Way, then, is not a set of human principles, but the course which all things follow in their regular successions of day and night, birth and death. One generalization about it which Lao Tzu reaffirms in metaphor after metaphor is that in all pairs of opposites the positive is transient and in due course reverts to the negative, the higher to the lower, strength to weakness, life to death, existence to nothingness. To be positive is to exert oneself, and all exertion tires. The yielding, the soft, the female, the tenuous, is at once the bottom into which everything sinks and the root from which it incessantly but temporarily grows. By most standards of value this is a profoundly pessimistic insight, and the equanimity with which it is presented (as though there were nothing depressing about the Second Law of Thermodynamics) is one of many indications that we are being asked to view the world from a startlingly unusual angle.

But the manner in which Lao Tzu applies this observation is neither optimistic nor pessimistic. Ordinarily when we recognize something as inimical we exert ourselves to resist it. The Taoist however sees it as having a fixed term with beginning, growth, climax, deterioration. If he discerns it at its inception, while it is still weak, he is prompted to crush it before it develops. If he misses the opportunity, he yields as it grows stronger, bows to prevailing circumstances, is satisfied to survive until it passes its peak, then as it weakens he advances. This is the strategy of the Japanese wrestling called *Judo* ("Way of Weakness"), a name taken directly from Lao Tzu. One might object that if this is the Way then one has only superficially forgotten self to accord with it; in the Biblical phrase, has cast one's bread upon the waters and got it back again. Lao Tzu is perfectly aware of that:

> Therefore the sage
>   In putting himself behind finds himself ahead,
>   In putting himself outside finds himself surviving.
> It is because he is without selfishness that he is able to be successful in his selfishness.[4]

For Lao Tzu all formulations are inadequate: even the least inadequate can contradict each other, therefore language is most enlightening and least misleading when one centers attention on the contradictions and speaks in paradoxes. Perhaps the ultimate paradox of the book is to discover the sublimity of the Way in the unmoral and the unheroic, in the evasions and compromises to which we are compelled by life.

Lao Tzu has attracted attention in the West for little more than a century. Voltaire and the other *philosophes* who admired China in the eighteenth century knew only the Confucian tradition, the one which interested the Jesuits on whom they depended for information. Perhaps Rousseau would have thought better of China if he had known something of Taoism. Since the French translations of the early nineteenth century, however, *Lao Tzu* has become the most frequently translated of all Oriental classics. One might suppose that a Chinese book in which obscurity is almost a matter of principle, and pitted with textual and linguistic problems invisible to the amateurs and cranks who from the first have almost crowded out the qualified translators, would be nearly inaccessible to ordinary Western readers. But the riddle of why certain books translate well and others do not remains as mysterious as the fiction-writer's puzzle of what makes a book a best-seller. For example *Chuang Tzu*, although some of its stories are famous (such as Chuang Tzu dreaming he is a butterfly and waking to wonder whether he is a butterfly dreaming he is a man), has never over most of its length been a live book in English, yet *Lao Tzu* keeps much of its enigmatic power even in the weakest versions. It may even be a point in its favour that readers do not, as with the English Bible, have the illusion of reading the original; many have shared Bynner's sense of a greater book looming behind the English words, one which they could have translated better themselves, one which, with little Chinese or none, they *will* translate themselves.

Lao Tzu does not appeal to everyone, but on temperaments sympathetic to it exerts a peculiar force. Readers of Robert Pirsig's semi-autobiographical *Zen and the Art of Motorcycle Maintenance* will remember that it was in reading *Lao Tzu* and discovering in it his own half-formed philosophy that the hero plunged into his psychotic episode. On the other hand Ezra Pound, most sinophile of poets, was impressed only by the Confucian side of Chinese civilization. Bynner is annoyed by the unimaginativeness of "pedant Giles," the nineteenth century sinologist who said that he would have barely mentioned the book in his *Chinese Literature* "were it not for the attention paid to it by several more or less eminent foreign students of the language."[5] But Giles, pedant or not, enjoyed and translated *Chuang Tzu*; and it happens that I myself find *Chuang Tzu* one of the most exhilarating books in the world, yet in the case of *Lao Tzu* remain unexcited by a force which I recognize. It has occurred to me in reflecting on this difference of taste that *Lao Tzu* appeals especially to those who experience a tension between the claims of the mystical and the practical. Pirsig is one, as may be known without reading more than his title, and Bynner was another (cf. his just remark that Lao

Tzu "fused mysticism and pragmatism").[6] Certainly an inclination to mysticism is not by itself either a necessary or a sufficient condition for going overboard for Lao Tzu. Aldous Huxley preferred the unworldly Hindus, while Brecht of all people found in Lao Tzu the wisdom of the common man, the knowledge of when to bend to superior force and how to elude it and survive. The attraction of Chuang Tzu on the other hand is rather to those of us in whom the tension is between the claims of the mystical and the rational (although the latter side of him is hardly visible in the translations).

Frank Lloyd Wright is another who demonstrates that *Lao Tzu* can mean all things to all men. He recognized in it his own idea that "the reality of the building lies in the space within to be lived in":

> When building Unity Temple at Oak Park and the Larkin Building in Buffalo, I was making the first great protest I knew anything about against the building coming up on you from outside as enclosure. I reversed that old idiom in idea and in fact.

> When pretty well puffed up by this I received a little book by Okakura Kakuzo, entitled *The Book of Tao*, sent to me by the ambassador from Japan to the United States. Reading it, I came across this sentence: "The reality of a room was to be found in the space enclosed by the roof and walls, not in the roof and walls themselves."

> Well, there was I. Instead of being the cake I was not even dough. Closing the little book I went out to break stone on the road, trying to get my interior self together. I was like a sail coming down; I had thought of myself as an original, but was not.[7]

The reference is to *Lao Tzu* 11:

> Thirty spokes share one hub: just where it does not exist is the wheel's use. Knead clay to make a vessel: just where it does not exist is the vessel's use. Cut out doors and windows to make a room: just where it does not exist is the room's use.

> Therefore we find it beneficial that they exist, find them useful where they do not exist.

What interests Lao Tzu of course is not architecture but conduct in general. It is one of his themes that we remain open to new situations and capable of fresh responses only as long as we can empty ourselves of the knowledge of things and the names under which we classify them, reverting to the nothingness out of which all that exists is born. But Wright does not misunderstand him; indeed, this is one of those stanzas in which Lao Tzu perfectly achieves his own kind of clarity, which almost excludes the possibility of misunderstanding. What he is presenting is not a vague idea but a highly organized system of lucid metaphors which illuminate any situation with a corresponding structure. The passage does mean what an architect reads into it, and whatever else you or I find ourselves reading into it.

Most translators of *Lao Tzu* have known some Chinese, and Bynner's casual remark that he cannot read the language[8] may surprise readers unaware of the force of the Lao Tzu obsession. Bynner is not the only or the most eminent of the writers who have refused to be deterred by this handicap. Tolstoy, who revered the Chinese sages and Lao Tzu in particular, made a Russian translation in 1893–94, based on the current French, English and German versions. The clash with those soulless pedants who so disgust Bynner is easily imagined. Tolstoy was especially attracted by the theistic interpretation of Victor von Strauss, who understood "Tao" as "God," and consulted the librarian V. V. Stasov about him:

> Stasov's reply of Nov. 6 was unequivocal and (as any scholar of Chinese will agree today) entirely correct: "The Professor of Chinese in our University, Ivanovski, says that Strauss is a *third-rate* sinologist and that he cannot be trusted"...Undaunted by Stasov's adverse reports, Tolstoy continued working on his translation until the middle of May 1894, apparently using Strauss as a basis.[9]

Tolstoy did not publish his version, but in 1913 sponsored and edited another by the Japanese D. P. Konishi.

In this sort of courage or rashness Bynner is the peer of Tolstoy:

> And perhaps I shall be taken to task for using two or three times an unorthodox interpretation of text. But might not Lao Tzu's expression, for example, to "stand below other people," usually translated to "humble oneself below them," have been an ancient origin of our own word "to understand"?[10]

The longest answer that question will get from any sinologist is "No." However it would be pointless to criticize Bynner for such details. We can do him justice only by treating his work as an American poem inspired by *Lao Tzu*, belonging to that genre the 'Imitation' which Robert Lowell has more recently reinvigorated. As a sinologist it is not my business to assess its quality, but I should like to point out how radically Bynner's poetry differs from Lao Tzu's in kind. There is the superficial resemblance that both works are cycles of philosophical verses, some unrhymed and some rhymed, although not in the same places. (*Lao Tzu* is not conceived as poetry by the Chinese, but that is a matter of differently classified genres.)

But the bareness, terseness, concentration of the Chinese is quite foreign to Bynner; the more recent, scrupulously scholarly version by D. C. Lau in *Penguin Classics* is much closer not only to the sense of the original but to its skeletal poetry. Bynner is always reluctant to risk obscurity by presenting naked insights without explaining, abstracting, qualifying, diffusing. He likes a smooth flow, not the abrupt confrontations and juxtapositions of the Chinese. Altogether he is much less "modern" than Lao Tzu. It is especially remarkable that a lover of *Lao Tzu* should take so little delight in the enigmatic and the paradoxical. When Lao Tzu utters an aphorism about aphorisms, "Straight words seem twisted" (a word-for-word rendering), Bynner replaces it by "They seem to twist the truth," referring to the sayers of a particular paradox.[11] Bynner's goal is a poem such as he supposes *Lao Tzu* to be, "neither occult nor complex but open and simple, neither pontifical nor archaic but lay and current."[12] But if he neither perceives complexity in Lao Tzu nor much cares for it where he does perceive it, it is plain that he is setting out on a very different enterprise.

To illustrate the difference we may take Stanza 6, which exhibits both our poets at their best. In the Chinese it consists of a couplet (with the rhyme lost in standard modern pronunciation) and a quatrain rhymed throughout:

KU 谷 Valley (low ground in contrast with high)	SHEN 神 spirit	PU 不 not	SSU 死， die,
SHIH 是 This	WEI 謂 call	HSÜAN 玄 dark/unfathomable	P'IN 牝。 female (of animals).
HSÜAN 玄 Dark	P'IN 牝 female	CHIH 之 's	MEN 門， gate,
SHIH 是 This	WEI 謂 call	T'IEN TI 天地 heaven earth	KEN 根。 root.
MIEN-MIEN 綿綿 Dim (?)		JO 若 as though	TS'UN 存， present,
YUNG 用 Use	CHIH 之 it	PU 不 not	CH'IN 勤。 exhaust.

> The spirit in the valley never dies.
> Call it the dark she-animal.
> The gate of the dark she-animal

Call the root of heaven and earth.
Dim, dim, you almost see it,
Inexhaustible however much you use.

Bynner's version is as follows:

The breath of life moves through a deathless valley
Of mysterious motherhood.
Which conceives and bears the universal seed,
The seeming of a world never to end,
Breath for men to draw from as they will:
And the more they take of it, the more remains.

The Chinese crowds together some of the most vibrant images in the book. At the bottom of things is an inexhaustible power likened to a nature-spirit of the valley (in contrast with the mountain), to a womb out of which heaven and earth are born, to a gate out of which they come, to a root out of which they grow. Its relation to heaven and earth is that of female to male and subhuman to human, lower, humbler, more fundamental. Bynner's verse rationalizes the valley spirit into "the breath of life," abstracts "mysterious motherhood" from the dark she-animal, abolishes her "gate," generalizes heaven and earth (with their antithesis of higher and lower) as "the world," replaces their "root" by the function of conceiving and bearing the universal seed. The purpose is to write a clearer poetry, but the coherence of Lao Tzu's metaphorical structure is to some extent obscured; instead of life growing up from the bottom of things the breath of life moves *through* the valley, and a "universal seed" has intruded somewhere between us and our ultimate mother. It is a pretty verse none the less; Bynner's rhythmic sense seems to thrive on imagery of reduced intensity, and here informs the most shapely and melodious stanza in his book.

Let us look at what Bynner does with the opening of Stanza 5 (unrhymed in the Chinese).

T'IEN 天	TI 地	PU 不	JEN 仁,		YI 以	WAN 萬
Heaven	earth	un-	feeling/, -kind/, -benevolent,		with	myriad
WU 物	WEI 爲	CH'U 芻	KOU 狗	SHENG -JEN 聖人		PU 不
Things	make	straw	dogs.	Sage		un-
JEN 仁	YI 以	PAI 百	HSING 姓	WEI 爲	CH'U 芻	KOU 狗
-feeling,	with	hundred	clans	make	straw	dogs.

Heaven and earth are ruthless, they treat the myriad things as straw
dogs. The sage is ruthless, he treats the people as straw dogs.

Bynner:

Nature, immune as to a sacrifice of straw dogs,
Faces the decay of its fruits.
A sound man, immune as to a sacrifice of straw dogs,
Faces the passing of human generations.

Bynner's second and fourth lines are not quite as disconnected from
the Chinese as they appear. The straw dogs were used in sacrifice; they
were honoured during the ceremony, afterwards tossed away as worthless
straw. The point is not that the sage values men only as means to his
ends—he does not think in terms of ends anyway—but that he values
them in relation to their time, forgetting them when their time is past, as
heaven and earth foster our birth and growth and then leave us to decline
and die. It is a bleak observation, and it was not surprising to meet it in the
cinema some years ago, before the credits of Sam Peckinpah's *Straw dogs*.
The moral of the film, if my memory has not distorted it, was a very un-
Taoist one, that life compels us all sooner or later to prove our manhood
by discovering in ourselves a proper zest to fight and kill. Elsewhere, in
Stanza 31, Lao Tzu says: "There is no glory in victory, and to glorify it is
to delight in killing men," and "Victory in battle, conduct with the rites of
mourning," quotations which would have been much less apt.

The difference here is that Bynner, accustomed to mean only one
thing at a time, cannot bear to risk being misunderstood, while Lao Tzu
never apologises and never explains. The "Straw dogs" passage is naked
vision defined with perfect economy, and is no more "misunderstood" by
Peckinpah than the passage about the room was misunderstood by Frank
Lloyd Wright; Lao Tzu does not qualify it, he leaves you to go in your
own direction when you notice its collisions and interactions with other
parts of the book. Bynner on the other hand is anxious to make it quite
plain that Lao Tzu is recommending indifference, not to the welfare of
other people, but to our common mortality. It is as though a translator of
Blake's "Sooner murder an infant in its cradle than nurse unacted desires"
were to adapt his phrasing to avoid the impression that he condones infan-
ticide.

It may be noticed that this time Bynner replaces "heaven and earth,"
not by "world" but by the abstraction "Nature." More interesting is his re-
placement of *sheng-jen* (commonly translated "sage") by "sound man,"

maintained consistently throughout the book. This is no abstraction. Bynner has a very concrete picture of the sound man, demystified, practical, democratic and American, exemplified by Lao Tzu himself, who was "as natural, as genial, as homely as Lincoln."[13]

As our third example we may take the famous opening lines of the book:

TAO 道	K'O 可	TAO 道	FEI 非	CH'ANG 常	TAO 道 。
Way	can-be	told	is-not	constant	way.
MING 名	K'O 可	MING 名	FEI 非	CH'ANG 常	MING 名 。
Name	can-be	named	is-not	constant	name.
WU 無	MING 名	T'IEN 天	TI 地	CHIH 之	SHIH 始 ，
Have-not	name	heaven	earth	's	beginning,
YU 有	MING 名	WAN 萬	WU 物	CHIH 之	MU 母 。
Have	name	myriad	things	's	mother.

> A way that can be told
> Is not the constant Way.
> A name that can be named
> Is not the constant name.
> The nameless is the beginning of heaven and earth,
> The named is the mother of the myriad things.

Bynner:

> Existence is beyond the power of words
> To define:
> Terms may be used
> But are none of them absolute.
> In the beginning of heaven and earth there were no words,
> Words came out of the womb of matter;

Bynner rejects any translation which "stays by expressions significant to Eastern and not to Western readers," and says that "Lao Tzu should, I am convinced, be brought close to people in their own idiom."[14] To this end he represents *Tao* in practical contexts by "way of life," but in the metaphysical flights by "existence." He cannot have understood that by this single substitution he not only transforms Lao Tzu's metaphysic but divorces it from his practical teaching. It can be seen from his preface that Bynner thinks of the metaphysics as incidental, as speculation about "the origin and meaning of life"[15] which will from time to time exercise the mind of the sound man but has nothing much to do with his sound instinct for living. He conceives it in Western terms as an ontological quest for that which he calls "existence," no doubt preferring the word to "being" as relatively closer to the earth. But Lao Tzu's quest is for that ultimate Way which is beyond all formulated ways of life. Existence and non-existence belong among his pairs of lower and higher: things we see, hear and touch exist, the Way is discovered by withdrawing into the nothingness from which they emerge. (Later Taoists indeed explicitly identified the Way with Nothing.) His metaphysic and his practice are thus a perfect unity. We need not go into the controversial issues which the stanza raises (characteristically confronting us without explanation with both a Name beyond names and the Nameless), but on one level it says merely that no way formulable in words is adequate to live by. If he had understood it better Bynner might have achieved a less prosaic opening to his poem. He finds nothing in the stanza to stimulate his own kind of talent; all he can do is try to make Lao Tzu sound sensible, and hover uncomfortably between triteness ("In the beginning of heaven and earth there were no words") and incoherence ("Words came out of the womb of matter").

The modern tradition of literary translation from Chinese stems from Pound's *Cathay*, but Bynner seems never to have assimilated Pound's lessons. To quote with approval some trivial observations about rendering "the spirit rather than the letter of the text," and translations being more obscure the more literal they are,[16] is surprisingly old-fashioned for a man who had been in touch with the avant-garde of his time. If the "spirit" of Lao Tzu can be caught in English, it is by channeling all insights, sympathies and inspirations by assigning to the key words the equivalents which will be at once nearest in sense and interrelated in a most nearly corresponding structure (the pairs of opposites with positive and negative members, the metaphors from the "Way" itself to the "gate," "valley," "mother," "ancestor," "uncarved block"), and then approximating as closely as possible to the patterning of both the prose and the verse, to allow such words their proper relative weight and exhibit analogies and contrasts. In Lao Tzu the thinker and the poet are one, and so in the translator are the discrimination which elucidates the ideas and the sensitivity which activates the images. To insist that Lao Tzu speak to readers "in their own idiom" is to deny them, not only the opportunity of deeper understanding, but the pleasure and adventure of thinking in metaphors new to them. Bynner must have heard that dictum of Mallarmé that a poem is written not with ideas but with words, but at bottom he does think that Lao

Tzu wrote his poem with ideas, that the metaphors are decoration, that you catch his spirit by expressing the thought in the form most natural in English.

Bynner was in a muddle about the art of translation, but in the writing of the book he knew what he was doing. There is much in *Lao Tzu* to interest readers who will not, initially at least, grant it the intellectual and imaginative effort which the ideal literary translation would require. Bynner could sense it through the existing versions, obscured by mysterious *chinoiserie*, which he decided to clear away for the sake of readers the book had not yet reached. Probably the result would not have been much different if he had known Chinese. In such an enterprise misleading interpretations hardly matter. To learn something from Lao Tzu is a gain to anyone, to make demonstrable mistakes about him is no great loss unless you are a sinologist. One culture learns from another only by such imperfect understanding and creative misunderstanding (even in the last resort within the circle of specialists with the duty of understanding as well as they can). However, a reader whom Bynner has roused to an interest in Lao Tzu had better move on to more demanding translators such as D. C. Lau. If he afterwards returns to Bynner it should be for his qualities as an American poet, and because the varied reactions of Westerners sympathetic to Lao Tzu have so often been interesting in themselves.

CHUANG TZU AND THE RAMBLING MODE[17]

My life has a limit, but my knowledge is without limit. To drive the limited in search of the limitless is fatal; and the knowledge of those who do this is fatally lost.

In striving for others, avoid fame. In striving for self, avoid disgrace. Pursue a middle course. Thus you will keep a sound body and a sound mind, fulfill your duties, and work out your allotted span.

Prince Hui's cook was cutting up a bullock...

This is how chapter 3 of *Chuang Tzu* opens in H. A. Giles's version. A lay reader will perhaps wonder at the mysterious workings of the Oriental mind, so alien to all Western standards of reason and continuity. In fact of course this extraordinary style, which drifts inconsequentially between sense and nonsense with an air of perfect confidence, is an invention of translators, to which we resort when losing our grip and meandering from sentence to sentence without any sense of direction. I have got into the habit of thinking of it as the "Rambling Mode," although there must be a better name for it. It has nothing especially Oriental about it (it pervades the current English version of Levi-Strauss's *La pensée sauvage*, for example); but its truly exemplary achievements, for reasons which it may be worthwhile to explore, have been in the realm of Oriental wisdom.

The verbiage we have just quoted is characteristic of all complete translations of *Chuang Tzu*. One of the great men of Chinese literature has always in English turned into a very bad writer, who except when telling a story can hardly put together three sentences without wandering off into banality or nonsense. He has some marvelous stories of course, an amiable personality, the occasional illuminating aphorism or argument, and suggestions of an individual vision of life which he is too careless and insensitive with words to establish for us—but could one not claim as much for any number of bad English writers?

If there has never yet been a viable English *Chuang Tzu* the reason is not that the book has been unlucky in its translators, which include Legge, Giles and Burton Watson, each the best of his generation. The trouble is that Chuang Tzu demands from us rather more than scholarship combined with sound literary instincts. There are many different factors which unite to drag us down into the Rambling Mode, and until we make a deliberate effort to identify and combat them even the best of us are bound to misrepresent him fundamentally. Let us briefly examine seven of them.

(1) Much of *Chuang Tzu* is unintelligible at the present stage of research. Waley, who was always faithful to the principle that one should translate only what one thinks one understands, limited himself in the case of Chuang Tzu to the extracts in *Three Ways of Thought in Ancient China*; all who profess to translate the whole book violate this principle. What seems to be the rambling style of the great Taoist is in the first place an evasive tactic of the scholar who has lost the thread, who is trudging from sentence to sentence with his dictionaries and commentaries hoping for the best.

Unfortunately one cannot transfer from one language to another the possibility of a passage becoming intelligible in the future. The Chinese text often looks like nonsense, although at every re-reading one sees more light; but once prematurely turned into English it *is* nonsense, in which no amount of re-reading will discover anything which the translator himself missed.

(2) The translators present each chapter as a continuous stream of paragraphed prose. This is appropriate, for example, to the "Primitivist" chapters (chapter 8 to half way through chapter 11), which really are consecutive essays, probably from about 205 B.C. But the "inner chapters" (chs. 1–7)—attributable to Chuang Tzu himself—are scrap-books of brief anecdotes, dialogues, aphorisms, pensées, verses, loosely grouped by theme. Far from emitting an unending stream of verbiage Chuang Tzu is a writer with a very short breath, and what he is saying emerges only when one makes definite decisions as to where a section begins and ends. To disguise the abrupt discontinuities between sections, and consequently submerge the real continuities in a spurious continuity of chapters read as wholes, is a procedure which leads inevitably to the Rambling Mode.

It may be noticed that translations of *Lao Tzu*, which is traditionally divided into very short sections, generally escape the Rambling Mode. We know that the thread of thought will break off at the end of the section, and however disconnected the aphorisms inside the section may seem the mind finds itself playing with elusive interrelations between them; we may be tantalised by Lao Tzu's obscurity, but we do not feel ourselves sinking into an interminable stream of nonsense. If *Lao Tzu* has firmly established itself as a document in world literature while *Chuang Tzu* has not, this is surely one of the reasons.

(3) Chuang Tzu writes in various literary forms, but even the fundamental difference between verse and prose disappears in the complete translations (although not in Waley's selection). Thus the doggerel ballad with which the madman of Ch'u mocks Confucius at the end of chapter 6 comes through in English as just another piece of meandering Taoist discourse. The effect of assimilating the verse to prose is almost always catastrophic. For example the first four exchanges of the "Autumn floods" dialogue (chapter 17) function even in English as an exceptionally coherent exposition of Taoist relativism, but by the fifth exchange one notices with a sinking heart that the lucid interval was too good to last, and the author has again collapsed into characteristic Taoist driveling:

河伯曰。然則我何爲乎。何不爲乎。吾辭
受之。趣舍。吾終奈何。北海若曰。以道觀
之。何貴何賤。是謂反衍。無拘而志。與
道大蹇。何少何多。是謂謝施。無一而私
行。與道參差。嚴乎若國之有君。其無私
德。繇繇乎若察之有社。其無所畛域。泛泛
乎其若四方之無窮。其無所畛域。兼懷萬
物。其孰承翼。是謂無方。萬物一齊。孰其
短孰長。道無終始。物有死生。不恃其
成。一虛一滿。不位乎其形。年不可舉。
時不可止。消息盈虛。終則有始。是所以
語大義之方。論萬物之理也。物之生也。
若驟若馳。無動而不變。無時而不移。何
爲乎。何不爲乎。夫固將自化。

(Harvard-Yenching 43/17/41)

"Well then," said the Lord of the River, "what should I do and what should I not do? How am I to know in the end what to accept and what to reject, what to abide by and what to discard?"

Jo of the North Sea said, "From the point of view of the Way, what is noble or what is mean? These are merely what are called endless changes. Do not hobble your will, or you will be departing far from the Way! What is few, or what is many? These are merely what are called boundless turnings. Do not strive to unify your actions, or you will be at sixes and sevens with the Way! Be stern like the ruler of a state—he grants no private favor. Be benign and impartial like the god of the soil at the sacrifice—he grants no private blessing. Be broad and expansive like the endlessness of the four directions—they have nothing which bounds or hedges them. Embrace the ten thousand things universally—how could there be one you should give special support to? This is called being without bent. When the ten thousand things are unified and equal then which is short and which is long?

"The Way is without beginning or end, but things have their life and death—you cannot rely upon their fulfillment. One moment empty, the next moment full—you cannot depend upon their form. The years cannot be held off; time cannot be stopped. Decay, growth, fullness, and emptiness end and then begin again. It is thus that we must describe the plan of the Great Meaning and discuss the principles of the ten thousand things. The life of things is a gallop, a headlong dash—with every movement they alter, with every moment they shift. What should you do and what should you not do? Everything will change of itself, that is certain!"

—Burton Watson 181 (cf. Giles 208, Legge 39/382, Ware 112)

What has gone wrong here? Or is the reader perhaps so punch drunk on Taoist English that he doesn't see anything wrong? In the original the Seagod, who had been answering in prose, has shifted to verse. He is no longer offering an answer to the Lord of the River's philosophical question, he is using poetry to guide him towards the ineffable *Tao*. He returns to prose at the sentence translated "It is thus that we must describe the plan of the Great Meaning...," which one may take as referring as much to the verse form of the description as to the content. I suggest that the proper way to approach the translation of this passage is as follows:

> "If that is so," said the Lord of the River, "What shall I do and what shall I not do? On what final consideration am I to refuse or accept, prefer or discard?"

> > "If you observe them in terms of the Way," said Jo of the North Sea,
> > "What shall we think noble, what shall we think mean?
> > This is called drifting with the flow.
> > Don't narrow the range of your intent,
> > Or you'll be too lame to walk the Way.

> > What shall we belittle, what shall we make much of?
> > This is called letting their turns come round.
> > Don't walk always on one course,
> > You'll be at odds and evens with the Way,

> > Stern!
> > As a lord to his state, no private favours.
> > Generous!
> > As the earth-god at the sacrifice, no private blessing.
> > Pervading everything!
> > As the infinite in the four directions, no fenced enclosures.

> > Embrace the myriad creatures every one,
> > Does any deserve your special help?
> > This is called being open in every direction.
> > All the myriad creatures are one and equal,
> > Which of them is short, which of them long?

> > The Way has no end and no start,
> > Every creature is born and dies,
> > Put no faith in the prime of life,

Now it empties, now it fills,
There's no reserved seat for its shape.

The years cannot be warded off,
The times cannot be made to stop.
Dwindling and growing, filling and emptying,
When one thing ends another begins.

This is how to tell of the range of the grand summing-up and to sort
out the patterns of the myriad things. A thing's life is like a stam-
pede, a gallop, at every prompting it alters, there is never a time
when it does not shift. What shall we do? What shall we not do? It
is inherent in everything that it will transform of itself."

From this illustration we can see why Chuang Tzu's verse when
turned into prose inevitably declines into the Rambling Mode. A statement
is much less dependent on immediate context in verse than in prose, because a verse line has, besides its place in a linear sequence, relations with
other lines organized by the overall pattern. Here, for example, every line
in the second quatrain connects with the corresponding line of the first in
both syntax and vocabulary. But once the form is dissolved we are left
only with a linear sequence too loose for consecutive prose, giving that effect of inconsequential drifting which we call the Rambling Mode. In the
case of *Lao Tzu* modern translations generally do reproduce verse by
verse, which is another reason why in spite of all obscurities they escape
the unfocused effect.

It will be seen too that it is the divisions organized by rhyme and distinguished by rhyme change which make verse translation obligatory, not
rhyme as such. We observe them only when lines are approximately equal
in length, characteristically the 4-syllable line of the *Odes*. But
Chuang Tzu uses rhyme freely in writing which by all other tests is prose.
In the following passage the rhymes and part-rhymes no doubt contribute
to the music of the Chinese but they have no organizing function except in
the opening quatrain:

無為名尸。無為謀府。無為事任。無為知
主。體盡無窮。而游無朕。盡其所受乎
天。而無見得。亦虛而已。至人之用心若
鏡。不將不迎。應而不藏。故能勝物而不
傷。

(Harvard-Yenching 21/7/31)

Don't be a medium for reputation's ghost,
Don't be a stockroom for schemes.
Don't take the weight of affairs on your shoulder,
Don't be the man-in-charge of wisdom.

Wholly embody the limitless and roam where there is no fore-
boding of anything. Exhaust what you received from Heaven and
never have gain in sight; simply keep yourself empty. The utmost
man uses the heart like a mirror: he does not escort things as they
go or welcome them as they come, he responds but does not retain.
Therefore he is able to conquer other things without suffering a
wound.

(4) The different literary forms of the sections of a chapter need to be distinguished typographically. For example in chapter 6 we find a rhymed
sequence of rhapsodic exclamations on the True Man immediately followed by a passage of uncertain topic which is in the dry-as-dust manner of commentary; each clause of a sentence is annotated in turn, a
form to be observed for example in the opening section of chapter 27.
The second passage has never been plausibly explained, but I am inclined to take it as a misplaced comment on a story in chapter 5 about a
disciple of Lao Tzu who has had a foot chopped for a crime, recognizes
that to keep out of trouble he must learn the conventions, and comes to
study under Confucius.

古之眞人。其狀義而不朋。若不足而不
承。與乎其觚而不堅也。張乎其處而不已
華也。邴邴乎其似喜乎。崔乎其不得已
乎。漻乎進我色也。與乎止我德也。厲乎
其似世乎。警乎其未可制也。連乎其似
好閉也。悗乎忘其言也。以刑爲體。以禮
爲翼。以知爲時。以德爲循。以刑爲體
者。綽乎其殺也。以體爲翼者。所以行於
世也。以知爲時者。不得已於事也。以德
爲循者。言其與有足者至於丘也。而人
眞以爲勤行者也。

(Harvard-Yenching 15/6/14)

The true man of old:
    His figure looms, suffers no landslides,
    Seems insufficient, has no needs.
    Unyielding! his aloneness, not hard.

Pervasive! his emptiness, not displaying itself.
Radiant! his seeming joys!
Resolute! his inevitable moves!
Impetuously! advancing what he shows of himself,
Apprehensively! stilling the virtue within himself.
Smooth of tongue! in his seeming worldliness,
Bold of tongue! in his independence of everyone,
Lax! in his seeming love of idleness,
Bemused! He forgets whatever he says.

He thought of the punishment as a feature of his body, of the rites as his supports, of knowing what to do as a matter of timeliness, of virtue as the capacity to stay on course.

"He thought of the punishment as a feature of his body": he did not mind its truncation.

"Of the rites as his support": as the means to conduct oneself among the worldly.

"Of knowing what to do as a matter of timeliness": of doing whatever is inevitable in the circumstances.

"Of virtue as the capacity to stay on course" means (yen 言) that he went to old Confucius with the people who still had their feet, and that the others genuinely thought of him as careful in his conduct.

The first passage has an almost unintelligible vocabulary, and I am not in the least proud of the near gibberish of my translation; but the point is that unless the two sections are contrasted formally we find ourselves back in the Rambling Mode, which absorbs first the rhymed verse, then the piece of commentary, and digests them so completely that they become successive paragraphs of prose indistinguishable in style:

God's Men of old, on the other hand, were quite proper in their attitude, but they were not partisan. They looked dissatisfied with themselves, but they did not cringe. They were independent, but not rigid. Their uncommittedness was quite evident, but they put on no airs. Their relaxation gave them an air of joy. Their action was inevitableness. Their sheen attracted esteem. Their calm stilled action. All-embracing, they resembled the whole world of men. They seemed so far removed that they were not to be controlled. They were so bland that they seemed to prefer the door closed. They were so sad that they forgot their own words.

They looked upon the penal code as a general framework, ceremony as their wings, know-hows as a time element, and their high action as compliance. Therefore, they executed sentences of death with indulgence, acted with ceremony in the world of men, considered know-how inevitable in affairs, and (looking upon their high action as compliance) climbed the hill of eminence with anybody who had the necessary feet. But people really think that God's Men were diligent workers in their own personal interest!

—Ware 47 (cf. Giles 72, Legge 39/240, Watson 79)

(5) The text of Chuang Tzu has come down to us in a very battered condition, disfigured by glosses, lacunae, transpositions. An editor of the Chinese text is entitled to be cautious in deleting or transposing without firm evidence; the problem remains visible in the text before the reader's eyes, whether or not the editor proposes a solution. A translator however has to be more adventurous, because breaks and parentheses will be smoothed over in the English, and the unsolved problem will disappear from sight.

There is a minor example within the first few sentences of the book:

北冥有魚。其名爲鯤。鯤之大不知其幾
千里也。化而爲鳥。其名爲鵬。鵬之背不
知其幾千里也。怒而飛。其翼若垂天之
雲。是鳥也。海運則將徙於南冥。南冥
者。天池也。齊諧者。志怪者也。諧之言
曰。鵬之徙於南冥也。水擊三千里。搏扶
搖而上者九萬里。去以六月息者也。

(Harvard-Yenching 1/1/1)

In the North Ocean there is a fish, its name is the K'un; the K'un's girth measures who knows how many thousand miles. It changes into a bird, its name is the P'eng; the P'eng's back measures who knows how many thousand miles. When it puffs out its chest getting ready to soar, its wings are like clouds hanging from the sky. This bird when the seas are churning has a mind to travel to the South Ocean. (The South Ocean is the lake of Heaven.) (The *Drolleries of Ch'i* is a record of marvels.) In the words of the *Drolleries*, "When the P'eng travels to the South Ocean, it leaves the water thrashing for 3,000 miles, spirals into the air 90,000 miles high, and does not stop to rest for six months"...

The two parenthetic phrases look like glosses. An editor of the Chinese text does not have to make up his mind on this point, but for a translator it is urgent. If he rejects them he has a plain consecutive text and can start off the book with a swing. If he keeps them, either he must break the rhythm with a patch of clumsy English (the two parentheses without even the brackets with which we have marked them), or he must cheat. Giles for example quite frankly reorganizes the material in new sentences:

> ...At the equinox this bird prepares to start for the southern ocean, the Celestial Lake. And in the *Record of Marvels* we read that...
>
> —Giles 1

There is a much more drastic example in chapter 24, which like several other of the "mixed chapters" ends with a string of fragments. At one place it can be seen that the compiler has simply put together scraps which happened to begin with *Ku* 故 "Therefore"; we get no less than six *Ku* (which should at least establish enough connection for an English "So" or "Thus...") linking passages quite disconnected in theme. How is a translator to deal with them? If he has committed himself to the quite meaningless enterprise of translating entire a book much of which no one pretends to understand, he cannot take the obvious course of omitting them as unintelligible. Nor can he choose the philologist's solution of marking lacunae with rows of dots, because Chuang Tzu is a great writer and we have to be able to read them as literature, don't we? What the translators in fact do is to continue the stream of arbitrarily paragraphed prose right to the end of the chapter, but avoid the impression that the author was actually insane by omitting some of the "Therefores." (Watson omits three out of six, Giles four, Ware all but one.) One is again impressed by the extraordinary capacity of the Rambling Mode to assimilate the most diverse material; there seems to be as much or little continuity here as in many parts of the book where the text is sound. The secret is that what characterizes this style is not that it is obscure or difficult (a translation is entitled to be obscure and difficult if the original is) but that it is quite unfocused, so that unless there is a word like "Therefore" to give the game away we simply do not know whether sentences follow on to each other or not.

It should be recognized that such a problem forces the translator to be a radical textual critic whether he likes it or not. He must look for contexts elsewhere in *Chuang Tzu* where the fragments belong and make sense, and if he does not find them, either discard them or present them explicitly as scraps which are uninterpretable in the absence of context. I believe in fact that most of the chapter 24 fragments belong to mutilated parts of chapters 3 and 5 (one of which we quoted in Giles's translation at the start of this paper), so that they can be used to reduce the confusion instead of adding to it.

(6) Chuang Tzu is a mystical writer, and presents those who like myself are not mystics with the problem that often the choice of Chinese words is determined by a kind of experience which we have never shared. The irreverent will perhaps object that since the mystic vision is ineffable mystical writing has to be in the Rambling Mode anyway. But this would be as unjust to Chuang Tzu as to St. John of the Cross. From the translator's viewpoint the problem is no different from that raised by such a down-to-earth sentence as the following (about the advantages of being a cripple):

上徵武士，則支離攘臂而游於其間。

(Harvard-Yenching 12/4/84)

When the authorities are levying troops the cripple strolls in the middle of them baring his arms.

Here I have not translated, have merely strung together the dictionary equivalents of words; my difficulty is to visualize the gesture of *jang pei* "baring the arms" and grasp the significance of the cripple making it. D. C. Lau explained it to me with a cheeky gesture of alternately bending his arms at the elbow and flipping back the top of the sleeve with the other hand, which I recognize as something I have seen in Hong Kong streets or Bruce Lee films. With this information I can start to think how to translate it: "...strolls in the middle of them cheekily flipping back his sleeves," perhaps, or can I afford to drop that "cheekily"? The problem raised by another sentence from the same chapter is of just the same sort:

夫徇耳目內通，而外於心知，鬼神將來
舍，而況人乎。

(Harvard-Yenching 9/4/32)

If you are inwardly fluid guided by the ears and eyes, and expel the heart's knowledge, the spirits of the air and the earth will come to rest in you, not to mention other men!

The first half of the sentence suggests to me LSD experiences in which I ceased to will and conceptualize and attention roamed freely over sights and sounds. I may well be misunderstanding it, but at any rate the reference to concrete experience enables me to pick words with a confidence which fails later in the sentence. I have no idea what it feels like to have the *kuei* and *shen* settling in me, or on what literal or metaphorical level to interpret the message. And when I render *kuei shen* by "spirits of the air and the earth" rather than Watson's "gods and spirits" or simply "spirits" I am making a blind choice which for all I know may be taking away from rather than nearer to the relevant associations of the Chinese words.

It must be admitted that in the parts of *Chuang Tzu* which describe interior experience most of us are bound to be stringing together the dictionary equivalents of words without catching their real connexions. Among our seven factors compelling us towards the Rambling Mode, No. 6 is the one that we shall never quite beat. The ideal translator of *Chuang Tzu* would be, among other things, a Bodhisattva who has put off Buddhahood until he gets to the end of the book.

The fact that most of an English-speaking mystigogue's literary models are available to him only in rambled English has had one very curious consequence. The Rambling Mode is essentially translator's English, our last resort when we are cracking under the strain of the multiple problems of our craft; but in mystical writing we do find it actually employed in original composition. This in turn modifies the expectations of the student of Eastern wisdom, so that it comes to seem entirely natural to assume that a Chinese mystic would be thinking in rambled Chinese.

(7) The problem of finding acceptable equivalents for the key terms is the most familiar and intractable of the difficulties of philosophical translation. What concerns us here is the danger, not so much of misrepresenting Chuang Tzu, as of making him talk gibberish.

How far is it practical to stick to a regular English equivalent for a Chinese word? Whatever one's decision there can always be circumstances in which it has to be revised. For example no one will deny that one has a general right to render *pi shih* 彼 是 as "that" and "this" but *shih fei* 是 非 as "right" and "wrong." But in chapter 2 the continuity of the thought disappears from sight unless *shih* is treated consistently in both combinations. In my own translation of chapter 2, the only one of my experiments to beat the Rambling Mode so far entrusted to print, I used "other" and "it" for *pi shih* and "That's it" and "That's not" for *shih fei*. The device has disadvantages of its own, but without some such desperate expedient much of chapter 2 lapses irremediably into the Rambling Mode.

One of the many advantages of Burton Watson's over earlier versions is that the major terms have regular and viable equivalents which appear in the index: *Tao*, "Way": *T'ien*, "Heaven": *te*, "virtue." These provide a firm framework of concepts which the reader can trust; he is not tempted to suppose them identical with any Western concepts and can grapple with them and get the feel of them. The trouble is that even in the best translation this is possible only with a limited number of words. In general the reader cannot collate instances as a sinologist can collate characters in the *Chuang Tzu* concordance, will be unsure just how much weight he can afford to give a word, and from time to time will lose himself in that wilderness of unfocused English where the only law is the translator's will to get past the next few sentences without publicly making a fool of himself.

A recurrent nightmare is the string of rhetorical definitions with one term deriving from another; however carefully one has chosen equivalents their inadequacy is painfully exposed by their refusal to function in combination:

不離於宗，謂之天人。不離於精，謂之神
人。不離於眞，謂之至人。

(Harvard-Yenching 90/33/2)

He who does not separate from the source is one with God. He who does not separate from the essence is a spiritual man. He who does not separate from the reality is a perfect man.

—Giles 437

When contact is maintained with Primal stock, one is Natural Man. When contact is maintained with gods one is a god (once a man). When contact is maintained with True (God), one is man in his highest form.

—Ware 223

He who does not depart from the Ancestor is called the Heavenly Man; he who does not depart from the Pure is called the Holy Man; he who does not depart from the True is called the Perfect Man.

—Watson 362

All these, at first sight seem to verge on nonsense, but cannot be judged outside their contexts in the three books. In Burton Watson's, the most literal and accurate, one might be inclined to think that "He who does not depart from the True is called the Perfect Man" would mean one thing in a Greek context, another in a Christian, nothing at all in a Chinese. However Watson is using "True" and "Perfect Man" consistently for *chen* and *chih jen*, he marks them with capitals and includes them in his index, through which one finds a discussion of Truth on pp. 349–50 and "Perfect Man" used in the same context on p. 351. "Holy man" is also in the index; from the instances one gets the impression that he intends "holy" in the pre-moral sense for which Otto in his *Idea of the Holy* coined the word "numinous." So the second clause does not mean that moral purity leads to moral holiness; but what does it mean? One misses "Pure" in the index and finds the words slipping through one's fingers. The same applies to the first clause, where "Ancestor" is unindexed. But here the trouble is not in the phrasing of the clause, but in the inconsistency that Watson elsewhere renders *tsung* not by "ancestor" but by "source" (indeed he does so again in his next sentence on p. 362). The word *tsung* belongs to a common metaphorical structure with such words as *sheng* 生 "engender, be born" and *pen* 本 and *mo* 末 "root" and "tip." Provided that such words have been represented by co-ordinated equivalents throughout the book the reader will be aware that Heaven has 'engendered' man with the rest of the "myriad creatures," that the spontaneous in man "grows" from a "root" in him behind which is an "ancestor," and that it is by not detaching himself from spontaneous process to make objective analytic judgments that he accords with Heaven. Against this background Watson's "he who does not depart from the Ancestor is called the Heavenly Man" assumes a definite sense which in its present context it lacks.

Among the current versions of *Chuang Tzu* Burton Watson's is by ordinary standards of scholarship and English style a very good translation, perhaps the best possible without coming fully to grips with the problems of the Rambling Mode, especially notable for his gift for picking the apt and vivid word. Certainly readers sympathetic to Chuang Tzu do get some glimpse of his genius through Watson (through Giles too), and some may be indignant at my assertion that the English Chuang Tzu has always been a very bad writer. Such readers have I think a sound instinct to respond only to the live English and refrain from judging the vast tracts in all the translations which if they had been original English composition would be taken as symptomatic of senile dementia. But to do this one must be a little overawed, like the Bible reader who where the King James version loses the thread of the Hebrew or Greek supposes that God has said something too deep for his present understanding. The translator's literary art may actually help to convince more skeptical readers that Chuang Tzu was a bad writer, for the effect of smoothing and refining the Rambling Mode is to weave the sense and the nonsense into a seamless robe. One would like to see an English *Chuang Tzu* which could be taken quite seriously even by readers not habituated to making charitable allowances for Oriental wisdom. It would often be enigmatic, elliptical, disjointed, like the original or like Blake's *Marriage of Heaven and Hell* or Nietzsche's *Beyond Good and Evil*, but it wouldn't ramble.

Notes

Originally published as item no. 63 in appended Bibliography

[1] Witter Bynner, *The Way of Life according to Lao Tzu* (New York: Capricorn Books, 1962).

[2] Ibid., 9.

[3] *Lao Tzu*, 48. The sentence is nowhere recognizable in Bynner's paraphrase.

[4] Ibid., 7.

[5] Bynner, 11.

[6] Ibid., 20.

[7] Frank *Lloyd Wright: Writings and Buildings*, selected by Edgar Kauffmann and Ben Raeburn (Cleveland, Ohio, 1960), 300.

[8] Bynner, 14.

[9] Derk Bodde, *Tolstoy and China* (Princeton, 1950), 241.

[10] Bynner, 15.

[11] Stanza 78. The passage was misunderstood in this way by at least one of Bynner's authorities, I. W. Heysinger, *The Light of China* (Philadelphia, 1903), 97.

[12] Bynner, 21.

[13] Ibid., 20.

[14] Ibid., 15.

[15] Ibid., 20.

[16] Ibid., 15.

[17] This paper, reprinted from *The Art and Profession of Translation* (edited by T. C. Lai [Hong Kong, 1976]) is earlier than my *Chuang Tzu: The Inner Chapters* (London, 1981). If a version of my own had been available for comparison with those I criticize I would not perhaps have written with the same fine swagger. The paper on Bynner's *Lao Tzu*, some of which will be commonplace for sinologists, was written for a wider audience about the same time, but left unpublished.

Chapter 5

Taoist Spontaneity and the Dichotomy of "Is" and "Ought"

A. C. GRAHAM

Even among the philosophies commonly called "mystical," there can hardly be one more resistant to an analytic approach than Taoism. By mocking reason and delighting in the impossibility of putting his message into words, the Taoist seems to withdraw beyond reach of discussion and criticism. No doubt one may try to pin him down by translating "Live according to the Way" into some more manageable imperative such as "Live spontaneously," and then laboriously explain to him that either he is expressing a taste for spontaneity which others may not share, or he is making a covert inference from "I am spontaneously inclined to do X" to "I ought to do X," an instance of that illogical jump from "is" to "ought" to which Western philosophers have been objecting ever since Hume. But since all the great Taoists are poets as much as they are philosophers, would it not be more to the point to approach Taoism as a view of life to be imaginatively explored and approved or rejected to the extent that one finds it fruitful? However, in the present essay I shall refuse to be deterred from trying to run down that elusive imperative behind the denial of imperatives, the implicit logic behind the derision of logic, in the most sophisticated of the Taoist writers, Chuang Tzu. Instead of accepting him on his own terms—as a poet only incidentally interested in logic, who by aphorism, verse, and anecdote guides us towards his view of life—I shall perversely insist on confronting him in Western terms. The enterprise has turned out, for me at least, to be a more stimulating experience than might be anticipated. It will be seen that, instead of ending up with a take-it-or-leave-it imperative or a trivial example of a fallacious inference, I find myself colliding with an unexpectedly firm logical structure which forces me to approach the fundamental problems of moral philosophy from an unfamiliar direction.

It is unlikely that Chuang Tzu, who lived in the times of King Hui of Liang (370–319 B.I.E. [Before International Era]) and King Hsüan of Ch'i (319–301 B.I.E.), wrote more of the book that bears his name than the "inner chapters" (ch. 1–7) and some of the fragments assembled in certain of the "mixed chapters" (ch. 23–27, 32). However, we are exploring a structure common to all Taoist thought (and perhaps to much of Oriental philosophy), so that questions of authorship do not much concern us. We may note in the first place that what logic there is in *Chuang Tzu* is directed against reason itself, in particular against rational choice between one course of action and another. The book goes counter to the whole trend towards increasing rationality which had begun with Mo Tzu late in the fifth century B.I.E. Confucius (551–479 B.I.E.) had never needed to give reasons for his dicta; he presented himself simply as a man of mature judgment trying to restore the moral and cultural tradition of the dying Chou dynasty. But Mo Tzu's doctrines, universal love, rejection of fatalism, opposition to aggressive war, promotion on grounds of merit rather than of birth, were novelties which it was necessary to defend in public debate. With the emergence of Mohism, and soon of other rivals to Confucianism, debate intensified, and it became habitual to argue one's case, define one's terms, look beyond moral and political disputes to metaphysical problems such as the relation between morality and human nature, and at last, among sophists such as Hui Shih and Kung-sun Lung, to ponder logical puzzles for their own sake. Chuang Tzu was himself a disciple or younger friend of Hui Shih; he himself displays an intermittent delight in logical subtleties, and in his turn he becomes the target of criticism in the most logically sophisticated document which survives from the period, the *Canons* of the Later Mohists (ca. 300 B.I.E.).[1] Chinese civilization, for the first and last time, was independently envisaging the prospect which unknown to it was already being opened up by the Greeks, that in the last resort all differences of opinion might be resolved by appeal to indisputable principles of reason. It did not sustain this vision, and to the extent, little or great as it may be, that individual thinkers do affect the course of history, much of the responsibility is Chuang Tzu's.

In his time the crucial debate was still between Confucians and Mohists, and the issues on which it centered were moral. Confucians understood the word *yi* 義 ("righteousness, duty") in terms of the customary "appropriateness" (another and etymologically related *yi* 宜) of conduct to status, as ruler or subject, father or son, elder brother or younger brother. Thus it is appropriate for a son to mourn his father for three years. The Mohists exposed all traditional standards to the tests of whether or not in practice they benefited the people; in the case of mourning, they argued in detail that such a long period is not beneficial but harmful to everyone concerned. In the *Canons*, which start with seventy-five definitions and twelve analyses of ambiguous words, *yi* is given a radically new definition: "To be 'righteous' is to benefit."[2] But with increasing care in definition, it became all the more obvious that every argument started from definitions which might be peculiar to the school. It happens that the Chinese words which established themselves as technical terms attract attention to this point, since the art of *pien* 辨 ("disputation, arguing out alternatives") was conceived in terms of fitting names to objects, and the customary words for judging between alternatives were basically demonstrative, *shih* 是 ("that's *it*" [an ox, a horse]) and *jan* 然 ("that's *so*" [that the horse is white, that one rides it]). Clearly, whether one is talking about oxen and horses or about morality, no argument can prove that something is *it* without agreement as to what the name refers to.

Chuang Tzu has plenty of reasons for denying reason, but let us concentrate on his point that all disputation founders on the fact that words mean what the debaters choose to make them mean:

> Saying is not blowing breath, the sayer says something; the trouble is that what he is saying has never been fixed. Has he really said something? Or never said anything? If you think it different from the twitter of fledglings, can disputation show the difference? Or can't it show the difference?[3]

He takes full advantage of the demonstrative nature of the key words in disputation, which show that the argument always depends on the initial choice of standpoint:

> *It* is also Other, Other is also It. There they say "That's it, that's not" from one point of view, here we say "That's it, that's not" from another point of view. Is there really It and Other? Or really no It and Other?[4]

When I choose a name, am I not free to call anything or everything "X" and therefore to affirm or deny of anything whatever that it is X?

When the sophist Kung-sun Lung went to such trouble to prove that "The meaning is not the meaning" and "A white horse is not a horse," he was wasting his time:

> Rather than use the meaning to show that the meaning is not the meaning, better use what is not the meaning; rather than use the horse to show that the horse is not a horse, better use what is not the horse. Heaven and earth are the one meaning, the myriad things are the one horse.[5]

As far as factual questions are concerned, Chuang Tzu's skepticism is well answered in one of the *Canons*. Provided that different things are indicated differently, it does not matter which of them is picked out as "this" or "that" (or as "horse" or "nonhorse"); the debaters, if they understand how each is using the words, will recognize that they are saying the same thing.[6] However, both Chuang Tzu and the Mohist are primarily concerned with issues of conduct; and in the case of moral terms the disputants cannot simply agree to differ, they must insist that their definitions are the right ones. To understand Chuang Tzu's criticism of disputation, it may be useful to stick to the instance of a Confucian and a Mohist debating whether it is one's duty to mourn a father for three years, each knowing that they disagree over the definition of "righteousness" yet compelled to insist on his own:

> You and I having been made to engage in disputation, if it is you not I that wins, is it really you who are on to it, I who am not? If it is I not you that wins, is it really I who am on to it, you who are not? Is it that one of us is on to it and the other not, or that both of us are on to it and both are not?[7]

We cannot break out of the deadlock unless we can find an independent standpoint from which to judge whether the righteous is the appropriate or the beneficial, but there is none:

> Who shall I call in to decide it? Suppose that someone of your party decides it, already being of your party how can he decide it? Suppose that someone of my party decides it, already being of my party how can he decide it?

Nor are we on any firmer ground if we appeal to someone whose general position differs from or agrees with both of ours (in the former case, we would simply reject his principles; in the latter, he would share principles of ours by which the issue could he settled for us both, but not necessarily for others):

Suppose someone of a party different from either decides it, already being of a party different from either how can he decide it? Suppose someone of a party embracing both decides it, already being of a party which embraces both how can he decide it?

Elsewhere Chuang Tzu goes several dizzying steps further. He concedes, as an *argumentum ad hominem*, that the search for an independent standard might indeed arrive at something on which there is universal agreement:

"Would you know something of which all things agreed 'That's it?'"

"How would I know that?"

"Would you know what you did not know?"

"How would I know that?"

"Then does no thing know anything?"

"How would I know that? However, let me try to find words for it. 'How do I know that what I call knowing is not ignorance, how do I know that what I call ignorance is not knowing?'"[8]

Universal agreement that the righteous is the appropriate or is the beneficial would merely eliminate finally the possibility of an independent standpoint from which to judge. I would not know whether the righteous is really the beneficial, but would not I at least know what I did not know? That, however, would be a contradiction (or so Chuang Tzu thinks, a position also found in Plato's *Meno*; the Mohist *Canon* takes him up on this point).[9] But then at any rate surely I know that no thing in the world knows anything? Another contradiction. One can never get further than the doubt expressed in the form of a question, "How do I know...?"

Skepticism and relativism as extreme as Chuang Tzu's are not in themselves unfamiliar to a modern reader, far from it. What is perhaps strange to him is that there is no vertigo in the doubt, which pervades the most rhapsodic passages of a philosophical poet who seems always to gaze on life and death with unwavering assurance. But there is anguish in ethical skepticism only if one feels bound to choose in spite of having no grounds to choose. For Chuang Tzu, to pose alternatives and ask "Which is beneficial, which harmful?" or "Which is right, which wrong?" is the fundamental error in life. People who really know what they are doing, such as cooks, carpenters, swimmers, boatmen, cicada-catchers, whose instruction is always available to any philosopher or emperor who has the sense to listen to them, do not go in much for analyzing, posing alternatives, and reasoning from first principles. They no longer even bear in mind any rules they were taught as apprentices. They attend to the total situation and respond, trusting to a knack which they cannot explain in words, the hand moving of itself as the eye gazes with unflagging concentration.

A craftsman is not of course "thoughtless" in the sense of "heedless"; on the contrary, he is attentive in the highest degree. As the cicada-catcher is represented as saying to Confucius:

> I settle my body like a rooted stump, I hold my arm like the branch
> of a withered tree; in all the vastness of heaven and earth, in all the
> multitude of the myriad things, it is only the wings of a cicada that
> I know. I don't fret or fidget, I would not for all the myriad things
> exchange the wings of a cicada.[10]

Indeed the craftsman may do a lot of hard thinking before he makes his move. Although Chuang Tzu detests *pien*, the arguing out of alternatives, there is another word for a kind of thinking, *lun* 論 ("sort out, grade, arrange") which throughout the book is used in a favorable sense.[11] And of course the craftsman does have to go on asking "What shall I do next?" until he has mastered his art, like the apprentice Taoist. But however long even the sage may take to sort out the elements of his situation in their interactions and interrelations, his move when he makes it is "spontaneous" (*tzu jan* 自 然 "so of itself"), as immediate as echo following sound or shadow following shape. In terms of the traditional dichotomy of "man," who thinks and chooses, and "Heaven," which is responsible for everything independent of man's will, his motions derive not from the man but from Heaven working through him. Even in governing the empire he is like Cook Ting, who when he comes to an especially intricate knot of bone and muscle, pauses until he has assimilated all the information, and then cuts through with a single deft stroke.[12]

The many stories about craftsmen in *Chuang Tzu* (of which, however, only the story of Cook Ting comes from the "inner chapters") are always especially illuminating to a Westerner grappling to understand Taoism. He learns from them that the Taoist art of living is a supremely intelligent responsiveness which would be undermined by analyzing and posing alternatives, a point easily appreciated in the case of physical skills—the tightrope walker who pauses to ask "Where do I put my foot next?" would fall from the rope. He comes to perceive also that the Taoist's refusal to lay down the Way in words is not mere evasiveness about a metaphysical truth which, since he is so coy about it, is probably nonsense anyway. Grasping the Way is a matter of "knowing how," not of "knowing that." As the wheelwright says to Duke Huan in one of the "outer chapters," the "Way of Heaven,"

> Chisel the wheel too slow and it slides and does not grip, too fast and it jams and will not enter. Not too slow, not too fast; you feel it in the hand and respond from the heart, the mouth cannot say it, there is a knack in it somewhere which I cannot convey to my own son, which my own son cannot get from me.[13]

Even the most rationalistic Westerner then has his times of accord with the Way, if he can drive a car with effortless grace. But he will probably spoil it all by supposing that this exercise in intelligent responsiveness owes its value to something else, that he must justify it either as a means to the end of arriving at his destination or as a source of pleasure. Not at all, says Chuang Tzu. This is one of the few activities that the rationalist conducts as he should be running his whole life, in the very manner in which the sage ruler governs the empire. That concentration on the total scene forgetful of self, in which one ceases to analyze and make considered choices, yet responds to variations so fine that one would not know how to analyze them, differs only in degree from the illumination in which all distinctions lapse, self and other, life and death, and it is no longer *I* that acts but Heaven. However, we are concerned here not with the depths of Chuang Tzu's thought but with its logical structure. It is enough for us to note that while Confucians and Mohists, like Westerners, would tend to think of the intelligent spontaneity exhibited on a humble scale by craftsmen as being no more than a means to ends for which reasons must be given, for Chuang Tzu it is the one and only end in itself.

Taoists speak of spontaneity in a vocabulary curiously like that of behaviorist psychology; the crucial pair *kan* 感 ("stir, rouse") and *ying* 應 ("respond" [primarily "reply" in dialogue]) recall the Pavlovian "stimulus" and "response":

> He will not, to gain an advantage, make the first approach:
> He will not, to escape misfortune, start things off.
> Only when stirred will he respond,
> Only when pressed will he move,
> Only when it is inevitable will he rise up.[14]

The implication is not of course that the sage delays until the last possible moment; he waits without premeditation until the situation is ripe. The man who reacts with pure spontaneity can do so only at one moment and in one way; by attending to the situation until it moves him, he discovers the move which is "inevitable" (*pu te yi* 不得已, the one in which he "has no alternative") like a physical reflex. But he hits on it only if he perceives with perfect clarity, as though in a mirror: "The utmost man uses the heart like a mirror. He does not escort things as they go or welcome them as they come, he responds but does not retain."[15]

For the ancient Chinese the heart, not the brain, is the organ of thought. Most men use it to plan ahead, but the sage uses it only to reflect the situation as it objectively is, before he responds. Like a mirror, it reflects only the present; it is not stuffed with past information which it "retains" (*ts'ang* 藏 "stores, hoards") at the cost of being trapped in obsolete attitudes. The sage perceives and responds to every situation as new:

> Within himself, no fixed position:
> Things as they take shape disclose themselves.
> In his motions, he is like water,
> In his stillness, like a mirror:
> He responds like an echo.[16]

The first couplet relates the sage's inner freedom from a fixed standpoint to the objectivity of his vision; the external situation as it takes shape presents itself from moment to moment as it objectively is. He is as fluid as water which is unimpeded because it adapts to the contours of the ground; his response is as immediate as the echo to the sound. The metaphor of the mirror is developed farthest in a prose passage in the "Way of Heaven":

> As for the stillness of the sage, it is not that he is still because he says "It is good to be still"; he is still because nothing among the myriad things is sufficient to disturb his heart. When water is still its clarity shows up the hairs of beard and eyebrows, its evenness coincides with the water-level—the greatest of carpenters takes his standard from it. If mere water clarifies when it is still, how much more the stillness of the quintessential and daemonic, the heart of the sage! He is the reflector of heaven and earth, the mirror of the myriad things.

> Emptiness, stillness, calm, serenity, Doing Nothing, are the even level of heaven and earth, the utmost reach of the Way and the Power; therefore the emperor, king, sage, comes to rest in them. At rest he empties, in emptiness is filled; and what fills him sorts itself out. In emptying he is still, in stillness he is moved; and when he moves he succeeds.[17]

The essential point here is that, in responding, the sage's heart is not subject to the agitations that obscure the common man's clarity of vision, to which Chuang Tzu himself is represented as confessing in one anecdote ("I have been observing in muddy water and have gone astray from the clear depths").[18] He keeps the heart empty and lets the external scene fill it, sort itself out in its own objective relations, and then "move" him (*tung* 動). His heart has the "evenness" (*p'ing* 平), the neutrality to all human ends, of the universe itself. Having achieved this mirror-like lucidity, he no longer has to evaluate, even to judge that "It is good to be still"; it is enough that he does *not* value anything in the universe above his own clarity of vision (nothing is "sufficient to disturb his heart"). At this ultimate degree of awareness of his situation, his response is perfectly apt to the goal to which at that moment he spontaneously tends; "when he moves he succeeds." His response hits exactly on the Way, the *te* 德 ("Power" [his aptitude, his knack]) is perfected.

It will by now be clear that from the Western point of view there is something very peculiar about the Taoist attitude. We are accustomed to think in terms of a dichotomy: either as a rational agent I detach myself from nature, study the objective facts about it, make my own choices, resist becoming the plaything of physical forces like an animal, or else I welcome the Romantic idea of spontaneity, as the free play of impulse, emotion, subjective imagination. The Taoist is somewhere where this dichotomy does not apply. He wants to remain inside nature, to behave as spontaneously as an animal, to be caused rather than to choose, and concepts resembling those of stimulus and response come easily to him without the science which for us provides their context; on the other hand, he has a contempt for emotion and subjectivity, a respect for things as they objectively are, as cool and lucid as a scientist's.

Let us try then to identify that ultimate Taoist imperative, for which in the opening paragraph we tentatively proposed "Live spontaneously." Very evidently Chuang Tzu does not recommend a surrender to emotion and subjective imagination. The craftsman, far from welcoming temperamental upheavals, knows that if he gets flustered he will lose his knack, and the sage can never allow the clear mirror of his mind to be obscured by the turbidity of passion. The Taoist ideal is a spontaneity disciplined by awareness of the objective. Let us say then that "Follow the Way" is translatable as "Respond with awareness (of what is objectively so)." The awareness will be, not only of the mirrored situation, but of how as a matter of objective fact things can be done (not of what on prudential or moral grounds ought to be done), knowing how, knack, skill, art. Of how much one has to be aware may be left vague. Presumably the Taoist should be aware of everything relevant to his intent. But he has no fixed ends, only fluid goals to which he spontaneously tends, which will accord with the Way to the extent that he is indeed aware of all factors relevant to them. The more aware he is, the more likely he is to attain them ("When he moves he succeeds"). There would no doubt be some persuasive force in the claim that conversion to Taoism would help me to my goals (which would, however, change in the process of conversion). But within the logic of the Taoist position, the value of awareness will not depend on the value I set on any particular goal; it is assumed only that, to the extent that responses are purposive, it is valuable to move towards goals intelligently, with awareness, whatever they may happen to be.

The stories of craftsmen may seem to make only the minor point (quite interesting as far as it goes) that in some circumstances we do better if we don't think than if we do. This however is a side issue. The implicit logic of Chuang Tzu's position has two steps:

1. all the reasons for which men depart from the spontaneity of the rest of nature to make choices between alternatives are logically baseless;

2. in reverting to spontaneity one remains bound by a single imperative, which we identify as "Respond with awareness."

Now if "Follow the Way" is equivalent to "Respond with awareness (of what is objectively so)," we need no longer be exasperated that Chuang Tzu should speak of following the Way as though its value were self-evident. "Respond with awareness" is an imperative which we all take for granted but hardly bother to formulate because it seems trivial; it comes as a surprise that a whole philosophy of life can be based on it. Whether I am deliberately acting or spontaneously reacting, I recognize that I ought to be aware of circumstances, of myself, of how to attain my goals, and sometimes I have to be recalled to attention by imperatives, "Face facts," "Know thyself," "Think what you're doing." In deliberate action such imperatives do not take me very far, since I can go on adding to the information forever without beginning to know what I ought to do. (If I doubt that, I confuse "is" and "ought"). But a spontaneous reaction has a merely causal connection with the perception which it follows, so that it can be judged without taking into account more than that the person is being insensitive or highly perceptive or has his facts right or wrong. Westerners are not accustomed to evaluating human beings by "Respond with awareness," only animals (as when comparing their sensitivity and adaptability to their surroundings, to rank them higher or lower on the "vast chain of being" or the evolutionary ladder). However, if like Chuang Tzu we sweep away all moral and prudential standards, certainly "Respond with awareness" will remain in force. Nothing is involved after all but preferring intelligence to stupidity, reality to illusion; of the traditional Western values, Truth, Good, and Beauty, only the first is assumed. If I am in the way of a car coming suddenly round a bend in the road, the intelligent reaction for me, as for a dog, will be to jump for the sidewalk before I know what I am doing. To stand paralyzed by shock, unaware of what is happening to me, or be aware of the danger but too confused to know how to escape in the instant available, would be reacting stupidly. This judgment, it may be noticed, has nothing to do with any value set on self-preservation. Even if I have made a firm decision to commit suicide, and have been pondering for weeks how to cheat the insurance company, the failure to jump would accord with my intention only by chance. It would be highly intelligent to take in the situation instantaneously and choose to stand waiting for death, but that would be not a reaction but a deliberate act.

But it would be an insult to Chuang Tzu to suggest that there is anything subhuman about obeying the injunction "Respond with awareness." Suppose that I am sitting by a bowl of fruit: my hand hovers over a pear, then a peach catches my eye: their distinctive flavors revive in memory and pull against each other, then my hand moves over and picks up the peach. Let us assume nothing but a causal connection between the imagined sensations and the motion of the hand. I responded like a monkey to what I saw and smelled, but in full awareness of the two flavors, in obedience to "Respond with awareness." Could I in fact have taken one rather than the other in a manner more worthy of my human dignity as a rational agent? Perhaps it will be said that I should have combined some principle of conduct with propositions about the flavors. But I do not even have a vocabulary to describe the distinctive tang of a pear or a peach. The best I could do would be to say "I prefer peaches" or "I get more pleasure from peaches," but in the first place to derive "Choose the peach" from these psychological statements would involve a jump from "is" to "ought"; in the second place, reliance on a generalization about my preference could get me into a habit that would dim my awareness of the tastes, until I fail to notice that I no longer like peaches as much as I did or that at this moment I hanker after a change, so that the abortive try at rationalization would make my choice *less* intelligent. Or suppose that I am eating escargots for the first time and cannot bring myself to forget the disgustingly slimy look and feel of snails in the garden. You reproach me for being stupidly repelled by a taste of which I never dared to become fully aware. As a gourmet, you certainly think of yourself as a product of high civilization, as far above the animal as a scholar or a scientist is. Perhaps I am myself no gourmet and think of food as a matter in which the rational man can excuse himself from making a fully considered choice. However, if I accept your demand for a considered choice, can I deny the justice of your reproach? If I reply that it does not matter whether or not one confounds a present taste with remembered sight and touch, whether one responds to reality or illusion, I plunge into a skepticism deeper than Chuang Tzu's. But since in practice I do admit that one ought to be on the lookout for perceptual error, ought to be aware of things as they objectively are (whatever metaphysical problems may incidentally arise), I have a principle for evaluating spontaneous behavior in general, which if I were a Taoist would supply me with all the ethics I need. Odd as it may seem, Taoism is a philosophy of life which, though of course criticizable as incomplete, assumes no more than is assumed in the sciences, depends only on a respect for things as they objectively are.

By interpreting "Follow the Way" as "Respond with awareness," we can dispose of an apparent contradiction in Taoist relativism. The "Autumn floods," one of the "outer chapters," presents what looks like the most extreme moral relativism:

> Observing from the standpoint of the Way, no thing is either noble or base. Observing from the standpoint of the things, they judge themselves noble and each other base. Observing from the standpoint of custom, whether one is noble or base is independent of oneself.[19]

It continues by asking us to accept with neutrality that "Yao [for Confucians a sage] and Chieh [for Confucians a tyrant] judged themselves right and each other wrong." Yet Taoists certainly do not treat their own evaluations as relativistic in this sense. A few lines later, after some historical instances of men who yielded or fought for a throne with differing results, we are told that "as for the propriety of fighting or yielding, the conduct of Yao or of Chieh, whether they are noble or base is a matter of timeliness, they are not to be adopted as norms." This is relativism in a more limited sense; there is no constant rule to apply to both Yao and Chieh because they lived in different situations, yet a Taoist does prefer the former to the latter. One can pronounce absolutely that a particular man in a particular situation did or did not accord with the Way. There is no contradiction here; as stock examples of the good ruler and the bad, Yao would be conceived by a Taoist as responding in awareness of the conditions of his time, Chieh as not.

Since Western philosophy has almost given up hope of finding logical grounds for imperatives, it may seem a little unfair that a Chinese antirationalist should, without looking for it, have stumbled on such a firm rock bottom for his philosophy of life. Unfortunately it appears that a rationalized ethic cannot take advantage of Chuang Tzu's solution. If we accept the need for rational choices between alternatives, and allow only marginal importance to the realm of spontaneity, what can we do but note that among the exotica of remote civilizations there is at least one philosophy which escapes our dichotomy of fact and value?

But are we perhaps still underestimating Chuang Tzu? Nothing forbids us to take over the model of man as a basically spontaneous being bound by the imperative "Respond with awareness (of what is objectively so)," but still insist against Chuang Tzu that rationality is a positive help in becoming aware. It might turn out that there are advantages in approaching the problems of moral philosophy from this direction. Let us explore this possibility. We shall continue to speak of awareness without bothering over the details of what degree or kind of awareness is appropriate to any particular situation, which might distract us from the main thrust of the argument.

At the start of my life I was behaving as spontaneously as the animals from which my species descends. Like a young animal, I became progressively more aware of my surroundings, and my reactions developed accordingly—a change for the better, for our imperative recommends it. Being human, I learned also to reason about questions of fact and so became more widely and accurately informed; but by itself such information could still serve only to make my reactions more intelligent. I also became more rational in choosing means to the goals that attracted me; but so far our only grounds for preferring one goal to another as a rational end will be that it is the one towards which I spontaneously inclined when most aware of the conditions, so that it was backed by the authority of "Respond with awareness."

In the course of this evolution I was being taught a varied assortment of imperatives by parents, teachers, other children. As I learned to choose in the light of imperatives, did my actions disconnect themselves from spontaneous motions? Let us suppose that a child at dinner wants to eat another helping but knows that he will be sick if he does. He remembers what it is like to vomit, and appetite is momentarily overwhelmed by nausea; but present sight and smell act on him more urgently and submerge the memory. His mother says to him, or he says to himself, "Don't or you'll be ill." A crisis of choice has arisen, and the issue is which of two suspended reactions is to be allowed to run its course. The more intelligent of them is in this case the weaker, and the force of the imperative is the force of the argument for preferring the weaker:

> Your choice is whether to respond in diminished awareness of the consequences and eat or in full awareness and refrain.
> Respond in awareness of what is objectively so.
> Therefore refrain.

(This is quite different from fallaciously inferring the imperative "Don't eat" from the factual premises "Eating will make you sick" and "You don't like to be sick.")

Since the situation recurs in his own and other's experience, he can generalize the injunction as the principle "One ought not to eat too much." A Taoist sage can no doubt dispense with such principles, since he has trained himself not to let local reactions distract him from his mirroring of the total situation. But the rest of us do need them, like Confucius, whom Chuang Tzu represents as saying, "They are the sort that travel outside the guidelines, I am the sort that travels inside the guidelines.... I am one of Heaven's convicts."[20] (He recognizes that he can never himself become a Taoist sage and cease to depend on rules.) For us, if we are rationalists, the Taoist sage will serve rather as a theoretical limit in ethics, and the significance of "Respond with awareness" will be, not so much that it requires us to become more aware and responsive, as that it has a corollary, "Prefer the response in fuller awareness," which can generate prudential imperatives on the model of "One ought not to eat too much." Since any collection of imperatives must be logically consistent if all are to be obeyed, we have to try to organize them in a coherent code. But even the most highly articulated system of standards will never, unless some new logical basis for it can be found, become more than an apparatus for criticizing and judging between conflicting reactions, in ultimate dependence on "Respond with awareness."

The imperative we took as example is prudential; what of moral standards? Chuang Tzu declares that the sage "has no self"[21] and always implies that in perfectly mirroring the affairs of the world the sage responds on behalf of all men. "The benefits of his bounty extend to a myriad ages, but he is not deemed to love mankind."[22] At first sight one might suppose that he is overlooking man's spontaneous egoism. But in submitting to "Respond with awareness" I have to admit that awareness from my own viewpoint has no privileged status. This raises the interesting possibility that the concept of awareness might prove to be a bridge over which the equal status of self and other in objective knowledge transfers itself to ethics. Let us examine this possibility, first noting that there is a close analogy between awareness from personal and from temporal viewpoints.

Suppose that I have a sudden impulse to settle when I retire in the village where I was born; but reality breaks in, I recognize that I had better try to remember it not as a nostalgic vision but as I indeed saw it before experiencing the city, try to anticipate living in it not as I am now but as an old man who no longer easily makes friends, try to see myself through the villagers's eyes as already a stranger who may not deserve a welcome. I respond in awareness of what is objectively so to the extent that I become independent of my individual and present viewpoint, reducing it to the level of other viewpoints. Whether the considerations that move me are prudential or moral, my whole understanding of the world of men requires that in thought and imagination I am constantly shifting between and responding from different viewpoints, remembered or anticipated, individual or collective, my own or another's (when I "put myself in his place" by an incipient mimicry), hypothetical, fictional, or simply indefinite; it is only in action that I have to settle in a present viewpoint, whether personal ("I") or social ("We"). There is of course the asymmetry that from other viewpoints I do not perceive but imagine. But I am still responding to what I suppose to be the objective situation, and it is of crucial importance that although I am imagining it, I am not imagining the response itself. This is the case just as much with personal as with temporal viewpoints. When trying to guess where someone went when I missed him at the airport I do not imagine his thoughts, I try to imagine his situation as someone like him would see it, and think; if he tells me that he has just learned that he has cancer, I may hear in imagination the doctor's grave voice, but I do not imagine the fear, I feel the chill of it; if I see him cut his finger, I do not imagine the pain as something objective before my "mind's eye," either I look on as though the knife were slicing through cheese or I incipiently wince.

This viewpoint-shifting to other times or persons is not an ethical but a cognitive act, by which I explore how I might, would, or shall feel or how other persons feel. However, to perform it I do have to feel; and my reactions, for example, to a pain which I expect to suffer in the future or which I see another person suffer differ only in degree from my reactions to a present pain of my own. I may harden myself not to feel it, or take measures to relieve or avoid it, or even (if I am sadomasochistic) be sexually excited by it. The difference of degree is of course considerable, and there is no assurance that the forebodings for myself or the sympathies for others which stir in me when I am most vividly aware will be strong enough to move me to action. But even if I am moved only a little, our imperative will oblige me to resist stronger impulses and choose to act on the prompting, as my response when most aware. The child experiencing a moment of nausea from an anticipated viewpoint was able to do that, and made a considered prudential choice; a moral choice following a faint tremor at someone else's pain, which one acknowledges without letting the mind uselessly dwell on it, will be closely analogous, and similarly grounded in "Prefer the response in fuller awareness."

Do we have here the groundwork of a new anti-egoist argument? We can claim at least that the Taoist conception of man as a basically spontaneous being is revealing an important advantage. Philosophers are accustomed to start from the idea of a rational agent pursuing his own ends; at once the question arises, "Why should I prefer anyone else's ends to my own?" and until it can be answered the advantage lies with the egoist. The moralists—as it seems to many of us who have worried over that question—either shirk the answer or botch it. Yet if we start by thinking of man as a spontaneous but intelligent being, obliged to pursue an awareness independent of viewpoint, recognizing if he is wise that all his behavior starts from responses which come about by causation, though able to suspend and choose between responses, the burden of proof is shifted. The egoist's question becomes, "Why shouldn't I prefer the responses from my own viewpoint?" and invites the answer, "That would be like preferring the response from your present viewpoint. Awareness is neutral as to viewpoint, and you cannot be aware from any viewpoint without responding." The egoist may now make his stand: "Well, I am *not* neutrally aware from all viewpoints, and neither are you. I am most aware from my own, and it is my selfish reactions which are the strongest. Why shouldn't

I choose to act as I please and numb myself to the hurt I do to others, resisting any enlargement of awareness which might arouse inconvenient sympathies in conflict with my present desires?" But now he is in open rebellion against "Respond with awareness." In the course of our argument we have found no rational grounds on which he could have chosen his present ends except that they were the ones to which he spontaneously inclined when most aware; on what grounds can he now prefer these ends to a further advance in awareness which might undermine them? He is assuming something which is indeed commonly assumed, but which a consideration of Chuang Tzu is forcing us to question, that it is possible to choose in a void, and ordain one's ends by an arbitrary fiat; but can one do anything else but choose, in lesser or greater awareness, between goals towards which one is already spontaneously tending? Moreover he is no longer maintaining a coherent egoistic position. He began by preferring his own response to anyone else's; now he is preferring his own as it is now to his own as it would become with greater awareness.

At its theoretical limit, to respond with awareness would be to attain full awareness from every viewpoint and react with sympathies and antipathies as impartial as those with which I read a play of Shakespeare or a novel of Tolstoy. The ideal sage of Taoism can presumably do that, so no more requires moral standards than I require that "Vengeance is mine, I will repay" which Tolstoy put under the title of *Anna Karenina*. The rest of us however are relatively unaware from other viewpoints, with the consequence that our altruistic reactions are relatively weak; like the child wondering whether to risk another helping at dinner, we need an "ought" to recall us to the reaction in fuller awareness when it is the weaker. But in moral as in prudential choices, it remains basic to our position that imperatives can serve only for judging between spontaneous reactions. Certainly duty can pull against one's strongest inclination, but could one recognize the force of a moral imperative without feeling some inclination, however slight, towards the course which it commands? It seems reasonable to claim that a man without the capacity to put himself in another's place could not understand a moral appeal (even if he should happen to be a law-abiding man who accepts commands and prohibitions on external authority), just as someone incapable of temporal viewpoint-shifting could not understand an appeal to his own future interests. On the present analysis, a reduced capacity for either kind of viewpoint-shifting is not a moral but a cognitive defect. It is a relevant psychological fact that insensibility both to moral appeals and to appeals to future interests, imprisonment in both "I" and "Now," often appears in the same person, and that the combination is widely accepted as the strongest criterion for classing him as psychopathic and exempting him from moral judgment.

The question now arises: Can that rational animal Man ever become more than an animal which criticizes its own spontaneous tendencies in the light of its awareness of objective conditions? Perhaps I think it beneath my dignity to let myself be carried on the spontaneous flood, employing my divine gift of reason only to navigate on the course of greatest awareness. I wish to be wholly responsible for my acts, to be master of my fate; I shall make my own choice of ends, distance myself from my own reactions, and learn to manipulate them like external events. There is something paradoxical about this aspiration to lift myself out of nature by the use of reason, since I cannot without setting arbitrary limits to reason forbid the sciences of physiology, psychology, and sociology to reincorporate me into nature, as a phenomenon in principle explainable and predictable like everything else. However, this has long been a Western ideal, at its most intransigent in Sartre's *Being and Nothingness*, which treats even emotion as a matter of choice, to the point of explicitly denying the distinction between genuine and willed feeling.[23] The ideal would indeed be attainable if a self-contained system of imperatives could be reestablished on foundations independent of "Respond with awareness." Philosophers have of course tried to do so, by deducing a priori a Categorical Imperative, or by deriving imperatives from theological, psychological, or sociological premises at the cost of leaping from "is" to "ought." It is now widely recognized that all such attempts have failed, yet it continues to be assumed that the rational agent has somehow pulled himself up by his bootstraps out of reach of his own spontaneity. This is to mistake the will for the deed. As long as the scope of reason is confined to refining and systematizing imperatives and deducing them from each other, how can it ever change their relation to the spontaneous?

The illusion that in rational choice I detach myself from the spontaneous and reduce it to the status of external events can be sustained for a long time through a stable life adequately covered by a system of principles. But then perhaps some goal at which I have been aiming for years loses all its appeal, the energy to pursue it dries up, and suddenly it is the rational project which seems external to me, a mechanism of means and ends in which I have been trapped. It becomes clear in retrospect that what I judged to be the right goal was at best the one to which I then spontaneously inclined after full consideration of the conditions; now, if no other ends or principles are involved, a whole galaxy of reasons for saying "I ought" has been annihilated by the waning of the ambition. Or I am caught in a dilemma between conflicting standards, deliberating whether to tell a truth which will do harm, or in the classic conflict between Love and Duty. I fall asleep pondering and wake the next morning knowing what I will do, like a compass needle that was swinging and has finally settled. Even assuming that I was conducting logical operations in my sleep, it was not like arriving at a balance of probabilities, for the conflicting principles were incommensurable. Nor was it like tossing a coin, for the preliminary reasoning was not a waste of time. Shall I dignify it by saying that I made an existential choice from the depths of my being? But that would only be a rhetorical way of saying that I responded intelligently, settled in the direction in which I spontaneously tended after taking account of every relevant consideration, with perhaps a further suggestion that it is by this kind of choice, not fully derivable from already acknowledged imperatives, that I learn and grow.

I may try to shrink myself to an infinitesimal point of thinking Ego to which all spontaneous process is external, but the spontaneous is always springing up at the center of me, thrusting me forward or dragging me back, and it is only at the periphery that I can take full control of it. Nor is it sensible to wish that it were otherwise, since raptures, aesthetic, erotic, intellectual, mystical, in which the spontaneous floods the whole of consciousness, can lift us to heights of awareness beyond our ordinary capacities. They can also delude us, of course, and the obscured line between revelation and illusion is a distinction to cling to as best one can, to be clarified by reason in retrospect or not at all. But if I insist on forcing the spontaneous towards an end which I already deem rational, I remain imprisoned within a circle of old concepts, reason goes on doing the same kind of sums, there can be no novelty except the discovery of unnoticed implications of the familiar. In poetry such a transport is evoked by a pattern of words (selected by the poet perhaps with the most intense thought and effort), which stabilizes it and allows me to evaluate it at leisure. The reader of a poem may find himself "responding" (a word as fully at home in some dialects of literary criticism as in behaviorist psychology or as the Chinese *ying* in *Chuang Tzu*) with an extraordinary expansion and enhancement of awareness. To a degree unknown in any other use of language, he finds himself not only attending to what is said, but simultaneously hearing the words as textures of vowels and consonants, noticing rhythm, rhyme, assonance; meanings refuse to be tied down, disclose associations and nuances of which he has never been conscious; sights and sounds which he has never heeded become sensuously precise and vivid in imagination; emotion assumes a peculiar lucidity, undisguised by what he habitually feels or has been taught that he ought to feel; truths about life and death which he follows social convention in systematically evading stand out as simple and unchallengeable. (Chuang Tzu himself is that kind of a poet, very much more than he is a Westerner's idea of a philosopher, so that his writing is a practical illustration of a response which veers with the unanticipated bends of the Way.) Or it might be a poem which has the opposite effect, lulling him in established habits of perception and feeling, or fascinating with some novel and appealing fashion in self-deception. A literary critic devotes much of his space to analyzing such effects. We may raise, although this is not the place to answer, the question: Does he need any aesthetic standards which cannot be treated as implications of "Respond with awareness?"

Among the wildest of the ecstatics who float themselves on the spontaneous, comparable only to the lover and the mystic, is the man of reason possessed by a new insight. When a routine problem arises he perhaps assembles the information and pursues his inferences to the conclusion almost as tidily as he would on paper. But on other occasions, to use a phrase of Nietzsche,[24] "a thought comes when 'it' wants, not when I want," explodes and opens out too fast and in too complex ramifications to be disciplined, takes bold analogical leaps in defiance of logical rigor; the problem on which it centers is obscure, defining itself in the process of being solved, and as he struggles to formulate it the thought is running in another direction, yet he yields to the flow out of a vague intimation that it will circle back; for the final effort to force the argument into a coherent and publicly testable form—the only assurance even for himself that he is illuminated and not deluded—he waits until the time comes to complete it on paper. Even for the creator of a philosophy of life, one may suspect, it is not the philosophy but these episodes which give meaning to his own life. It is curious that thinkers should explore the logic of rational conduct without coming to terms with this phenomenon at the very center of their own experience. It has after all become a commonplace that the creative imagination of a philosopher, mathematician, or scientist is not much different from that of a prophet or poet; what distinguishes him is how he treats his findings in retrospect. A great formula has been known to appear to a scientist ready-made in a dream as though he were a Siberian shaman, but unlike the shaman, he accepts it not on the authority of the dream but because afterwards it satisfies his most stringent tests. But if even in the sciences rationality is no more than the capacity to criticize the spontaneous, where can we expect it to be anything else?

If we are right in arguing that the underlying logic of the Taoist position escapes the dichotomy of fact and value, because the spontaneous unlike the willed can be evaluated solely in terms of awareness, it is important to find a place for it in Western philosophy. But although we can do so without becoming Taoists, it sets limits to rationality which not everyone will welcome. It implies that however rational I become I can only suspend and choose between processes within me which are spontaneous, not themselves initiated by my own decisions. This is not easy to reconcile with the faith that a man is master of his destiny, can be wholly responsible for what he becomes, which from the seventeenth to the nineteenth century inspired the triumphs of rationalism in the West, and has shifted us to the opposite pole of thought from Chuang Tzu's. Not that there is anything essentially new about it; most of mankind throughout most of history seems to have taken it for granted that they were moved by forces beyond them and mysterious to them, which might lift them above or drag them below the capacities of which they could presume to be in command (in Chuang Tzu it is the flooding of man by "Heaven" or his inexplicable crippling by "Heaven's punishments," in Christian theology the unpredictable visitations of divine grace assisting a will otherwise impotent to resist the temptations of the Devil), and in the present century, ever since Freud demonstrated that the same conception of man could be translated from a religious into a psychological language, we have found ourselves thinking our way back to it. The man of reason is becoming reconciled to admitting that the function of his reason is critical, that it is not itself the initiator of what it judges to be best in him. He can make this concession without allowing any limits to the scope of reason as a critical tool. Is this perhaps the only conception of rationality which is viable in the twentieth century? A rationalism which imprisons in systems of means and ends, in which the ends are both disconnected from spontaneity and without rational foundations, resting on nothing, summons up irrationalism as its nemesis.

The argument has digressed a long way from Chuang Tzu. But what higher compliment can we pay him than that he forces us to philosophize for ourselves?[25]

Notes

Originally published as item no. 46 in appended Bibliography

[1] Translated by A. C. Graham, *Later Mohist Logic, Ethics and Science* (Hong Kong: Chinese University Press, 1978). For criticisms of Chuang Tzu, cf. *Canons* B 35, 48, 68, 71, 72, 79, and 82.

[2] *Canon* A 8.

[3] Textual citations from the *Chuang Tzu* are taken from the edition in *Chuang Tzu yin-te*. Harvard-Yenching Institute Sinological Index Series no. 20 (Peking, 1947; hereafter: *HYCT*). They follow the format "page x/chapter y/line z." *HYCT* 4/2/23–24.

[4] Ibid., 4/2/29–30.

[5] Ibid., 4/2/31–33.

[6] *Canon* B 68. "One cannot treat 'this' as 'that' without interchanging 'this' and 'that.' Explained by: 'the difference.' *Explanation:* "It is admissible for the man who uses names rightly to interchange 'this' and 'that.' When treating only that as 'that' and only this as 'this,' it is inadmissible to treat this as 'that.' When that is about to be treated as 'this,' it is likewise admissible to treat this as 'that'; you treat only this or only that as 'this' or 'that,' and if accepting this condition you treat this as 'that,' that will likewise be treated as 'this.'"

[7] *HYCT* 7/2/84–86. After a brief ellipsis, the following two quotations (7/2/87–88 and 7/2/88–89) continue this passage.

[8] *HYCT* 6/2/64–66 (names of interlocutors omitted).

[9] The Mohist appeals to the distinction between knowing names and knowing objects (laid down in *Canon* A 80). One can know that a name refers to something without knowing what it refers to. *Canon* B 48: "Knowing what one does not know. Explained by: 'picking out by means of the name.'" *Explanation:* "If you mix what he knows with what he does not know and question him, he is sure to answer 'This I do know, this I do not.' To be able both to pick out the one and dismiss the other is to know in both cases."

[10] *HYCT* 48/19 ("outer chapter")/19–21.

[11] For the meaning of *lun*, cf. *Later Mohist Logic*, 28.

[12] *HYCT* 8/3/10–11.

[13] Ibid., 36/13 ("outer chapter")/71–73.

[14] Ibid., 40/15 ("outer chapter")/11.

[15] *HYCT* 21/7/32–33.

[16] Ascribed to Kuan-yin, the friend of Lao Tzu. *HYCT* 93/33 ("mixed chapter")/56–57.

[17] *HYCT* 33/13 ("outer chapter")/2–6.

[18] Ibid., 54/20 ("outer chapter")/66.

[19] Ibid., 43/17/29–30.

[20] Ibid., 18/6/66, 71.

[21] Ibid., 2/1/21–22. Cf. also 28/11/66 and 43/17/28.

[22] Ibid., 15/6/11.

[23] Jean-Paul Sartre, *Being and Nothingness,* tr. Hazel E. Barnes (London: Methuen, University Paperbacks, 1969), 462.

[24] Friedrich W. Nietzsche, *Beyond Good and Evil,* tr. R. J. Hollingdale (London: Penguin Classics, 1973), 28.

[25] This paper has benefited from the detailed criticisms of Henry Rosemont, Jr.

Colophon

An Appraisal of Angus Graham's Textual Scholarship on the *Chuang Tzu*

HAROLD D. ROTH

Angus Graham's philosophical insights into the *Chuang Tzu* were founded upon his methodical criticism and analysis of the text. In what follows I will attempt to analyze and assess Graham's scholarship on the text of the *Chuang Tzu* by trying to understand the perspective from which he approached the text, the perspective that led to his many important and controversial insights. I will also attempt to expand upon his achievements by offering answers to a number of questions that Graham's research raised, but did not answer, including that of how the various intellectual voices that he identified came to be incorporated into the text.

INTRODUCTION

When Angus Graham's almost complete translation of the *Chuang Tzu* was published in 1981 it represented a radical break with all complete English translations extant at that time.[1] Rather than translate the entire book as a whole as his predecessors James Legge, Herbert Giles, and Burton Watson had done, with the implicit assumption that it was the creation of one person (*as per* the *Analects* of Confucius or the *Way and its Power* of Lao Tzu), Graham treated the text as a collection of distinct (and mostly Taoist) philosophical positions, which he carefully identified and contextualized. This was part of a deliberate strategy on his part to confront the realities of the text as he saw them and we cannot appreciate his singular contributions to our understanding of what is arguably the most significant work of foundational Taoism without grasping how he saw the problems of the text and what to do about them.

Basing himself on the work of a number of contemporary East Asian scholars—the most important of whom was Kuan Feng 關 鋒[2]—and upon his own research on the text, Graham implicitly applied the principles of form, redaction, and composition criticism that he learned during his undergraduate studies in theology at Oxford.[3] He saw that the *Chuang Tzu* was far from the homogenous product of a single author but was rather a heterogeneous product that embraced at least five distinct philosophical positions that could be identified as Taoist or related to Taoism. These were:

The historical Chuang Tzu of the "inner chapters";

The "school of Chuang Tzu": his followers;

The Primitivist, a "pugnacious" thinker philosophically related to the *Lao Tzu*;

The Yangists: followers of the "hedonist" philosopher Yang Chu;

The Syncretists: early Han eclectic Taoists distinct from the Huai-nan circle.

He further concluded that most of the original scrolls of the text were neither separate essays nor chapters in what we would call a "book" but were instead compilations of various literary forms including narratives, prose, aphorisms, songs, and poetry that were initially put together in the early Han by someone from the final "Syncretist" stratum. He recognized that the extant recension of Kuo Hsiang (fl. ca. 300 A.D.) in thirty-three chapters was not the original recension of the text listed in the "Bibliographical Monograph" of *The History of the Former Han* (which consisted of fifty-two chapters) and that its many textual corruptions and dislocations resulted at least in part from Kuo's editing as he attempted to fit fragments of the chapters he excised into those he retained. He also asserted that the text contained a series of philosophically subtle and significant technical terms that had to be clearly elucidated by understanding their intellectual context before they could be accurately translated.

For Graham the principal failing of all previous complete translations—including that of Watson, which he admired for its outstanding literary qualities—was a failure to come to grips with these outstanding textual, linguistic, and philosophical problems. He reserved praise solely for the work of Arthur Waley who, in *Three Ways of Thought in Ancient China*, had attempted to translate only those passages whose problems he felt he was able to resolve rather than translate continuously through them to create an English prose style Graham labeled as the "Rambling Mode." In "Two Notes on the Translation of Taoist Classics" included herein, Graham defines this translation style as that "which drifts inconsequentially between sense and nonsense with an air of perfect confidence." It results from the translator's attempt to render the entire text as if it were constituted of unified and integral chapters while ignoring the various literary forms, shifting philosophical positions, and corrupt passages that in reality constitute it. "What seems to be the rambling style of the great Taoist," Graham writes, "is in the first place an evasive tactic of the scholar who has lost the thread, who is trudging from sentence to sentence with his dictionaries and commentaries and hoping for the best."

In order to avoid this problem, Graham made the following decisions:

1. to offer (in the spirit of Waley) integral translations of only those "blocks of text" that are homogeneous. These are: the "inner chapters"; the Primitivist essays that constitute chapters 8–10 and the first part of 11; the Yangist chapters 28–31; the complete Syncretist essays in 15 and 33; chapter 16 (which Graham failed to link with any known philosophy); and any complete episode extracted from miscellaneous chapters.

2. to provide a clear intellectual context for each of these.

3. to differentiate between the various literary forms in the translation. This involved distinguishing between verse, songs, aphorisms, propositions, provisional formulations, and comments and treating only "true essays," such as those of the Primitivist, as consecutive paragraphed prose.

4. while striving to retain the order of material in the extant recension, to rearrange and patch in those fragments from the textually heterogeneous "mixed chapters" (23–27) that could plausibly be relocated into the "inner chapters."

5. to translate only those philosophically significant passages from the "outer" and "mixed" chapters that can be classed as "school of Chuang Tzu" material and to group them by theme such as those that present, for example, tales of Chuang Tzu and meetings between Confucius and Lao Tan.

By following these guidelines Graham attempted to provide a translation that was intellectually nuanced and linguistically precise, that never fell into the "Rambling Mode," yet did justice to Chuang Tzu as both philosopher and poet. The foundation for these guidelines and for the translation that was shaped by them was Graham's research on the various aspects of the text of the *Chuang Tzu* and it is to this that I shall now turn.

TEXTUAL CRITICISM

Imagine publishing Wang Shu-min's 王叔岷 masterful *Chuang Tzu chiao-chu* 莊子校註 as an edition of the text without Wang's detailed textual notes that make all his emendations comprehensible.[4] That is essentially what Allen and Unwin did when they published *Chuang Tzu, the Seven Inner Chapters: and other writings from the book 'Chuang Tzu'* without the textual notes that Angus Graham so painstakingly compiled. Of course few if any publishers were including Chinese characters in their books two decades ago, especially not trade presses. Nevertheless without these notes—previously available only in a typescript of extremely limited circulation—we had only a glimpse of the research and reasoning that went into Graham's distinctive translation.

In looking over these notes again I am struck by the similarities between the works of Graham and Wang. Most certainly Wang's entire project was different: he attempted to establish a critical edition by an exhaustive search for and analysis of all the important extant editions, early commentaries, parallel passages in other early works, the indirect testimony, and the work of the major Ch'ing dynasty textual scholars;[5] Graham was primarily concentrating on translation and utilized other editions and textual critics to a much lesser extent and in the service of his translation. Nonetheless, Graham's work drew on the best examples from these same five categories that are the proper scholarly basis for establishing a critical edition. He made extensive use of the early commentaries to the *Chuang Tzu*, of parallel passages in the *Huai-nan Tzu* and the *Lieh Tzu*,

and of the scholarship of the best Ch'ing and modern textual critics, including Chu Kuei-yao 朱桂曜, Ch'en Ku-ying 陳鼓應, and Wang
himself.[6] As to the indirect testimony to the text, Graham drew heavily
from two of the most important sources: Ch'en Ching-yüan's 陳景元
Chuang Tzu ch'üeh-wu 莊子闕誤 and the fragmentary Kōzanji manuscript.[7] Graham can perhaps be criticized for his choice of the Harvard-
Yenching concordance edition that is itself based upon the flawed critical
text of Kuo Ch'ing-fan, 郭慶藩 *Chuang Tzu chi-shih* 莊子集釋,
published in 1894.[8] Yet in terms of general accessibility of his work to the
widest scholarly audience, Graham chose the edition that is still the most
extensively circulated in Europe and North America. So while Graham's
textual notes are by no means as thorough as Wang's, he does adhere to
solid text-critical principles in establishing and emending his basic edition.

The greatest value of Graham's textual notes is not their comprehen-
siveness but the way in which they augment and complement his distinctive translation and demonstrate a number of his intellectual strengths: an
extensive knowledge of the grammar of classical Chinese; his deep understanding of the contemporary philosophical milieu; and his creativity and
insight into reconstructing fragmented and separated passages of text.

To begin with, many of his textual notes expand on the brief notes he
was able to include in the translation. See for example, how note 1/2 explains the rationale for the parenthetically enclosed sentences and paragraphs on pages 43–44 in the translation, or how note 3/19 to page 65
provides a much more detailed rationale for his understanding of the final
sentence of *Chuang Tzu* chapter 3. Throughout these notes we see how
Graham's command of classical Chinese led him to many inspired and
original understandings of words and phrases in the text. See, for example,
notes 1/5 on the limits of the P'eng's flight or note 3/12 on the "singular-
ity" of Kung-wen Hsüan. His approach to the frequent and otherwise un-
attested binomes and compounds in the *Chuang Tzu* is also insightful: for
example, 1/19 on Sung Jung's failure to "break clean away," and notes
2/75 and 84 where Confucius thinks a saying is a "flight of fancy" but
which the narrator concludes is "a flight into the extraordinary." We also
find in these notes detailed explanations for his unique understanding and
translations of a variety of phrases. See, for example, his rationale in note
4/32 for the phrase "The about to be does not stay still" on page 69 and
note 6/43 for his translation of "at home where it intrudes" from page 87.
Graham's philological and philosophical expertise coalesce in notes 2/27
and 2/29 where he offers an analysis of the meaning of two key technical

terms that Chuang Tzu seems to have borrowed from the *Canons*. These
are: *yin shih* 因 是 (the "contrived that's it" or the "that's it which
deems"), and *wei shih* 爲 是 (the "adaptive that's it" or the "that's it
which goes by circumstance"). Throughout these notes Graham draws on
the *Canons* for a number of new insights into Chuang Tzu's unique ideas
and this can readily be seen in his article "Chuang Tzu's Essay on Seeing
Things as Equal," which we have included in this volume.

REARRANGEMENT OF THE TEXT

Perhaps the most original and controversial aspect of Graham's scholarship on the *Chuang Tzu* is his reconstruction and rearrangement of the
text. The reconstruction involves putting passages back together that he
felt were originally whole but had been fragmented due to textual corruption and to the drastic editorial work of the fourth century commentator
Kuo Hsiang. The rearrangement involves his establishment of thematically
based reconstituted redactions of whole passages from the "outer" and
"mixed" chapters that were distributed randomly throughout these sections
of the work. I will analyze each of these in turn.

There are seven significant textual reconstructions accomplished by
Graham in his translation of the *Chuang Tzu* and these are detailed and
justified in the textual notes:

1. chapter 2, p. 49: adding the poem, "Heaven turns circles..." from
   14/1–4.[9]

2. chapter 3, pp. 62–63: adding "Hence as the ground which the foot
   treads...we do not know how to put our questions to *it*" from 24/105–
   111; 32/50–52; 24/103–105.[10]

3. chapter 5, p. 79: adding a bracketed commentary misplaced in 6/17–19
   but relevant here

4. chapter 5, pp. 79–82: a major reconstruction involving rearrangement of
   5/41–52 and the insertion of fragments from the end of chapters 24 and
   23.

5. chapter 6/1–20, p. 85: a major reconstruction involving

   - relocation of 6/11–14 to after 6/89 (p. 91): "...when the sage goes to
     war"

- relocation of 6/17–19 to chapter 5 as in item 3 above

- relocation of 6/22–24, the little episode of the fish on dry land, to after 6/73

- insertion of fragments from 24/97 and 96 on the True Man after poem at 6/17

6. chapter 17/1–53, pp. 144–149: a reconstruction of the "Autumn floods" dialogue involving:

- relocating 17/24–28 as a separate "great man" fragment on p. 150

- insertion of 22/16–21 ("Heaven and earth have supreme beauty…") on pp.148–149

7. chapter 8, p. 202: insertion of a fragment at line 26 from 12/96–102: "Century old wood is broken to make a vessel…a leopard in its cage has got somewhere too."

In all the above cases, Graham makes cogent arguments based upon both meaning and upon grammar. He moves fragments from contexts in which their meaning seems out of place to those in which their meaning fits. He then justifies the move by detailing similarities in specific unique phrases, particle usage, and technical terminology between the relocated fragment and its new context. For example, in the first relocation he reconstructs what he believes to be the original ending to the Tzu-ch'i narrative by adding the introductory poem from chapter 14, "The Cycles of Heaven." He justifies this by an argument from meaning: "The poem carries on Tzu-ch'i's question about who it is that causes things to begin and end, with the same metaphor of a wind blowing through everything." He then follows up with an argument from grammar and terminology: "As in the first two episodes of chapter 2, the ending of things is described in terms of 'stopping of themselves' (14/2 自 止; similar to 2/9 自 已) and being 'sealed up' (14/2 緘, variant 咸 in Ssu-ma Piao's text; similar to 2/9 咸, 2/12 緘); we also find the metaphor of the trigger which starts things off (機14/2 cf. 2/11)." He also provides corroborating evidence in the form of a T'ang dynasty Buddhist source citing the poem as an example of the distinctive thought of the "inner chapters." He argues further that the poem must have been excised from chapter 2 by Kuo Hsiang because it duplicated the opening of chapter 14, which needed to be retained because the chapter title was taken from it.

In general Graham makes a reasonable case in favor of each recon-struction. A minor problem with all of them is that they are difficult to lo-cate in the translation, even by using the finding list on pages 36–39 of *Chuang Tzu: The Inner Chapters*, and the reconstructions make compari-sons between Graham's translation of these passages and all others virtu-ally impossible. My major hesitation in accepting all of them is that it is not clear how most of these textual dislocations actually took place. Gra-ham only provides such an explanation for the reconstruction of the end of the Tzu-ch'i narrative and it is a plausible one. The second, third, and fourth reconstructions could be explained if we assume that damaged ver-sions of chapters 3 and 5 were transmitted along with their missing pas-sages, which found their way into the ends of chapters 23, 24, and 32. If so however, was this the case in the original 52-scroll recension or in the ex-purgated Kuo Hsiang recension? Also how did 6/17–19 get displaced to this location in chapter 6 from chapter 5? The reconstruction in chapter 6 implies that several larger fragments were displaced from later to earlier in the chapter. Perhaps all could be explained if we assume that a series of bamboo strips simply became detached from their proper positions in the redaction ancestral to all extant editions, perhaps that created by Kuo Hsiang, and that the editor simply tacked them onto the ends of chapters 23, 24, 32, and 12 (in the seventh reconstruction) or found new places for them in chapters 5 and 6 (or in chapter 22, for the dislocated fragment from chapter 17). While this is certainly not impossible by any means, it does seem rather implausible. If true we should all have less confidence that the text we now have of the thirty-three chapters that survived Kuo Hsiang's excision is an accurate reflection of those chapters in the original recension.

Graham's thematically based textual rearrangements derive from his identification of the different philosophical positions in the text and upon topics within those positions. These rearrangements remind me of the scholarly practice of creating reconstituted redactions of lost works. Originating during Ch'ing dynasty with scholars like Ma Kuo-han 馬 國 翰 and T'ao Fang-ch'i 陶 方 琦, these redactions collected passages from the indirect testimony to lost works.[11] A superb modern example of this genre is Wang Shu-min's collection of lost fragments for the *Chuang Tzu*.[12] Of course the major difference is that Graham assembled passages from within one extant textual collection while these other scholars worked from a great variety of sources of indirect testimony; yet both were reestablishing lost works of distinct philosophical viewpoints.

The first of these rearrangements is the group of sixteen passages Graham assembles from chapters 23–27 and 32 that he considers directly related to the "inner chapters" by virtue of the fact that they contain themes and the highly specific technical terminology of logical debate that would "hardly have outlasted" the lifetime of Chuang Tzu. In addition to this principal rationale for their inclusion, Graham concluded that the chapters from which they were taken "include strings of miscellaneous pieces, some no more than fragments, which may come from any or all of the authors in the book" (page 100). He implies that the passages he includes in this section came from Chuang Tzu without explicitly stating so. Other scholars, such as Liu Hsiao-kan 劉笑敢, have taken the similarities in meaning and wording between these passages and those of the "inner chapters" to indicate that the chapters in which they are found are the product of later disciples attempting to emulate their master.[13]

In fact both these theories could be right. If we analyze, for example, chapter 23, "Keng-sang Ch'u," we see that it is made up of two distinct parts. The first is a long continuous narrative involving a quest for the Tao undertaken by a character named Nan-jung Chu who first studies with Keng-sang and later with his teacher Lao Tan. While it is arguable where this narrative ends, I see it continuing to line 42. The second part of chapter 23 is a collection of eleven different fragments with no discernable link to one another except for their being distillations of general Taoist wisdom. These fragments could have been added to an original narrative by the Syncretist compilers in the second century B.C. or to an original short chapter (recall that *Chuang Tzu* 15 has twenty-two lines and 16 has twenty-one) by Kuo Hsiang from material he wanted to save from chapters he was deleting. Without subjecting these chapters to a detailed composition criticism we cannot settle the issue.

Graham also provides a small collection of passages from the Syncretist position taken from chapters 11–14 and divides them into two sections, "Syncretist fragments" (pp. 268–270) and "Three rhapsodies on the Way" (pp. 271–273). These chapters are often taken together as representing a coherent viewpoint, although Graham sees them as miscellaneous collections containing some Syncretist material. Again I would argue that without a detailed composition criticism we cannot reach conclusions about which position is correct. I presented a partial composition criticism of chapter 12 in an earlier work, arguing that the presence of Syncretist and non-Syncretist material therein was not the result of tampering on the part of Kuo Hsiang but was part of the original version of this chapter but

I did not take it farther to see if I could find a rationale for the inclusion of each of the fifteen passages that make up the chapter.[14] I did conclude that this chapter was assembled by a later Syncretist than the author of its overtly "Syncretist" passages and that this person was a member of the Huai-nan circle of Liu An.

By far the most extensive collection of thematically rearranged passages is contained in Graham's "'School of Chuang-tzu' selection" (pp. 116–194). Drawn principally from chapters 16–22 but including passages from chapters 11–14, 23–26, and 32, they are organized into ten topical headings such as "stories about Chuang-tzu," "dialogues of Confucius and Lao Tan," "the advantages of spontaneity," and so on, and they constitute Graham's most significant reorganization of the text. This section results directly from his decision to translate only those passages that are clearly understandable, have a definite viewpoint, and are intellectually interesting, and from his conclusion that there was no organized school of Chuang Tzu surviving his death but rather a tradition of "thinking and writing in the manner of Chuang Tzu" that led to these writings. There are a number of problems however with this methodology.

To begin with, removing these many passages from their contexts within specific chapters makes it impossible to perform a composition criticism of how each of the chapters was assembled. This in turn makes it impossible to derive any shred of historical evidence about who might have written the material in these chapters and who might have assembled them into these units. Furthermore without this kind of information we have little idea of how the "inner chapters" might have been transmitted after the death of their author. Indeed, I would argue that it makes more sense to see at least some of these chapters—particularly 17–22—as the products of the followers of Chuang Tzu who were attempting to continue writing in his style and practicing the meditative inner cultivation techniques he advocates in the "inner chapters." Certainly this is the position of many Chinese scholars, including Liu Hsiao-kan, and of the recent doctoral thesis of Brian Hoffert.[15] Graham's decision to rearrange this material also fails to give any evidence for why the various philosophical positions that he accurately identifies actually became assembled into a text and in many ways leaves us with more questions than it answers. Of course, when he did this research, Graham was not primarily concerned with such historical issues; he was concerned with providing a clear and coherent translation, first and foremost. Nonetheless, I would argue that their resolution will only augment the insights into the philosophical positions in the text that he identifies. In addition, this radical rearrangement of the material in these chapters makes comparison with other translations impossible, except for the very short chapter 16 which he translates as a whole.

REDACTION CRITICISM

Graham's expertise in both philosophy and philology come together again in his influential study, "How Much of *Chuang Tzu* did Chuang Tzu Write?," which we have included in this collection. This work, which implicitly adheres to the principles of redaction criticism, was the first in the West to differentiate the distinct philosophical positions in the text and provide a detailed rationale for so doing. He begins with the question that many have taken for granted: can we provide evidence that the "inner chapters" were written by one person? In the most thorough analysis in this article Graham proceeds to identify four general categories of linguistic tests through which he compares the "inner chapters" with the "outer" and "mixed" chapters:

1. *idioms:* for example, those concerning life and death, perfection, and distinctive turns of phrase such as "How do I know?" 惡乎知 and "it is caused by Heaven//man" 爲人 // 天使.

2. *grammar:* for example, "never yet" 未始 and "only now" 乃今.

3. *philosophical terms:* for example, "that which fashions and transforms" 造化者 and "lodging place" 寓.

4. *persons and themes:* for example, the madman of Ch'u as a spokesman for the author of the "inner chapters" and the absence of any textual parallels to *Lao Tzu* in the "inner chapters."

Acknowledging that these tests are heterogeneous, of unequal value, and in need of refinement, Graham nonetheless maintains that they indicate a sufficient consistency in philosophical outlook, technical terminology, and literary style so that we need not seriously question that they were written by a single hand. He also uses these tests to identify fragments in the "mixed chapters" that can be used to reconstruct damaged passages in the "inner chapters" and he demonstrates this with a detailed reconstruction of the introductory essay to chapter 3.

Working independently of Graham but using similar kinds of linguistic tests—some more detailed, some less—Liu Hsiao-kan reached a similar conclusion on Chuang Tzu's authorship of the "inner chapters," and further argued that they are a "mid-Warring States" creation whose contents were written mostly by Chuang Tzu but compiled by his disciples.[16] One of the strengths of the latter's much more lengthy work—and a weakness of Graham's—is that Liu briefly summarizes and then criticizes the work of some other Chinese scholars who did not think that the "inner chapters" were all the creation of the hand of Chuang Tzu. While Graham indirectly disproves them, it would have been fascinating if he had directly taken on, for example, the theory of Wang Shu-min that the extant "inner chapters" were the creation of Kuo Hsiang's revised arrangement and that the true thought of Chuang Tzu can be found scattered throughout the collection.[17]

Graham uses similar but more limited linguistic tests to identify the distinctive thought and style of three other unique philosophical positions in the "outer" and "mixed" sections of the text. First, we have the "Primitivist" (chapters 8–11/line 28), whom he identifies with some confidence as a single author who takes the view that civilization and its attendant devices and values have destroyed the essentially pure nature of human beings. Thus man's innate tendency to perceive things clearly and to realize the Power (*Te*) that emerges from the spontaneous attainment of the Way is blocked, and disorder and chaos reign. Graham concludes that this individual was an exponent of Lao Tzu's ideal of a minimalist government and only incidently interested in Chuang Tzu, who lived at a particular moment during the Ch'in- Han interregnum very close to 205 B.C.

While recognizing that the only four chapters with thematic titles outside the "inner chapters" are a group (chapters 28–31) that share a number of important similarities with the Primitivist material (e.g. figure of Robber Chih, vitriolic criticism of Confucians and Mohists, fondness for a primitive agrarian Utopia, criticism of the damaging influences of culture, the equal harmfulness of moralist and criminal), Graham sides with Kuan Feng in concluding that they are attributable to the later followers of the philosopher Yang Chu. He finds that they contain a number of the key phrases and ideas that other sources attribute to his distinctive philosophy, including: "keeping one's nature intact"(*ch'üan-hsing* 全 性), "protecting one's genuineness" (*pao-chen* 保 真), not risking life and health for the sake of material possessions. Although he sees a similar, but more pronounced, nonmystical side to these chapters and the Primitivists, he attributes the similarities between these two groups of chapters as their being products of the same general time period.

Liu Hsiao-kan treats the commonalities between these two groups of chapters not as an indication of temporal proximity but as an indication of a common philosophy. Basing himself on the presence of several similar phrases and narratives between these groups, he links them together under the title of the "Anarchist school," which he takes from passages with a similar point of view in the much later *Pao-p'u Tzu*.[18] This is one of Liu's weaker arguments. He totally fails to examine whether or not these two groups of chapters share the same underlying philosophy and does not seriously examine Kuan Feng's assertion that the second group is Yangist. He also concludes that the second group, despite its close ties with the first group, "are not products of the legitimate branch of Chuang Tzu's later followers" but were influenced by Chuang Tzu and his school.[19] Yet he fails to tell us why he reached this conclusion. Indeed, the relationship between these two groups is essential to understanding why the latter group—the most anomalous chapters in the entire work—were even included. (I will return below to a more detailed consideration of these two closely related groups of chapters).

Graham applies linguistic criteria to identify the final philosophical position in the text, which he calls "the Syncretists." This group advocated a comprehensive Taoist social and political philosophy they called "the Way of Heaven and Earth" governed by an enlightened sage-king who embodies the spontaneous workings of the Way commended in the "inner chapters." He includes whole chapters 15 and 33 in this group but only adds the opening sections of chapters 12–14 and various other fragments. By contrast Kuan Feng and Liu Hsiao-kan see these chapters as solid blocks advocating a similar point of view, one whose central philosophy is similar to that identified by Graham. Kuan sees them as the products of the school of Sung Hsing 宋 鈃 and Yin Wen 尹 文, identified as Huang-Lao philosophers in the *Shih chi*; Liu thinks they represent the ideas of Huang-Lao Taoists.[20] Their differences with Graham point to a methodological contrast to which I will return.

One of the main criteria Graham uses for his conclusion that only the introductory sections of chapters 12–14 were written by the Syncretists is the absence of post-verbal use of the particle *hu* 乎 common in the rest of *Chuang Tzu*. However this may not be as significant as he suggests. I have checked for the use of post-verbal *hu* and post-verbal *yü* 於 (the preposition it is often seen as synonymous with in these usages) in two clearly datable works of this general time period, the *Lü-shih ch'un-ch'iu* (ca. 240 B.C.) and *Huai-nan Tzu* (139 B.C.). In both works post-verbal *hu* and *yü* seem to be used interchangably, even with the same verb. The ratio of their use seems to shift between these two works. In the former, *hu* is used after verbs about 27% of the time (*yü* follows verbs about 73%) and in the latter it is used about 10% of the time (with *yü* occurring about 90%).[21] This could suggest that the distinctions between their usages were becoming blurred by the time of the *Lü-shih ch'un-ch'iu* as *yü* was gradually eclipsing *hu* in these post-verbal positions. Whatever the case, I would conclude that the absence of post-verbal *hu* is not a reliable indicator of anything more than perhaps the style of a particular Syncretist writer, if that. Using it to determine authentically Syncretist passages, as Graham did, may eliminate some that are.

One final point to note is that Graham says little more in this article about the "School of Chuang Tzu" material. He does not feature it as a subject of any of his linguistic tests beyond the tests for authorship of the "inner chapters" because it seems he has already concluded that its linguistic contrasts with them indicate a later group of followers of "Chuang Tzu's own branch of Taoism." By contrast Liu sees these chapters and Graham's "rag-bag" chapters as the creations of the "Transmitter School" of Chuang Tzu's followers.[22] As to this latter group, Liu presents phrases or terms from each of these "mixed chapters" that are similar to or identical with phrases or terms in the "inner chapters." While these may be true, they cannot be used to establish that the entire chapter shares the same philosophical position. Graham's work clearly demonstrates that these chapters do contain material related to the "inner chapters" as well as material related to all other philosophical positions found in the book. Now that he has put forth his arguments only a detailed redaction and composition criticism of them will establish their provenance.

THE PROBLEM OF *CHUANG TZU'S* SYNCRETISTS

One of the distinctive characteristics of Graham's identification of the philosophical positions in the text, in contrast to the scholarship of others such as Kuan and Liu, is that he makes little attempt to link these positions with other contemporary intellectual lineages and shows little interest in the questions of how the text came to be constituted with so many differing intellectual positions. What he does say about its textual history is simple and straightforward:

> Chuang Tzu wrote the seven "inner chapters" and related passages in the late fourth century B.C.;
>
> 1. later followers who wrote in his style created chapters 17–22;
>
> 2. a single Primitivist author influenced by the *Lao Tzu* wrote chapters 8–11/28 in about 205 B.C.;
>
> 3. the Yangist miscellany is roughly contemporaneous with the Primitivist writings;
>
> 4. the Syncretists who wrote parts of chapters 12–14 and all of 15 and 33 also compiled the entire text sometime in the early Han.

In an article in the *festschrift* for Graham, I argued that it was possible to link the group he identified as the Syncretists with a series of other works under the rubric of "Huang-Lao" or syncretic Taoism.[23] Working with three categories of technical terms, "cosmology, psychology/self-cultivation, and political thought," I found distinct commonalities between the *Chuang Tzu*'s Syncretists and the authors of three of the "Techniques of the Mind" essays in the *Kuan Tzu*, the *Huai-nan Tzu* and in Ssu-ma T'an's definition of the Taoist lineage. I concluded that these commonalities indicated all belonged to the same lineage of practice and thought and that this constituted the sole surviving Taoist lineage in the early Han. In his reflections on this piece Graham largely agreed with these conclusions although he took exception to my identification of this lineage as "Huang-Lao" and to my argument that members of the Huai-nan circle actually compiled the *Chuang Tzu*.[24] Graham's comments suggest agreement with linking the Syncretists from *Chuang Tzu* with these other syncretic Taoist works as the lineage that first defined "Taoism." I think it is possible to extend these links even farther.

Andrew Meyer has argued that there are four books in the *Lü-shih ch'un-ch'iu*—3, 5, 17, and 25—that are largely made up of essays written by members of this Syncretic Taoist tradition.[25] Since, as Wang Shu-min and Liu have argued, there a significant number of common passages between the *Chuang Tzu* and this work, it is important to examine its possible relationship to the *Chuang Tzu* and possible role in its transmission. Using the terms identified by Graham and myself as characteristic of Syncretic Taoism I have constructed the following table based on a preliminary investigation:

Table 7
Syncretic Taoist Technical Terms in the *Lü-Shih Ch'un-Ch'iu*

Categories and Terms	Books 3, 5, 17, 25	Remainder of Text
1. Cosmology		
天之道	3 (3x); 25 (1x)	Book 7 (1x); Book 20 (1x)
天地之道	none	none
無爲	3 (2x); 17 (3x) 25 (3x)	Book 12 (1x) in Postface Book 13 (1x)
無形	17 (1x)	Book 18 (2x)
理	3 (3x); 5 (5x) 17 (12x); 25 (4x)	43x
2. Psychology		
靜 mental tranquillity	3 (2x); 5 (5x) 17 (13x); 25 (4x)	none
虛 mental emptiness	17 (3x); 25 (3x)	none
去智與故	3.4 去巧故 17.5 去想去意 17.3 棄智	none
去欲	17.5 去愛惡之心	none
心術	none	none
精(氣)	3 (9x)	9x
精神	3 (2x)	Book 8 (1x)
性	3 (3x); 5 (2x) 17 (10x); 25 (3x)	48x (including 15x in Book 1)
壽 desire/techniques for	3 (2x); 5 (2x); 17 (1x); 25 (1x)	Book 1 (3x); Book 2 (1x); Book 4 (1x)
神明	none	none
3. Political Thought		
因	17 (4x)	none
應	3 (3x); 17 (7x) 25 (3x)	59x

Categories and Terms	Books 3, 5, 17, 25	Remainder of Text
循	25 (2x) 理 3 (2x) 順性 17 (1x) 順天	Book 12 (1x) in Postface
宜	17 (1x)	none
育萬物	none	Book 21 (1x)
畜下	17 (1x) 畜人	
王天下	none	Book 2 (1x); Book 8 (1x)
(五)帝(三)王	17 (1x)	Book 2 (2x); Books 6, 13, and 19 (1x each)
4. Additional		
黄帝 (favorable)	3 and 5 (1x each)	15x

NB: In the tables "x" stands for "times."

This table shows that there are a significant amount of shared technical terms between the Syncretic tradition of the *Chuang Tzu*, the "Techniques of the Mind" texts in the *Kuan Tzu*, the later *Huai-nan Tzu*, and now these four books of the *Lü-shih ch'un-ch'iu*. Of particular importance are the psychological terms from the inner cultivation tradition that advocates a meditation practice that involves the removal of thoughts, desires, and prior intellectual commitments of all kinds, in an attempt to create a condition of tranquillity and emptiness needed to act selflessly and successfully in the world as characterized by phrases such as *wu-wei erh wu pu-wei* 無爲而無不爲 (take no action yet nothing is left undone). Such terms as *jing* 靜 and *hsü* 虛 (tranquillity and emptiness) and phrases such as *ch'ü ch'iao-ku* 去巧故 (casting off cleverness and precedent— or casting off thoughts and ideas//wisdom// and the mind of love and hate) are definitely part of the technical vocabulary of those who followed this practice.[26] It is clearly commended to the ruler in essays from these four books such as 17.2, 17.8, and 25.3. A further similarity with *Chuang Tzu's* Syncretists is that in these *Lü-shih ch'un-ch'iu* essays, inner cultivation is first and foremost to be practiced by the ruler, who maintains a similar hierchical structure to that found in, for example, *Chuang Tzu* 13:[27]

> As a general principle, a lord should dwell in tranquillity and quiescence and depend on the transforming influence of his Power in order to hear what is essential. In this way his bodily frame and inborn nature will gather an ever-greater harvest and his ears and eyes will have ever more energy. The hundred officials will all be careful in their duties, and none will dare be lax or remiss. It is by doing his job a man satisfies the meaning of his title.

> When title and reality match
> This is called "knowing the Tao."

Lü-shih ch'un-ch'iu 17.4, "Not Personally" (*Wu-kung* 勿 躬)[28]

These books also show a degree of use of other philosophical concepts such as the matching of name and reality here taken from the Legalists that is another hallmark of the Syncretic Taoist tradition. Other important Syncretist ideas such as *yin* 因 (adaptation) and *hsün-li* 循 理 (compliance with natural patterns), and *ying* 應 (spontaneous responsiveness) are also found here. To be sure, such terms as *wu-hsing* 無 形 (formlessness), *t'ien-ti chih Tao* 天 地 之 道 (the Way of Heaven and Earth), *yü wan-wu* 育 萬 物 (nurturing the myriad things) and several others do not have the same importance in these *Lü-shih ch'un-ch'iu* writings as in other Syncretist works. Nonetheless, there is enough evidence in these tables to support further research on the theory that Syncretic Taoists wrote these books and that they were part of a larger intellectual tradition that not only included the Syncretists who wrote the material Graham identified in the *Chuang Tzu* but also led directly to them.

THE PROBLEM OF *CHUANG TZU'S* PRIMITIVIST

There is considerable evidence from the Primitivist and Yangist sections of the *Chuang Tzu* of certain intriguing parallels with the *Lü-shih ch'un-ch'iu* that warrant further examination and that could present a challenge to Graham's conclusions that these two sections were written at a moment during the Ch'in-Han interregnum. Indeed, Liu Hsiao-kan lists a total of twenty-six parallel passages between the two texts, eleven of which come from chapter 28, "Yielding the Throne."[29] He uses them as evidence that the entire *Chuang Tzu* was already extant and served as the source for the *Lü-shih ch'un-ch'iu* parallels, yet his logic is flawed. He assumes without question and without establishing criteria for directionality of borrowing that the *Chuang Tzu* is always the source. He completely neglects the possibility that both texts were drawing on common oral or written sources or that the *Lü-shih ch'un-ch'iu* might have been the source for the *Chuang Tzu*. Indeed, Graham concludes that the only parallel with the Primitivist chapters (10/10 and *LSCC* 11.4) is from a common source.[30] Furthermore, the only parallel with the Syncretist chapters is a narrative at *Chuang Tzu* 12/33–7 and *Lü-shih ch'un-ch'iu* 20.2 in which the latter's version is almost twice as long, thus making it more likely that it was the source and not *vice versa*.[31] Nonetheless, the fact that *Lü-shih ch'un-ch'iu* 9.5 shows an awareness of the Cook Ting narrative (which itself is much too specific to Chuang Tzu to have come from a common source) and the fact that *Lü-shih ch'un-ch'iu* 14.8 contains almost verbatim the narrative about Chuang Tzu and the mountain tree that begins chapter 20, indicates that some version of the *Chuang Tzu* text was present at the court of Lü Pu-wei and that it probably contained material from Chuang Tzu and his immediate disciples. If an early recension of the *Chuang Tzu* were present at the Ch'in court circa 240 B.C. and if it contained writings of Chuang Tzu and his disciples, then what of the other three sections of the text that Graham has identified and how might that affect his dating of them?

After dispensing with the possibility that *Lü-shih ch'un-ch'iu* 11.4 tooks its version of the Robber Chih narrative from *Chuang Tzu* 10, Graham provides two pieces of evidence to support his concusion that the Primitivist wrote during the Ch'in-Han interregnum. The first is the following phrase from the Primitivist chapter 10, "Rifling Trunks":[32]

然而田成子一旦殺齊君而盜其國...十二世
有齊國。

However T'ien Ch'eng-tzu in one morning murdered the lord of Ch'i and stole his state...and (his family) possessed the state of Ch'i for twelve generations.

The T'ien family ruled Ch'i until it fell to Ch'in in 221 B.C. Thus, Graham reasons, the Primitivist author must have written these words after the Ch'in unification. However since no tense for the verb *yu* is indicated, another possible reading is that "(his family) **has** possessed the state of Ch'i for twelve generations." Ch'ien Mu lists twelve formal changes of rulership in Ch'i, where the T'ien family effectively governed the state, beginning with T'ien Ch'i's 田乞 murder of the Yen family heir on the death of Duke Ching 景公 in 489 B.C. and continuing until the last Ch'i ruler, Wang Chien 王建, who ruled from 264 B.C. until the Ch'in conquest.[33] Thus the Primitivist could have been writing at any point after 264 B.C., when the last T'ien family member ascended the throne of Ch'i.

Additional evidence Graham provides for the interregnum date are several Primitivist references to a present age of death and destruction amidst which Confucians and Mohists "start putting on airs and flipping back their sleeves among the fettered and manacled." He argues that this must be a reference to the revival of philosophical schools during the period following the death of the First Emperor but there is another intriguing possibility that takes us to the decade during which the *Lü-shih ch'un-ch'iu* was written and compiled. According to historical sources, at the same period Lü Pu-wei was inviting scholars to come to the Ch'in court to write a philosophical blueprint for governing the empire to be, he was undertaking several campaigns against rival states. Between 249 and 243 B.C. he directed three successful campaigns against the states of Chao, Han, and Wei and effectively destroyed them as independent entities.[34] It is possible that the turmoil the Primitivist writes about is what he has seen in one of these three states, ironically victimized by armies directed by the man who at the same time was opening his court to scholars of all intellectual persuasions, including of course the Confucians, Mohists, and the Yangists who the Primitivist also detests. Indeed, the courts of Chao and Wei entertained numerous scholars of various schools before this time and some of the retainers who went to Ch'in could have easily come from one or both of these intellectual centers.

Furthermore there is intriguing textual evidence that places Graham's Primitivist at the court of Lü Pu-wei during this period. The one phrase that Graham demonstrates is the most characteristic of the Primitivist's writing—"the essentials of our nature and destiny" (性 命 之 情 *hsing-ming chih ch'ing*)—is found excusively in only one other Warring States philosophical work: the *Lü-shih ch'un-ch'iu*.[35] This distinctive phrase occurs nine times in the *Chuang Tzu*, all of which are in the Primitivist chapters or related passages.[36] In the *Lü-shih ch'un-ch'iu* there are twelve uses in six passages and they are distributed in an interesting fashion across the entire work: 1.3: twice in same passage (p.3/lines 12,13); 13.5: twice in same passage (67/5); 16.2: once (92/5); 17.4: once (103/6); 17.5: thrice in same passage (104/3,4); 25.3: thrice in same passage (162/9, 17).[37] It is important to note that the essay 1.3, "Giving Weight to the Self" (*Ch'ung-chi* 重 己) is one of the five essays in the *Lü-shih ch'un-ch'iu* that Graham follows Fung Yu-lan in identifying as Yangist and that essays 17.4 "Not Personally" (*Wu-kung* 勿 躬), 17.5 "Knowing the Measure" (*Chih-tu* 知 度), and 25.3 "Having the Measure" (*Yu-tu* 有 度) are in the group that I have earlier linked with Syncretic Taoism. These form an interesting pattern that we need to contextualize.

A distinctive theory of the inborn nature of human beings is completely absent from Taoist works written prior to 240 B.C. This includes

Kuan Tzu's *Nei Yeh*, *Chuang Tzu* "inner chapters" and most of the "school of Chuang Tzu" material, and the *Lao Tzu*.[38] The first enunciation of such a theory is in the Primitivist chapters of the *Chuang Tzu* and I have argued that it emerged from dialogue with the Yangists rather than the Confucians because it shares a similar—but not identical—vision of human nature. For the Yangists, the single most important of the spontaneous tendencies of human nature is longevity.[39] They argued that human beings tend to live long if they keep themselves from being disturbed by the "external things" of this world such as fame and profit. The second important aspect of human nature is the desire of the five sense faculties (eye, ear, nose, tongue, skin) for sense-objects. It is the senses's desire for their objects that in a fundamental way helps to maintain the health and the development of the organism, thus enabling it to realize its inherent tendency for longevity. However the senses themselves need to be regulated and limited to only the "suitable" amount of stimulation. Over-stimulation causes the senses to be impaired and eventually damaged. Thus there is a suitable amount of stimulation that is conducive to the health and development of the human organism and that suitable amount must be determined by Sages; the senses on their own do not have the ability to do this. Self-cultivation for the Yangists therefore consists of nourishing one's inherent nature by strictly limiting sense stimulation to the appropriate degree needed to maintain health and vitality. One of their principal practices was to prevent the loss of one's finite supply of *ching* (essential vital energy), which is lost due to over-stimulation of the senses. The Yangists shared an understanding of how the human organism functioned with the thinkers of the "inner cultivation" tradition and with early Chinese medical philosophers and practitioners who envisioned a body-mind complex made up of various systems of *ch'i* (vital energy).

The Primitivist understanding of "the essentials of our nature and destiny" seems to be an expansion of the Yangist position from within the Yangist model of human nature. Just like the Yangists, in their theory of human nature the Primitivists chose to focus on the senses. They argue that it is not merely the *desire* of our senses for sense-objects that constitutes our inborn nature, but, rather, their spontaneous *tendency* to perceive clearly and accurately that does. Furthermore, contra the other traditions that focus on human nature, the Primitivist argues that this spontaneous tendency can only be realized if the senses are unimpaired by either the Yangist rational attempt to limit their stimulation or the Confucian attempt to circumscribe them by the moral dictates of humanity and rightness or by cultural standards of beauty and taste. Thus, the Primitivist theory of human nature is based on a sense perception model just as is the Yangist and both differ distinctly from Confucian virtue models that entail the conquering of the senses because they easily lead to self indulgence.

An excellent contrast between Yangist and Primitivist theories can be seen in the following two passages:

Lü-shih ch'un-ch'iu 2.3, "The Essential Desires"

> Heaven generates human beings and causes them to have lusts and desires. Desires have essential aspects. These essential aspects have limits. The Sage cultivates these limits in order to regulate his desires. Thus they do not exceed what is essential to them. Therefore the ear's desire for the Five Tones, eye's desires for the Five Colors, the mouth's desire for the Five Flavors: these are the essentials. The noble and base, the foolish and the wise are not alike, but in desiring these they are as one. Even Shen Nung and the Yellow Emperor are the same as (the tyrants) Chieh and Chou when it comes to these. The reason that the Sage is different is because he attains the essentials....[40]

Chuang Tzu 8, "Webbed Toes"

> Moreover whomever keeps his nature subordinate to Humanity and Rightness, though as intelligent as Tseng and Shih, is not what I would call a fine man; and whomever keeps his nature subordinate to the Five Tastes, though as intelligent as Yü Erh, is not what I would call a fine man either. Whomever keeps his nature subordinate to the Five Tones, though as intelligent as Music-Master K'uang, does not have what I would call good hearing; and whomever keeps his nature subordinate to the Five Colors, though as intelligent as Li Chu, does not have what I would call good eyesight. When I call someone a fine man, it is not Humanity and Rightness that I am talking about, but simply the fineness in his Power; nor when I call someone a fine man is it the Five Tastes I am talking about, but simply a *trust in the essentials of our nature and destiny*. When I say someone has good hearing, I mean not that he hears something, but simply that he hears with his own ears; and when I say someone has good eyesight, I mean not that he sees something, but simply that he sees with his own eyes.[41]

The point being made here is further clarified in *Chuang Tzu* 16, "Menders of Nature": "If someone else lays down the direction for you, you blinker your own Power."[42] The Power is what develops from the spontaneous manifestation of our inborn nature to perceive things clearly. To do so spontaneously and harmoniously and completely without self-consciousness is what constitutes our innate nature. Perhaps borrowing images from *Lao Tzu*, the Primitivist argues in chapter 9, "Horses Hooves": "In the Simple and Unhewn the nature of the people is found."[43] The Confucians with their pre-established categories of morality and the Yangists with their rational determination of stimulation into such categories as Five Tones, and so forth, introduce a strong element of self-consciousness into the human psyche and destroy our innate ability to function spontaneously and harmoniously. And so the Primitivist laments in "Horses Hooves":

> In the time of the House of Ho-hsü (when Power was at its utmost), the people when at home were unaware of what they were doing, when travelling did not know where they were going...Then came the sages, bowing and crouching to Rites and Music...groping in the air for Humanity and Rightness...and for the first time the people were on tiptoes in their eagerness for knowledge. Their competition became centered on profit...This too is the error of the sages.[44]

If we return to examine the six passages in which the dozen oc-curences of the phrase, "the essentials of our nature and destiny" are found in the *Lü-shih ch'un-ch'iu*, an interesting pattern emerges. The initial use is in Chapter 1 and this is the only occurrence of this phrase in the first twelve chapters of the work (the "Almanacs"), the only ones that conform completely to Lü Pu-wei's original plan. The Postface to this first major division is dated August 11, 239 B.C., but then Lü's political difficulties grew as he became increasingly compromised by his involvement in the so-called "Lao Ai Affair." He was removed from the office of Prime Minister in 237 B.C. and committed suicide two years later when the future First Emperor exiled him to Shu. During this difficult period Lü must have had to increasingly concentrate on political affairs instead of his book, which seems to have been hastily finalized and could not follow his original plan for it.[45] Thus the initial use of our phrase is Yangist; both it and the theory of inborn human nature that includes it, seems to have been topics for debate and discussion in Lü's intellectual circle. The five remaining uses seem to either extend it or challenge it. Let us examine all these uses in their contexts:

> 1.3, "Giving Weight to the Self" argues that our individual life is our most precious possession that must be attentively guarded by the reasoned and moderate fulfillment of the senses and that whomever injures it "does not fathom the 'essentials of our nature and destiny'."

As we have seen, these essentials are the desire of the senses for sense objects and the need to rationally regulate them.[46]

13.5, "Carefully Listening" (*Chin-t'ing* 謹聽) argues that Yao found Shun worthy and Shun found Yü worthy because "They listened with their own ears" and thus relied upon "the essentials of nature and destiny." Thus this phrase must refer to the senses's tendency to perceive clearly and accurately.[47]

In 16.2, "Observing the Age" (*Kuan-shih* 觀世), Lieh Tzu refuses the gift of grain from Prince Yang of Cheng even though he is starving because the prince was only offering it based on someone else's recommendation and did not directly know of Lieh Tzu's abilities on his own: "Would he also kill me based on someone elses recommendation?" he reasons. Later Prince Yang was killed in a rebellion and Lieh Tzu, not being associated with him, survived. Because he declined after seeing how things might change, he "was well-versed in the essentials of our nature and destiny" states the author. Here it seems to entail using our inborn tendency to perceive and know things clearly rather than to rely on others as a basis for making decisions and is thus a similar use to that of 13.5.[48]

17.4, "Not Personally" argues that sage-kings, by nourishing their spirit and cultivating their Power, govern effectively because their inner cultivation prevents them from interfering with the work of their officials and meddling in the lives of the people. Thus "good rulers take care to preserve the essentials of nature and destiny," which here seems to refer to the inherent tendency for their spirits to be united with the Grand Unity (*T'ai-i*) a synonym for the Tao, and to thereby attain the Power. This implies that it is a natural human tendency for the mind to be tranquil and unbiased because at our deepest levels humans are grounded in the Tao.[49]

In 17.5, "Knowing the Measure," the essentials of according with the Tao are to be found in knowing the essentials of nature and destiny to which the superior ruler submits by relinquishing love and hatred and using emptiness and nonaction as his foundation for governing others. This use seems consistent with the prior one.[50]

25.3, "Having the Measure," quotes the teaching of Chi Tzu that all those who are able to penetrate (*t'ung*) "essentials of our nature and destiny" are able to govern effectively because they have controlled their selfish impulses and become impartial and selfless. Confucian and Mohist dicta of humaneness and morality are alien to nature: only by penetrating the essentials of nature and destiny will people become spontaneously humane and moral. Realizing these essentials involves holding fast to the One by an apophatic practice of emptying the mind. Again here the spontaneous tendency to become tranquil and realize our innate union with the Tao is meant by this phrase.[51]

It looks like the understanding of our phrase in the Syncretic Taoist essays in chapters 17 ("Not Personally" and "Knowing the Measure") and 25 ("Having the Measure"), directly contradicts that in the Yangist "Giving Weight to the Self." In the latter, the individual self is the focus of cultivation; it is the self that rationally regulates the natural desires of the senses for sense objects. In the former three essays the focus of self cultivation is on the ontological basis to human nature in the Tao that can only be attained when these selfish concerns can be set aside. Indeed, their position is similar to what emerged in the *Huai-nan Tzu* a century later but which the Syncretist authors in the *Chuang Tzu* were completely silent about.[52] Indeed, the concept of human nature is totally absent from their writings.

The uses of our phrase in the essays in chapters 13, "Carefully Listening," and 16, "Observing the Age," seem to be working within the same model we find in the Yangist understanding of human nature in "Giving Weight to the Self" and the three other early Yangist essays, 1.2, "Making Life the Foundation" (*Pen-sheng* 本生); 2.2, "Valuing Life" (*Kuei-sheng* 貴生); and 2.3, "The Essential Desires" (*Ch'ing-yü* 情欲). In these instances the model is that of sense perception. For the Yangists it is the desire of the senses for sense objects that is the inborn tendency of human nature and in these two other passages it is the tendency of the senses to perceive clearly that is this basis. In fact the understanding of human nature in 13.5 and 16.2 seems strikingly close to that in *Chuang Tzu*'s Primitivist in its assumption that this inborn nature consists of the spontaneous tendency of the senses to perceive clearly and accurately and that this must be the basis of an enlightened awareness.[53]

Given this theoretical similarity with the Primitivist and given the earlier argument that the Primitivist developed his theory of human nature by extending a Yangist model, I think it likely that the Primitivist developed his own unique theory in response to the four early Yangist essays of the *Lü-shih ch'un-ch'iu*. There are two possible scenarios for how this happened: he read the text at some later point in time (as Graham would have it); or he was present at the court of Lü Pu-wei and either participated in the disputations that led to the writing of the text or read the text perhaps when the initial twelve chapters were completed in 239 B.C. As for the former scenario, we have already noted the problems with Graham's justification for his late date of authorship. Furthermore, given the vagaries of textual transmission, especially during the latter half of the third century B.C., it is much more likely that the Primitivist formed his ideas in dialogue with the Yangists at the court of Lü Pu-wei than that he came across them in written form forty years later in some other place. Moreover, if the Primitivist had read the *entire Lü-shih ch'un-ch'iu* text he would have seen that the Syncretic Taoist authors of 17 and 25 had already given a Taoist response to the Yangist misunderstanding of "the essentials of our nature and destiny." And if he had read the entire text and then disagreed with the authors of 17 and 25, he would have been prompted to include a criticism of them in his attack. Yet this is not the case.

Therefore, I think it likely that the Primitivist wrote his essays in direct response to the early Yangist essays of the *Lü-shih ch'un-ch'iu* and before the authoring of the Syncretic Taoist challenges to the Yangist theory of human nature now found in chapters 17 and 25. This places him in Ch'in after Lü Pu-wei's last military campaign in 243 B.C., the devastation from which he seems to have witnessed, and before Lü was removed from office in 237. Furthermore, given what Graham describes as his "pugnacious attitude" in these writings, it would seem that he became disaffected with the entire enterprise and with its director. Indeed, if we look carefully at his representation of Robber Chih in "Rifling Trunks," one can almost see Lü Pu-wei: "The man who steals a buckle is put to death; the man who steals a state becomes a lord, and at the gates of a lord you'll see the humane and righteous."[54]

For a number of reasons I also think that the Primitivist was also a follower of the Chuang Tzu of the "inner chapters." First, his essays were included in the book; I think with further study we will find that all of the thirty-three chapters had some relationship to the first seven. Second, while social criticism predominates in these chapters, they are not totally without mystical concerns. For example, the exemplary person when forced to rule does so through nonaction (*wu-wei*) and "...sitting still as a corpse he will look majestic as a dragon; from the silence of the abyss he will speak with a voice of thunder...He will move with the numinous and proceed with the Heavenly, will be relaxed and nonacting...."[55] Third, as Graham notes in "How Much of *Chuang Tzu*..." the phrase *tsai yu* 在 宥 ("to locate and circumscribe [one's nature]") found in *Chuang Tzu* 11 is also present in the "inner chapters."[56] Finally, the Primitivist shares the same essential concern of the "inner chapters": the most important thing one can engage in in this life is the cultivation of the numinous and spontaneous qualities of one's being and the concomitant development of Inner Power and manifestation of the Way. The Primitivist embeds these qualities in human nature and argues that to first realize them and then fulfill them constitute "the essentials of our nature and destiny."

Therefore, I conclude that these Primitivist chapters were written during the debates that presumably occurred at the Ch'in court of Lü Pu-wei before and during the writing of the *Lü-shih ch'un-ch'iu* by a lineal descendant of the historical Chuang Chou who is also likely to have brought the extant writings of his teacher and his tradition to the court. This person responded particularly to the Yangists and from them adapted a number of unique concepts into early Taoist thought including the notion of inborn nature. However, due to the excessively combative and polemical nature of his writings, the Primitivist chapters were not included in the *Lü-shih ch'un-ch'iu*, if, indeed, they were ever even submitted for inclusion.

THE PROBLEM OF *CHUANG TZU'S* YANGISTS

This then brings us to a reconsideration of the four Yangist chapters and why they are included in the *Chuang Tzu*. Graham identifies them as Yangist because they contain many of the technical terms that independent sources say characterized their philosophy, terms such as "honoring life" (*kuei-sheng*), "giving weight to life" (*ch'ung-sheng* 重 生), and "keeping life (or nature) intact" (*ch'üan-sheng/hsing* 全 生 / 性). To be sure these terms also abound in the five Yangist essays in the *Lü-shih ch'un-ch'iu*. However if these *Chuang Tzu* chapters really are Yangist, as Graham would have it, then how did they find their way into the *Chuang Tzu*? If they are not Yangist, as Liu Hsiao-kan would have it, then why do they

contain so many Yangist ideas? Part of the explanation may be found in the eleven shared narratives between *Chuang Tzu* 28 and the *Lü-shih ch'un-ch'iu*:

Table 8
Shared Narratives in *Chuang Tzu* 28 and the *Lü-shih ch'un-ch'iu*

Narrative in Chuang Tzu 28	HYCT location; Graham Translation	Location in *Lü-shih ch'un-ch'iu*	Knoblock/ Riegel
1. Yao and Hsü Yu	28/1–3; ACG 224	2.2	80
4. Shun and farmer	28/8–9; ACG 225	19.1 longer	475
5. King Tan-fu	28/9–15; ACG 225	21.4	557–8
6. Prince Sou flees	28/15–18; ACG 226	2.2	81
7. Master Hua	28/18–23; ACG 226	21.4	558
8. Lu and Yen Ho	28/23–31; ACG226–7	2.2 slightly fuller	81–2
9. Master Lieh	28/31–35; ACG 227	16.2 has conclusion	380–81
14. Master Chan	28/56–9; ACG 229–30	21.4 omits conclusion honoring Mou of Wei	558–9
15. Confuc. trapped	28/59–68; ACG 230–1	14.6	325–6
16. Shun and Wu-tse 17. T'ang and Chieh	28/68–70; ACG 231 28/70–8; ACG 231–2	19.1 longer; has key variants and conclusion	475–78
18. Po Yi and Shu Ch'i	28/78–87; ACG 232–3	12.4 longer; many variants; approving	266–68

To begin with, six of the eleven shared narratives are found in Yangist essays of the *Lü-shih ch'un-ch'iu*. All of these are fairly close textually with only a handful of variants among them. Four of the remaining five vary rather more extensively from their *Chuang Tzu* counterparts and three of those have different conclusions. While Graham thinks that the *Lü-shih ch'un-ch'iu* was the source and Liu would have it the other way round, I find it difficult to determine a clear direction of borrowing between them. I would hypothesize that both texts draw on a common source, perhaps a Yangist collection of tales for use in disputation that could be used for different ends, depending upon one's ideological persuasion. Graham argues that the *Chuang Tzu* collection of these passages is Yangist but perhaps there is another explanation.

The last three narratives in "Yielding the Throne" are different from the rest, as Graham has noted. To him they they are examples of the wasting of life that the Yangists so detested but if we look to their *Lü-shih ch'un-ch'iu* parallels we see that they were put to different uses. *Lü-shih ch'un-ch'iu* 19.1, "Departing from the Conventional" (*Li-su* 離 俗) argues for an extreme Confucian position that we can track back to Mencius 6A10, that if one keeps life at the expense of what is Right one is not an ethical person. Here these men who killed themselves rather than dishonor their sense of "Reason and Rightness" (*yi li* 義理) are honored; the *Chuang Tzu* parallel omits this conclusion. In *Lü-shih ch'un-ch'iu* 12.4, "Sincerity and Purity" (*Ch'eng lien* 誠廉), the story of Po Yi and Shu Ch'i, who starved themselves to death rather than serve a corrupt (Confucian) Chou conquest, looks every bit a Mohist attack against the Yangists in its conclusion that it is more important to keep intact one's principles of benefit for all, rather than selfish gain even at the cost of one's life. Of course "Yielding the Throne" excoriates these men for their "lofty punctiliousness and harsh code of conduct."

Now while these narratives could have been collected by the Yangists, their use by Confucian and Mohist extremists in the *Lü-shih ch'un-ch'iu* suggests that such views were being argued in the Lü Pu-wei circle. The Primitivist is particularly harsh in his denunciation of both these groups and if, indeed, he was present there he could have also been interested in collecting these passages for use in arguing for a different vision. One possibility not envisioned by Graham and Liu is that *Chuang Tzu* 28, rather than being a Yangist compilation or the writings of a disciple of Chuang Tzu, is a collection of narratives for use in disputation against the Yangists, Confucians, and Mohists—but drawn from them—that was created by the Primitivist.[57] Indeed, this could have been inspired by the idea of practicing "saying from a lodging-place," which is advocated in a brief essay in chapter 27 Graham links to the "inner chapters."[58] On this theory then, the Primitivist would be the author of *Chuang Tzu* 29 and 31.[59] This would explain the commonality of the figure of Robber Chih to both chapters 29 and 10, and many other shared technical terms and metaphors such as their interest in inborn nature, their strong anti-Confucianism, their promoting of a primitive agrarian Utopia, the touches that Graham recognizes as "mystical" in "Robber Chih" such as the advice: "Return and seek what is from Heaven in you...Take your course from Heaven's pattern...and...In accord with the Way walk your meandering path."[60] It would also explain some of the Taoist sounding phrases in chapter 31, "The Old Fisherman," such as "Carefully guard the Genuine in you" and "The Genuine is the means by which we draw upon Heaven, it is spontaneous and irreplaceable" and "...it is from the Way that the myriad things take their course."[61] And it would also explain the six examples of shared narratives between the Primitivist essays and these "Yangist" chapters enumerated by Liu Hsiao-kan.[62]

If these four "Yangist" chapters were actually created by the Primitivist, they would have entered the *Chuang Tzu* along with his essays now found in chapters 8–11 and would have been included because the Primitivist was himself a follower of Chuang Tzu and was the person who brought what existed of the *Chuang Tzu* text to Lü Pu-wei's court. However if the Primitivist left the court in a huff, how then did his text get transmitted from there? Perhaps the answer is to be found in the resolution of another problem: the classification of chapter 16, "Menders of Nature."

THE PROBLEM OF *CHUANG TZU* 16, "MENDERS OF NATURE"

The classification of Chapter 16 "Menders of Nature" (*Shan-hsing* 繕 性) has been problematic. Liu Hsiao-kan links it to the "Huang-Lao" chapters of the text but Graham finds it unlike anything else in the entire work and refuses to classify it.[63] In my opinion this chapter is very close to the Primitivist material.

There are two principal reasons why Graham fails to link "Menders of Nature" to the Primitivist writings, although he does see some strong parallels. The first is that this chapter contains a series of Confucian definitions derived from Taoist concepts. These are found in the 38 (or 54: Ch'en) graphs found at 16/3–4.[64] The second is that chapter 16 does not have any of the expressions characteristic of the Primitivist's very distinctive style.

However, scholars since the Sung dynasty have questioned the authenticity of the Confucian definitions in these two lines. Recently they include Ch'ien Mu 錢 穆, Kuan Feng, and Ch'en Ku-ying.[65] Since, as Graham has pointed out, there are a number of other places in the text that appear to be glosses inserted by a compiler (see for example four quotations from *Lao Tzu* he feels were inserted into the Primitivist essays), there is every reason to believe that these sentences were written by a Syncretist editor who was contending that Taoists and Confucians weren't that different after all. This will be clearer if we examine the disputed passage (which contains thirty-eight graphs whose translation I have italicized) in context:

> The men of old who cultivated the Way used calm to nurture knowing. They knew how to live but did not use knowing to *do* anything; one may say that they used knowing to nurture calm. When knowing and calm nurture each other harmony and pattern issue from our nature. The Power is the harmony, the Way is the Pattern. *The Power harmonizing everything is Humaneness; the Way patterning everything is Rightness; when Rightness is clarified and we feel close to other things, this is Loyalty;...when something pure and real from within you gets expressed, there is Music; when trustworthy conduct has a harmonious embodiment that conforms to elegant patterns, there are Rites.* When Rites or Music are universally practiced, the world falls into disorder. If something else lays down the direction for you, you blinker your own power. As for the Power, it will not venture blindly; and things that do venture blindly are sure to lose their own natures.[66]

The most striking thing about this passage is the contrast between the problematic sentences and the two that immediately follow them. How can the author be advocating Rites and Music and other Confucian virtues in one breath and then criticizing them in the next? Criticism of the deleterious effects of culture, which would include such virtues, is the norm in this essay rather than the anomaly. Furthermore there are no—absolutely no—places in the entire essay in which Confucian values are advocated. If we take these thirty-eight graphs as an editor's gloss and remove them, then the essay can be definitively linked with the Primitivist chapters.

In addition to sharing the Primitivist interest in the Way and its Inner Power as we see in the above passage, the author of "Menders of Nature" shares the following themes with the Primitivist:

   i. Both advocate and defend the life of the hermit.
  ii. Both criticize cultural institutions for meddling with inborn nature:
     a. Confucian practices and ideas
     b. "wisdom"
     c. cultural norms of taste, beauty, etc.
 iii. Both harken back to primitive Utopias and use very similar descriptions.
 iv. Both detail the decline from this and see it as a loss of Power, which they concur in defining as the ability to act and live spontaneously in accord with the Way.
  v. Both are unique in the text for their being pivotally concerned with inborn nature and "nature and destiny."[67]

However there are a few differences. First, as Graham points out, the author of "Menders of Nature" does not use any of the distinctive expressions of the Primitivist author. Second, he is more positive about the possibility that certain kinds of knowledge (properly harmonized with quiescence; not used to *do* anything) can be beneficial. Third, he criticizes the Confucians and Yangists, as does the Primitivist, but not the Mohists, perhaps indicating he wrote at a slightly later time when they were no longer a viable intellectual rival. Finally he talks positively about *li* (pattern), an idea much further developed by the Syncretic lineages of early Taoism and, by the way, a particular concern of the authors of the *Lü-shih ch'un-ch'iu*.

For all these reasons I conclude that the author of "Menders of Nature" was a different person than the author of the Primitivist essays, but because of their shared perspective and opinions, this author was likely a disciple who wrote at a slightly later time. Like the Primitivist, he is a believer in the type of minimalistic government found in *Lao Tzu* and he uses technical terms from the latter, most importantly Tao, Te, the Unhewn (*p'u* 樸), and spontaneity (*tzu-jan* 自 然). On the theory that his teacher, the Primitivist author, left the Ch'in court a bitter man, he could very well have left his student in charge of his writings and of a copy of the extant *Chuang Tzu* text. This author of "Menders of Nature" might have found a home with the Syncretist Taoist authors of *Lü-shih ch'un-ch'iu* 17 and 25 and it was this group that continued to transmit the *Chuang Tzu* text, now expanded by the addition of the Primitivist essays in chapters 8–11 and his disciple's essay in chapter 16. On this theory, later members of this Syncretist tradition added the remainder of the *Chuang Tzu* text and transmitted all this material into the Han where it eventually ended up in Liu An's court in Huai-nan.[68] This theory, while admittedly tentative and in need of further corroboration, has the benefit of explaining how the different strata of the text that Graham aaccurately identified all came to be part of it.

CONCLUSION

Angus Graham's groundbreaking research on the different authorial voices in the *Chuang Tzu* stopped short of answering a number of key questions about the history of the text, the most important of which is how the diverse positions he correctly identified came to be considered part of the text. I have tried to answer some of these questions by focussing on the relationship of the Syncretist, Primitivist, and Yangist sections to material in the *Lü-shih ch'un-ch'iu*. Based upon the evidence and arguments evinced above, I would present the following theory of the early textual history of the *Chuang Tzu*:

By the time Lü Pu-wei announced the establishment of an intellectual center at the Ch'in court in about 250 B.C., the text consisted of the material now found in the "inner chapters" and most—if not all—of the "school of Chuang Tzu" material now found in chapters 17–22. In addition much of the material in chapters 23–27 and 32 could also have been written by this time. Future composition criticism of these conflated chapters will hopefully establish all the different viewpoints contained within them and how they were compiled.

This early recension was brought to the Ch'in court by a follower of Chuang Tzu who later penned the chapters Graham calls "Primitivist." He wrote them in response to Yangist ideas now found in the *Lü-shih ch'un-ch'iu* but left the court in disgust over the prevalence of Yangist, Confucian, and Mohist ideas there and over his contempt for Lü Pu-wei himself, whom he may have satirized through the figure of Robber Chih.

Before leaving, the Primitivist compiled the collection of narratives in "Yielding the Throne" and tried his hand at using some of them in "Robber Chih" and "The Old Fisherman."

After he left, his writings were added to the text, perhaps by his disciple, who penned "Menders of Nature." As the Lü Pu-wei circle collapsed after 235 B.C., this disciple may have left Ch'in with the Syncretic Taoist group that authored many of the essays in *Lü-shih ch'un-ch'iu* 3, 5, 17, and 25. I have elsewhere argued that the Syncretic Taoist intellectual tradition was the first to attempt to self-consciously build something that could be called a Taoist "school" and that they transmitted Taoist practices and texts into the Han dynasty.[69] At some point this group added their own ideas to the text of the *Chuang Tzu* and decades later brought it to the court of Liu An at Huai-nan (a theory Graham took to be "an attractive conjecture"). Thus the original recension of the *Chuang Tzu* was finally established.

Of course much of this is hypothetical and awaits further research. It is difficult to say how much the textual interference of Kuo Hsiang has altered the materials on which we may base our final conclusions. But there is no doubt that we would be much farther from a resolution of the many questions that have surrounded the text of the *Chuang Tzu* for over a millenium without the innovative scholarship of Angus Graham.

Notes

[1] A.C. Graham, *Chuang Tzu, the Inner Chapters* (London: George Allen and Unwin, 1981; reprint, Indianapolis: Hackett Publishing Co., 2001).

[2] Kuan Feng, *Chuang Tzu che-hsüeh t'ao-lun chi* 莊子哲學討論集 (Peking: Chung-hua, 1962), 61–98.

[3] These three types of literary criticism were developed in New Testament studies and were being propounded and debated during the 1930's and 40's while Graham was a college student. Form criticism is an analysis of the standard genres in which the oral and early written tradition is cast in the effort to interpret each in terms of its concrete historical setting. Redaction criticism is an analysis of the philosophical positions of the people who wrote and compiled texts and the application of this analysis to discover their historical circumstances. Composition criticism examines the literary techniques of the early redactors and how they assembled their inherited material to create unified works. All three criticisms overlap. For details see Stephen D. Moore, *Literary Criticism and the Gospels: The Theoretical Challenge.* (New Haven: Yale University Press, 1989), 179–83 and Michael LaFargue, *The Tao of the Tao Te Ching* (Albany: State University of New York Press, 1992), 179.

[4] Wang Shu-min, *Chuang Tzu chiao-chu.* Institute of History and Philology Monograph No. 88 (Taipei: Commercial Press, 1988). This is a revised and expanded redaction of Wang's 1947 study *Chuang Tzu chiao-shih* that Graham cited frequently in his textual notes. It includes the most complete collection of indirect testimony to the lost *Chuang Tzu*, those chapters in all likelihood deleted by Kuo Hsiang. Wang's book is a masterpiece of text-critical scholarship.

[5] The indirect testimony is the sum total of all the passages from a given work extant or lost that are found in other sources such as encyclopedias and commentaries. It consists of quotations and paraphrasings from that work, both acknowledged and unacknowledged, that are found in these other sources. It contrasts with the direct testimony, the total of all extant editions that have descended from the original authors manuscript. For these definitions see Harold D. Roth, *The Textual History of the Huai-nan Tzu* (Ann Arbor: Association for Asian Studies, 1992), 9–11.

[6] Chu Kuei-yao 朱桂曜 *Chuang Tzu nei-p'ien cheng-pu* 莊子內篇證補 (Shanghai, 1935); Ch'en Ku-ying 陳鼓應, *Chuang Tzu chin chu chin yi* 莊子今註今譯 (Taipei, 1975).

[7] Ch'en's *ch'üeh-wu* is an appendix to his *Nan-hua chen-ching chang-chü yin-yi* printed in 1084. It contains three hundred fourty-nine variant readings between

his basic text and seven other T'ang and Sung dynasty editions. These readings are very old indeed and many are preserved nowhere else. The Kōzanji manuscript is a Muromachi period (1392–1568) hand-written copy of what was in all probability an early T'ang edition. It contains seven complete chapters from the "outer" and "mixed" sections: 23, 26–28, 30, 31, and 33.

[8] Kuo's work was probably the most widely circulated edition of the *Chuang Tzu* until the publication of the Harvard-Yenching concordance in 1947. His base text was the *Ku-i tsung-shu* reprint of a Southern Sung edition that contained Kuo Hsiang's commentary, Ch'eng Hsüan-ying's sub-commentary, and the glosses from Lu Te-ming's *Ching tien shih-wen*. It's frequent copyists's errors were largely corrected in the emended edition, *Chiao-cheng Chuang Tzu-chi-shih* (Taipei: Shih-chien, 1974).

[9] Textual citations from the *Chuang Tzu* are taken from the edition in *Chuang Tzu yin-te*. Harvard-Yenching Institute Sinological Index Series no. 20 (Peking, 1947). They follow the format "chapter x /line number y ."

[10] This reconstruction is explained most completely in "How Much of *Chuang Tzu* did Chuang Tzu Write?"

[11] Ma's research is published in his collection, *Yü-han shan fang chi i-shu* 玉 函 山 房 輯 佚 書 (Ch'ang-sha, 1883); Tao's thorough collection of the lost Hsü Shen commentary to the *Huai-nan Tzu*, *Huai-nan Hsü-chu yi-t'ung ku* 淮 南 許 注 異 同 詁 was first printed in 1881. This genre of reconstituted redactions has largely been overlooked in Western scholarship and merits further examination.

[12] See, Wang Shu-min, *Chuang Tzu chiao-chu*, 1383–1414.

[13] Liu, like many Chinese scholars whose work he summarized, considers these chapters to be written by later followers of Chuang Tzu and he groups them together with chapters 17–22 as the products of the "Transmitter School" who continued the ideas of their founder. See Liu, *Classifying the Chuang Tzu Chapters*, Michigan Monographs in Chinese Studies no. 65 (Ann Arbor: Center for Chinese Studies, University of Michigan, 1994), 83–121.

[14] Harold Roth, "Who Compiled the *Chuang Tzu*?" in *Chinese Texts and Philosophical Contexts: Essays Dedicated to Angus C. Graham*, ed. Henry Rosemont, Jr. (LaSalle, Ill.: Open Court, 1991), 115–18.

[15] Brian Hoffert, "*Chuang Tzu*: The Evolution of a Taoist Classic" (Ph.D. diss., Harvard University, 2001).

[16] Liu, 1–45. This is a partial English translation of his 1985 doctoral dissertation at Peking University, *Chuang Tzu che-hsüeh chi ch'i yen-pien* 莊 子 哲 學 及 其 演 變 (Peking: Chung-kuo she-hui k'o-hsüeh ch'u-pan-she, 1988).

[17] Wang, *Chuang Tzu chiao-chu*, 1434–38.

[18] Liu, pp.134–47. Liu, like Kuan Feng, omits chapter 30 which he says bears no relationship to anything else in the text. However he fails to explain why it's there.

[19] Ibid., p.137.

[20] Ibid., 121–34.

[21] D.C. Lau and Chen Fong Ching, eds., *A Concordance to the Lü-shih ch'un-ch'iu* (Hong Kong: The Commercial Press, 1994), 379–83 and 872–81. Here I found 197 instances of post-verbal *hu* contrasted with 722 instances of post-verbal *yü*. In the *Huai-nan Tzu*, by contrast, I found 110 instances of the former and over 1100 instances of the latter. D.C. Lau and Chen Fong Ching, eds., *A Concordance to the Huai-nan Tzu* (Hong Kong: The Commercial Press, 1992), 511–14 and 954–66.

[22] Liu, 89–121. Liu presents phrases or terms from each of these "mixed chapters" that are similar to or identical with phrases or terms in the "inner chapters." While these may be correct, they cannot be used to establish that the entire chapter shares the same philosophical position. Graham's work clearly establishes that these chapters do contain material related to the "inner chapters" as well as material related to all other philosophical positions found in the book.

[23] Roth, "Who Compiled the *Chuang Tzu*?" 79–128.

[24] Graham, "Reflections and Replies" in *Chinese Texts and Philosophical Contexts: Essays Dedicated to Angus C. Graham*, ed. Henry Rosemont, Jr. (LaSalle, Ill.: Open Court, 1991), 279–83.

[25] Andrew Seth Meyer, "Late Warring States Daoism and the Origins of Huang-Lao: The Evidence from the *Lüshi chunqiu*" (Unpublished manuscript. 1996).

[26] For details of this practice see my *Original Tao: Inward Training and the Foundations of Taoist Mysticism* (New York: Columbia University Press, 1999), chapter 4 and my article "Evidence for Stages of Meditation in Early Taoism" *Bulletin of the School of Oriental and African Studies* 60:2 (June 1997): 295–314.

[27] The Syncretist theory of the hierarchical nature of government patterned after the greater paatterns of Heaven and Earth is most clearly presented in *Chuang Tzu* 13/27–36; Graham, 261–62.

[28] John Knoblock and Jeffrey Riegel, *The Annals of Lü Buwei: A Complete Translation and Study* (Stanford: Stanford University Press, 2000), 422.

[29] Liu, 50–61.

[30] Graham, *Chuang Tzu, the Inner Chapters*, 207; Knoblock and Riegel, 251.

[31] Ibid., 174 ; Knoblock and Riegel, 220.

[32] *Chuang Tzu yin-te*, 10/6–8.

[33] Ch'ien Mu, *Hsien Ch'in chu-tzu hsi-nien* 先秦諸子繫年 (1935; rev. ed., 1956; reprint, Peking: Chung-hua, 1985), 524–74. There is some disagreement about what this phrase "twelve generations" refers to. Ch'en Ku-ying *Chuang Tzu chih-chu chin-yi* 254–55, identifies T'ien Ch'eng-tzu as Ch'i Prime Minister Ch'en Heng 陳恆, who in 481 murdered Duke Chien 簡公 and stole the state. However to do this gives us only nine changes of rule until

the fall of Ch'i. If we identify him instead with T'ien Ch'i, who also murdered a Ch'i ruler and put a puppet on the throne, then we have an extra three changes of rule. Wang Shu-min, (*Chuang Tzu chiao-chu,* 348–49), shows that the character *shih* 世 (generations), is an error for *tai* 代 (dynasty, change of rule). Thus the passage is talking not about entire generational changes but changes of rule. Wang however, identifies T'ien Ch'eng-tzu with T'ien Chuang Tzu 田 莊 子 and argues that we should date these changes of rule from the latter's death in 411 B.C. Part of the problem is how to count twelve of these changes. The T'ien family held ministerial posts in Ch'i for generations before they committed regicide and established a line of puppet rulers in Ch'i starting in 489 B.C. They did not officially put themselves on the throne until 386 B.C. According to Ch'ien Mu's historical table, we can count twelve changes of rule from 489 B.C., including, of course, the puppet dukes who were the official rulers of Ch'i while the T'ien family really controlled the power. Wang seems to want to begin his count with the official T'ien ascent to the throne but then has to go back for two more T'ien family ministers in order to reach the proper count. This analogy to a powerful ministerial family controlling a weaker ruler may have been intentionally used by the Primitivist to satirize Lü Pu-wei's power over the young Ch'in king who eventually, after removing Lü from power, became the First Emperor. See below for a further discussion of this.

[34] Knoblock and Riegel, 11–13. While Han did not fall until 230 B.C., Chan until 228, and Wei until 225, Ch'in annexed large amounts of territory during these campaigns and killed many soldiers and civilians, thus seriously undermining the strength of these states and making them ripe for the final conquest.

[35] I have examined concordances to the following works and none contain the phrase in question: *Lun-yü, Meng Tzu, Hsün Tzu, Lao Tzu, Kuan Tzu,* and *Han Fei Tzu.*

[36] To be specific, the phrase is found three times in chapter 8 (in lines 8, 12, and 30) and four times in the first part of chapter 11 (in lines 8, 10, 11, and 14). The other two occurrences are in chapter 14 (14/73) and chapter 24 (24/2), both passages that Graham concludes are Primitivist. See his section "Episodes related to the Primitivist" (*Chuang Tzu, the Inner Chapters,* 214–15).

[37] The use in 17.5/104/6 is simply of *hsing ming* but the context implies the full phrase.

[38] There are six sporadic references to the term *hsing* in three "school of Chuang Tzu" chapters: 17/37; 19/11, 52, 53, 54; and 20/61. The last four are in passages that feature Confucius and seem to be borrowing the idea; the first is about the nature of all things and not human nature; 19/11. None of these even faintly suggest a unique Taoist theory.

[39] This summary of Yangist ideas is primarily based on five *Lü-shih ch'un-ch'iu* essays: 1.2, 1.3, 2.2, 2.3, and 21.4, and also draws on material in *Chuang Tzu* 28 and 30. It is taken from my article *"Zhuangzi," Stanford Encyclopedia of Philosophy* (November 2001).

[40] This translation from 2.3/8/20–23 is my own.

[41] *Chuang Tzu yin-te*, 8/26–31; Graham, *Chuang Tzu,* 202–3. I have modified it slightly.

[42] Ibid, 16/4, Graham, *Chuang Tzu*, 171.

[43] Ibid., 9/10–11, Graham, 205. The Simple and Unhewn are defined in *Lao Tzu* 19 as being selfless and desireless.

[44] Ibid., 9/16–19, Graham, 205–6.

[45] Knoblock and Riegel, 12–32, cover this in greater detail.

[46] Ibid., 67–68.

[47] Ibid., 292–93.

[48] Ibid., 380–81. I accept their emendation of the graphic error *yüan* 遠 to *ta* 達.

[49] Ibid., 419–21.

[50] Ibid., 423–25. The third use of our phrase lacks the final *chih ch'ing*, but I think it is implied by the context.

[51] Ibid., 630–32.

[52] Roth, "The Concept of Human Nature in the *Huai-nan Tzu*," *Journal of Chinese Philosophy* (1985): 1–26.

[53] The concluding paragraph to this narrative in the *Lü-shih ch'un-ch'iu* takes a Confucian turn towards Rightness that the Primitivist would not approve, but this does not mean that the understanding of "the essentials of nature and destiny" implied here could not have been taken from the Primitivist and then applied to a Confucian argument. This suggests he was part of debates in the Lü Pu-wei circle but that he did not write anything that was included in the final version of the text.

[54] *Chuang Tzu yin-te*, 10/19; Graham, *Chuang Tzu*, 208. Andrew Meyer presents a different interpretation of the symbolism of Robber Chih, suggesting instead that in *Chuang Tzu* 29 he represents the state of Ch'in itself with its pretesions to rule all of China. ("On the Trail of Robber Zhi: An Intra- and Intertextual Reading of *Zhuangzi* 29" [paper given at the 2002 meeting of the Association for Asian Studies].)

[55] Ibid., 11/15–16; Graham, *Chuang Tzu*, 212.

[56] Ibid., 2/55. For an interesting discussion of this phrase see D.C. Lau, "On the Expression Zai You 在 宥," in Henry Rosemont, ed., *Chinese Texts and Philosophical Contexts*, 5–20.

[57] In a paper he gave at a meeting of the Warring States Working Group in the fall of 1998, Andy Meyer first suggested that *Chuang Tzu* 28 is a collection of Yangist stories made by the Primitivist.

[58] *Chuang Tzu yin-te*, 27/1–10; Graham, *Chuang Tzu*, 106–7.

[59] Like most scholars I am still not sure what to make of chapter 30, "The Discourse on Swords."

[60] *Chuang Tzu yin-te*, 29/71–74; Graham, *Chuang Tzu*, 240–41. The term *hsing* is extremely rare outside the Primitivist chapters but it occurs thrice in "Robber Chih": 29/86, 89, 98.

[61] Ibid., 31/31, 37, 49; Graham, *Chuang Tzu*, 251–53.

[62] Liu, 138–39.

[63] Ibid., 125, 128, 133. Liu's links between "Menders of Nature" and the "inner chapters" are much more persuasive than his two extremely weak links between it and the "Huang-Lao" material.

[64] *Chuang Tzu yin-te*, 16/3–4; Graham, *Chuang Tzu*, 171.

[65] Ch'en Ku-ying *Chuang Tzu chin-chu chin-yi*. Taipei: Chung-hua, 1983, 403.

[66] This translation is based on Graham's but I have edited it to make it consistent with other translations of mine throughout this essay. The italicized text constitutes 38 characters; Ch'en would expand this to 54 by adding the sentence immediately before and the one immediately after this section but I see no reason to do this. He would also excise the passage as not the words of Chuang Tzu. See Ch'en, *Chuang Tzu chin-chu chin-yi*, 403.

[67] "Menders of Nature" 16/17 uses the partial phrase *hsing-ming*, rare outside the Primitivist essays and passages related to them.

[68] For details on this theory, see Roth, "Who Compiled the *Chuang Tzu*?"

[69] Roth, *Original Tao*, 198–203.

Bibliography

The Writings of Angus C. Graham

BOOKS

1. *Two Chinese Philosophers: Ch'eng Ming-tao and Ch'eng Yi-ch'uan.* London: Lund Humphries, 1958. Reprinted as *Two Chinese Philosphers: The Metaphysics of the Brothers Cheng.* LaSalle, IL: Open Court, 1992.

2. *The Book of Lieh-tzu.* London: John Murray, 1960. UNESCO Chinese translation series. Reprinted New York: Columbia University Press, 1990. Contains a new preface by Graham.

3. *The Problem of Value.* London: Hutchinson's University Library, 1961.

4. *Poems of the Late T'ang.* UNESCO Chinese translation series. London: Penguin Classics, 1965.

5. *Later Mohist Logic, Ethics and Science.* Hong Kong: Chinese University Press, 1978.

6. *Chuang Tzu: The Seven "Inner Chapters" and Other Writings from the Book Chuang Tzu.* London: Allen and Unwin, 1981.

7. *Chuang Tzu: Textual Notes to a Partial Translation.* London: School of Oriental and African Studies, 1982.

221

8. *Reason and Spontaneity.* London: Curzon Press; New York: Barnes and Noble, 1985.

9. *Studies in Early Chinese Philosophy and Philosophical Literature.* Singapore: Institute for East Asian Philosophies, 1986; Albany: State University of New York Press, 1990.

10. *Disputers of the Tao: Philosophical Argument in Ancient China.* La-Salle, IL: Open Court, 1989.

11. *Poems of the West Lake.* London: Wellsweep Press, 1990.

12. *Unreason within Reason: Essays on the Outskirts of Rationality.* Edited by David Lynn Hall. LaSalle, IL: Open Court, 1992.

ARTICLES

1. "A probable fusion word: WUH(勿) = WU(毋) +JY(之)." *Bulletin of the School of Oriental and African Studies* 14/1 (1952).

2. "Kung-sun Lung's essay on meanings and things." *Journal of Oriental Studies* 2/2 (1955).

3. "The final particle FU (夫)." *Bulletin of the School of Oriental and African Studies* 17/1 (1955).

4. "The composition of the Gongsuen Long tzyy (公孫龍子)." *Asia Major* 5/2 (1957). Reprinted in *Studies in Early Chinese Philosophy.*

5. "The relation between the final particles YU (與) and YEE (也)." *Bulletin of the School of Oriental and African Studies* 19/1 (1957).

6. "Confucianism." In *Concise Encyclopedia of Living Faiths,* edited by R. C. Zaehner. London: Hutchinson, 1959.

7. "Being in Western philosophy compared with SHIH/FEI (是 非) and YU/WU (有 無) in Chinese philosophy." *Asia Major* 7/1, 2 (1959). Reprinted in *Studies in Early Chinese Philosophy.*

8. "Observations on a new Classical Chinese grammar." *Bulletin of the School of Oriental and African Studies* 22/3 (1959).

9. "The dialogue between Yang Ju (楊朱) and Chyntzzy (禽子)." *Bulletin of the School of Oriental and African Studies* 22/2 (1959).

10. "The date and composition of Liehtzyy (列 子)." *Asia Major* 8/2 (1961). Reprinted in *Studies in Early Chinese Philosophy.*

11. "The prosody of the SAO (騷) poems in the Ch'u tz'u (楚 辭)." *Asia Major* 10/2 (1963).

12. With G. B. Downer. "Tone patterns in Chinese poetry." *Bulletin of the School of Oriental and African Studies* 26/1 (1963).

13. "Natural goodness and original sin." *Rationalist Annual* (1963).

14. "Reason in the Chinese philosophical tradition." In *The Legacy of China,* edited by Raymond Dawson. Oxford: Clarendon Press, 1964.

15. "The logic of the Mohist Hsiao-ch'ü (小 取)." *T'oung Pao* 51/1 (1964).

16. "Liberty and equality." *Mind* 74/293 (1965).

17. "Two dialogues in the *Kung-sun Lung tzu* (公 孫 龍 子)." *Asia Major* 11/2 (1965). Reprinted in *Studies in Early Chinese Philosophy.*

18. *Anthology of Chinese Literature,* edited by Cyril Birch. 2 vols. New York: Grove Press, 1965-72. Translations of poems and fu (賦). Vol. 1: Tu Fu (235-38); Han Yu (262); Li Ho (281-82); Lu T'ung (285-87); Li Shang-yin (324-29); Ou-Yang Hsiu (368-69); Su Shih (381-84). Vol. 2: Kuang Han-ch'ing (6-15).

19. "'Being' in philosophy and linguistics." In *The Verb 'Be' and its Synonyms,* edited by John W. M. Verhaar, 225-33. *Foundations of Language, Supplementary Series,* Part 5. Dordrecht, Holland: D. Reidel, 1972.

20. "The 'Hard and White' (堅 白) disputations of the Chinese sophists." *Bulletin of the School of Oriental and African Studies* 30/2 (1967).

21. "Chinese logic." In *Encyclopedia of Philosophy,* edited by Paul Edwards. Original edition 1967; reprint, New York: MacMillan, 1972.

22. "The background of the Mencian theory of human nature." *Tsing Hua Journal of Chinese Studies* 6/1, 2 (1967). Reprinted in *Studies in Early Chinese Philosophy.*

23. "'Being' in Classical Chinese." In *The Verb 'Be' and its Synonyms,* edited by John W. M. Verhaar, 1-39. *Foundations of Language, Supplementary Series,* Part 1. Dordrecht, Holland: D. Reidel, 1967.

24. "The archaic Chinese pronouns." *Asia Major* 15/1 (1969).

25. "Chuang Tzu's 'Essay on seeing things as equal' (齊物論)." *History of Religions*, 9 (1969/70).

26. "Some basic problems of Chinese syntax." *Asia Major* 14/2 (1969).

27. "Ch'eng Hao (程顥) and Ch'eng Yi (程頤)." *Encyclopedia Britannica*. Chicago: 1970.

28. "The grammar of the Mohist dialectical chapters." In *A Symposium on Chinese Grammar Held at the Scandinavian Institute of Asian Studies, Copenhagen, 27-29 August 1970,* edited by Inga-Lill Hansson. Lund, Sweden: Lund University Press, Studentlitteratur, 1971.

29. "China, Europe and the origins of modern science." *Asia Major* 16/1, 2 (1971). Reprinted in *Chinese Science,* edited by Shigeru Nakayama and Nathan Sivin, 45-70. Cambridge, Mass.: MIT Press, 1973.

30. "A new translation of a Chinese poet: Li Ho (李賀)." *Bulletin of the School of Oriental and African Studies* 34/3 (1971).

31. "Later Mohist treaties on ethics and logic reconstructed from the *Ta ch'ü* (大取) chapter of *Mo-tzu* (墨子)." *Asia Major* 17/2 (1972).

32. "The Classical Chinese topic-marker FU (夫)." *Bulletin of the School of Oriental and African Studies* 35/1 (1973).

33. With Nathan Sivin. "A systematic approach to the Mohist optics." In *Chinese Science,* edited by Shigeru Nakayama and Nathan Sivin. Cambridge, Mass.: MIT Press, 1973.

34. "The terminations of the Archaic Chinese pronouns." *Bulletin of the School of Oriental and African Studies* 36/2 (1973).

35. "The concepts of necessity and the 'a priori' in Later Mohist disputation." *Asia Major* 19/2 (1975).

36. "Chuang Tzu and the Rambling Mode." In *The Art and Profession of Translation,* edited by T. C. Lai. Hong Kong: n.p., 1976.

37. "The Chinese particle TZENG (曾)." *Early China* no. 3 (1977).

38. "The organization of the Mohist Canons." In *Ancient China: Studies in Early Civilization,* edited by David T. Roy and Tsuen-hsuin Tsien. Seattle: University of Washington Press, 1979.

39. "The Ch'eng Brothers (二程)." In *A Sung Bibliography,* edited by Yves Hervouet. Hong Kong: Chinese University Press, 1978.

40. "A post-verbal aspectual particle in Classical Chinese: the supposed preposition HU (乎)." *Bulletin of the School of Oriental and African Studies* 41/2 (1978).

41. "The Nung-chia (農家) 'School of the Tillers' and the origins of peasant Utopianism in China." *Bulletin of the School of Oriental and African Studies* 42/1 (1978). Reprinted in *Studies in Early Chinese Philosophy*.

42. "How much of *Chuang Tzu* did Chuang Tzu write?" In *Studies in Classical Chinese Thought,* edited by Henry Rosemont, Jr. and Benjamin I. Schwartz, *Journal of the American Academy of Religion Thematic Studies.* Chico, Calif.: Scholars Press, 1980.

43. "Structure and license in Chinese regulated verse." *Journal of Chinese Linguistics* 8 (1980).

44. "The origins of the Legend of Lao Tan (老聃)." In *Kuo-chi Han-hsueh, hui-yi lun-wen chi* (國際漢學會議論文集). Taipei: n.p., 1981. Reprinted in *Studies;* Revised and reprinted in *Lao-Tzu and the Tao-Te Ching*, edited by Livia Kohn and Michael LaFargue. Albany: State University of New York Press, 1998.

45. "Other Schools of Philosophy." In *The Cambridge Encyclopedia of China,* edited by Brian Hook and Denis Twitchett, 309-13. 2nd ed. Cambridge: Cambridge University Press, 1991.

46. "Taoist spontaneity and the dichotomy of 'is' and 'ought.'" In *Experimental essays on Chuang Tzu.* Edited by Victor H. Mair. Honolulu: University of Hawaii Press, 1983.

47. "YÜN (云) and YÜEH (曰) as verbs and as particles." *Acta Orientalia* (Copenhagen) (1984).

48. "Value, fact and facing fact." *Journal of Value Inquiry* 19 (1985).

49. "Divisions in early Mohism reflected in the core chapters of Mo-tzu." Institute for East Asian Philosophies, Occasional paper and monograph series no. 1. Singapore: National University of Singapore, 1985.

50. "The right to selfishness: Yangism, Later Mohism, Chuang Tzu." In *Individualism and Holism: Studies in Confucian and Taoist Values,* edited by Donald Munro. Ann Arbor: University of Michigan Center for Chinese Studies, 1984.

51. "Translation of Li Po, 'The hard road to Shu.'" in *A Brotherhood of Song,* edited by Stephen C. Soong. Hong Kong: Chinese University Press, 1986.

52. "What was new in the Ch'eng-Chu (程朱) theory of human nature?" In *Chu Hsi and Neo-Confucianism,* edited by Wing-tsit Chan. Honolulu: University of Hawaii Press, 1986. Reprinted in *Studies in Early Chinese Philosophy.*

53. "The disputation of Kung-sun Lung as argument about whole and part." *Philosophy East and West* 36/2 (1986). Reprinted in *Studies in Early Chinese Philosophy.*

54. "Yin-Yang and the nature of correlative thinking." *Philosophy East and West,* v. 36/6 (1986); Institute for East Asian Philosophies, Occasional papers and monograph series no. 6. Singapore: National University of Singapore, 1986.

55. "Vampiri in un solo morso." *Il Manifesto* (Rome) (Sept. 1, 1986).

56. "Poems of the West Lake." *Renditions* (Hong Kong) no. 25 (1987).

57. "Hsien-Ch'in Ju-chia tui jen-hsing wen-t'i ti t'an-t'ao (先秦儒家對人性問題的探討)." In *Ju-chia lun-li, yen-t'ao-hui lun-wen chi* (儒家論理研討會論文集), edited by Liu Shu-hsien. Singapore: Institute for East Asian Philosophies, 1987.

58. "A neglected pre-Han philosophical text: *Ho-kuan-tzu,* (鶡冠子)." *Bulletin of the School of Oriental and African Studies* 52/3 (1989).

59. "Conceptual schemes and linguistic relativism in relation to Chinese." *Synthesis Philosophica* (Zagreb, Yugoslavia) 4/2 (1989). Reprinted in *Culture and Modernity: East-West Philosophic Perspectives,* edited by Eliot Deutsch (Honolulu: University of Hawaii Press, 1991; *Epistemological Questions in Classical Chinese Philosophy,* edited by Hans Lenk and Gregor Paul (Albany: State University of New York Press,1993).

60. "Rationalism & Anti-rationalism in Pre-Buddhist China." In *Rationality in Question,* edited by S. Biderman and Ben-Ami Scharfstein. Leiden: Brill, 1990.

61. "Mysticism and the question of private access." In *Rules, Rituals, and Responsibility: Essays Dedicated to Herbert Fingarette,* edited by Mary I. Bockover, La Salle, IL: Open Court, 1991.

62. "Reflections and Replies." In *Chinese Texts and Philosophical Contexts,* edited by Henry Rosemont, Jr. LaSalle, IL: Open Court, 1991.

63. "Two Notes on the Translation of Taoist Classics." In *Interpreting Culture Through Translation: A Festschrift for D. C. Lau.* Edited by Roger T. Ames, Chan Sin-wai and Mau-Sang Ng. Hong Kong: Chinese University Press, 1991.

64. "Chinese philosophy of language" (Chinesische Sprachphilosophie). In *Sprachphilosophie: Ein internationales Handbuch zeitgenössischer Forschung* (Philosophy of Language: An International Handbook of Contemporary Research). Edited by Marcelo Dascal, Dietfried Gerhardus, Kuno Lorenz and Georg Meggle, 94-104. Berlin and New York: Walter de Gruyter, 1992.

Index

About the Editor

Harold D. Roth is Professor of East Asian Studies and Religious Studies at Brown University. A graduate of Princeton University (A.B.) and the University of Toronto (Ph.D.), he is the author of *The Textual History of the Huai-nan Tzu* (AAS, 1992), *Original Tao: Inward Training* (Nei-yeh) *and the Foundations of Taoist Mysticism* (Columbia,1999), and of numerous scholarly articles on the early history and foundational texts of Taoism. He met Angus Graham while doing interviews for a radio program on Chinese philosophy in 1981 and later worked with him at London University on a post-doctoral grant from the Social Sciences and Humanities Research Council of Canada.